THE RUNGLESS LADDER

There is a ladder to heaven, whose base God has placed in human affections, tender instincts, symbolic feelings, sacraments of love, through which the soul rises higher and higher, refining as she goes, till she outgrows the human, and changes, as she rises, into the image of the divine. At the very top of this ladder, at the threshold of Paradise, blazes dazzling and crystalline that celestial grade where the soul knows self no more, having learned, through a long experience of devotion, how blest it is to lose herself in that eternal Love and Beauty of which all earthly fairness and grandeur are but the dim type, the distant shadow. This highest step, this saintly elevation, which but few selectest spirits ever on earth attain . . . this Ultima Thule of virtue had been seized upon by our sage as the all of religion. He knocked out every round of the ladder but the highest, and then, pointing to its hopeless splendor, said to the world, "Go up thither and be saved!"

THE MINISTER'S WOOING

THE
Rungless Ladder

HARRIET BEECHER STOWE
AND NEW ENGLAND PURITANISM

BY

Charles H. Foster

COOPER SQUARE PUBLISHERS, INC.
NEW YORK
1970

Originally Published and Copyright 1954 by
Duke University Press
Published by Cooper Square Publishers, Inc.
59 Fourth Avenue, New York, N. Y. 10003
Standard Book Number 8154-0319-4
Library of Congress Catalog Card No. 79-114086

Printed in the United States of America

To the memory of
GEORGE FRISBIE WHICHER
1889-1954

A man may drop a remark,
In itself a quiet thing,
That may furnish the fuse unto a spark
In dormant nature lain.

Let us deport with skill,
Let us discourse with care,
Powder exists in charcoal
Before it exists in fire.

EMILY DICKINSON

PREFACE

HARRIET BEECHER STOWE may be characterized as the author everybody *almost* knows. Everybody has heard of *Uncle Tom's Cabin* and even those who have never read a chapter know just what to think about it and its author, and all for very obvious reasons. Not only was *Uncle Tom's Cabin* (1852) the most immediately famous and most immediately influential of nineteenth-century American books; but its plot, somewhat distorted, and its characters and meaning, even more distorted, were dinned into the minds of generations of Americans by the Uncle Tom plays and the Tom Shows. By 1878 *Uncle Tom's Cabin* was a separate branch of theatrical business. By 1890, when the United States was creating public buildings reminiscent of Imperial Rome, the Tom Show approximated a homemade gladiatorial contest. There was a parade with a Negro band and a white one and in leash the bloodhounds (really mastiffs or Great Danes) which Harriet had omitted from her book as impractical in hunting slaves in Kentucky. The main characters, known to all, were drawn through the streets in a wagon to the shouts and applause of the crowd.

Many must have told themselves that they had come to see the piety of Uncle Tom, Topsy's mischief, and Eva's literal ascent into heaven. But the violent elements highlighted in George L. Aiken's play of 1852, now raised to a higher pitch of sadism, must have furnished a strong attraction like that of lynching for the vulgar. Eliza and little Harry might escape across the icy river amid the yelping of the bloodhounds, George might make his way to Canada, but these incidents whetted the appetite. Ahead lay a promised feast for the darkest passions. Only wait and a black man would be whipped to death beneath the long, curling bull whip of a white giant. For the vicious, here was the wished-for moment like the slaughter of the victim before the howling Roman mob. For all, the spectacle meant immediately that the Negro had been defeated at the hands of the white man. Tom, to be sure, was welcomed into heaven by Eva and her father, Augustine St. Clare, in a celestial burst of radiance. But this was anticlimax to the vulgar imagination. Like showing the flag in fireworks on the Fourth of July, it was simply a justification for the preceding excitement. Undoubtedly these suggestions are unfair to many who pitied Tom, vibrated to the piety of Eva, and innocently enjoyed the humor of Topsy and other characters. Still it is significant that the universal popularity of the Tom Show coincided with the cynicism and the immorality of the Gilded Age. In the Show there was a ruthless exploitation of American sensibility matching the more obvious exploitation of the American continent.

Anyone who wishes to learn the depth of misunderstanding to which this almost complete distortion of *Uncle Tom's Cabin* can lead should consult James Baldwin's article "Everybody's Protest Novel" in the *Partisan Review* for June, 1949. Utterly confusing the book with the stage plays and the Tom Shows, Baldwin supposes that Harriet equated black with evil and white with good and that she found it necessary to robe Tom theologically in white before she could embrace him. Apparently blending Harriet Beecher Stowe with that degenerate New England spinster, Miss Joanna Burden, in Faulkner's *Light in August*, Baldwin refers to the "medieval morality" in terms of which Harriet, alias Miss Ophelia, postulates "black, white, the devil, the next world." Considered from this aspect, *Uncle Tom's Cabin* achieves "a bright, almost lurid significance, like the light from a fire which consumes a witch." Later he amplifies: ". . . the spirit that breathes in this book, hot, self-righteous, fearful, is not different from that spirit of medieval times which sought to exorcise evil by burning witches; and is not different from that terror which activates a lynch mob." "The aim of the protest novel," he further writes, "becomes something very closely resembling the zeal of those alabaster missionaries to Africa to cover the nakedness of the natives, to hurry them into the pallid arms of Jesus and thence into slavery."

Other more careful critics have given another verdict on Harriet Beecher Stowe and *Uncle Tom's Cabin.* In his review of the Modern Library *Uncle Tom's Cabin* in the *New Yorker* for November 27, 1948, Edmund Wilson wrote that to read Harriet's first novel for the first time today may be a "startling experience" and that "It is a much more remarkable book than one had ever been allowed to suspect." In addition to this essay, undoubtedly the most perceptive of all brief essays on *Uncle Tom's Cabin,* Mr. Wilson in other reviews has noted Harriet's "brilliant expression" of Puritan culture in her New England novels. Van Wyck Brooks has called attention to the charm and authority of *The Minister's Wooing* and *Old-town Folks.* George Frisbie Whicher has praised *The Minister's Wooing* as "a masterly revelation of the springs of Puritan character" valuable for "the light it throws on the inner life of an intensely native New England poet like Emily Dickinson." Perry Miller has written concerning a notable passage in *Old-town Folks* that Harriet Beecher Stowe understood the implications of Jonathan Edwards' thought "better than the theologians who endeavored to follow him, and could evaluate his achievement in terms that are fundamental for understanding American culture."

But these and other attempts to remind us that Harriet Beecher Stowe was a very different kind of author from that of rumor and popular biography have been made only in passing. The distorted image of an important American author persists; her books, which carry us vividly and authoritatively into the American past, are either misunderstood or ignored.

I have written this book in the belief that others might wish to share my excitement in discovering an author everybody *almost* knows and in the hope that I might make some penetration in long-established prejudice. Certainly there is surprise in a famous American social reformer who on close inspection turns out to have been an introspective novelist seeking to resolve through the strategy of fiction the peculiar and fascinating psychological adventures of New England Puritanism; and I have found, I believe, significant drama in the neglected inner history of a sensitive, imaginative, and intelligent woman driven by New England Puritanism to battle slavery, to flirt with spiritualism, to try out Catholicism in imagination, and ultimately to seek in the Episcopal Church a stay against religious and moral confusion.

But I regard Harriet's books themselves as my major discovery. As F. O. Matthiessen noted in *American Renaissance,* Hawthorne is "our one major artist in fiction yet to have come out of New England"; and when we subtract him, New England is left "with Harriet Beecher Stowe and Sylvester Judd and Edward Bellamy; with minor talents of great distinction like Sarah Orne Jewett, Mary Wilkins, and Thornton Wilder, who was not born there; with the recently discovered John W. DeForest of Connecticut, the author of *Miss Ravenel's Conversion* (1867), and with Robert Herrick, who was born in Cambridge, Massachusetts, but whose creative life was passed in Chicago." Despite its long and intense interest in thought and expression, New England, in short, has not produced major novelists as it has produced major theologians, preachers, essayists, and poets.

This fact endows Harriet Beecher Stowe's work with special significance. With the exception of Hawthorne, she is the only very important New England novelist and, when we remember how little of New England actually found expression in Hawthorne's exquisite achievement, she is New England's most revealing native novelist. Following her own practice I have used "Puritan" and "Calvinist," "Puritanism" and "Calvinism" interchangeably to avoid monotony, but she is most exactly described by another term I have used, "Edwardean Calvinism." Unlike Hawthorne, Harriet Beecher Stowe was precisely rather than loosely Puritan. Her whole life was a struggle with the premises Jonathan Edwards established with the authority of science and religion to return the spreading New England mind to those profound channels to salvation preached by Thomas Shepard and other seventeenth-century divines. Original sin, predestination, freedom of the will, the burning necessity for a sincere conversion, grace, heaven, and hell: these were her primary points of reference as she carried out "symbolic action" in writing her novels.

She spoke, therefore, from far more deeply within the New England tradition than Hawthorne. If as Mark Twain stated, "There is only one expert who is qualified to examine the souls and life of a people and make a valuable report—the native novelist," certainly she is worth our time and attention. I find the essence of her achievement her extraordinary talent for seeing Puritan New England steadily and for seeing it whole and for dramatizing it with vividly specific and often charmingly humorous detail. She can help us understand all varieties of New England character from the most granite-like stubbornness to the most mystical and loving submission; she can lead us credibly through the inner adventures of those blessed or cursed by Calvinism. Through her vigorously imagined world and through the inner history behind her fiction, we can experience afresh our New England past in its full human dimensions and its intellectual and emotional complexities.

I had hoped that this book might be read by my friend and teacher, the late George Frisbie Whicher of Amherst College, who first suggested that I read the novels of Harriet Beecher Stowe; I should have valued his comment more than that of anyone else. There are, however, other debts which I can acknowledge. In writing this book, I have been greatly aided by a leave of absence made possible through the co-operation of Grinnell College and the American Council of Learned Societies. My investigation of Puritan theology and New England intellectual history during that leave has been fundamental in illuminating the significance of many of Harriet Beecher Stowe's pages. My other important debt is to my wife, whose interest in my book has been indispensable and who has been the only audience for all my chapters as they have been written. But I wish to thank all those friends and acquaintances who, often in ways unknown to them, have contributed to this book.

C. H. F.

Grinnell College

ACKNOWLEDGMENTS

I wish to thank the following persons and publishers for permission to make quotations:

Mrs. Z. Boylston Adams for quotation from *Life and Letters of Harriet Beecher Stowe* (1897), edited by Annie Fields, and from *Letters of Sarah Orne Jewett* (1911), edited by Annie Fields.

Edmund Wilson for quotation from two book reviews in the *New Yorker: Uncle Tom's Cabin* (Modern Library Edition), Nov. 27, 1948, and *The Collected Works of Abraham Lincoln,* March 14, 1953.

American Council of Learned Societies, Charles Scribner's Sons and the New York *Times* for quotation from *The Dictionary of American Biography* (1928-1936), edited by Allen Johnson and Dumas Malone.

The American Book Company for quotation from *Native American Humor 1800-1900* (1937), by Walter Blair; *Jonathan Edwards: Representative Selections* (1935), edited by Clarence H. Faust and Thomas H. Johnson; *The Puritans* (1938), edited by Perry Miller and Thomas H. Johnson.

Appleton-Century-Crofts, Inc. for quotation from *American Fiction: An Historical and Critical Survey* (1936), by A. H. Quinn.

The Bobbs-Merrill Company, Inc. for quotation from *Saints, Sinners and Beechers* (1934), by Lyman Beecher Stowe, used by special permission of the publishers.

E. P. Dutton and Company, Inc. for quotation from the book *The Flowering of New England,* by Van Wyck Brooks, New American Edition of Everyman's Library, and from the book *New England: Indian Summer 1865-1915,* by Van Wyck Brooks, New American Edition of Everyman's Library.

Harper and Brothers for "A man may drop a remark" from *Bolts of Melody: New Poems of Emily Dickinson* (1945), edited by Mabel Loomis Todd and Millicent Todd Bingham, copyright, 1945, by Millicent Todd Bingham; for quotation from *The Writings of Mark Twain* (1903), published by the American Publishing Company; from *The Complete Works of Mark Twain* (1924); from *Letters of Emily Dickinson* (1931), edited by Mabel Loomis Todd; from *Mark Twain's Letters, Arranged with Comment by Albert Bigelow Paine* (1917), edited by A. B. Paine.

Henry Holt and Company, Inc. for quotation from "Blueberries" in *Complete Poems of Robert Frost* (1949); from "The Figure a Poem Makes," the preface to *Complete Poems of Robert Frost* (1949); from the preface by Robert Frost to *Memoirs of the Notorious Stephen Burroughs of New Hampshire* (1924), published by Dial Press, Inc.; from "Poverty and Poetry" by Robert Frost in *Biblia,* Vol. IX, No. 1, Feb., 1938, Princeton University Library; from the preface by Robert Frost to *King Jasper* (1935), by E. A. Robinson, published by the Macmillan Company.

Houghton Mifflin Company for quotation from *The Writings of Harriet Beecher Stowe* (1896), 16 vols.; from *Life of Harriet Beecher Stowe* (1890), by Charles Edward Stowe; from the works of Hawthorne, Emerson, and Holmes, now in public domain but formerly copyrighted by Houghton Mifflin.

J. B. Lippincott Company for quotation from *Crusader in Crinoline: The Life of Harriet Beecher Stowe* (1941), by Forrest Wilson; from *American Issues,* Volume II (1941), edited by Thorp, Curti, and Baker.

Little, Brown and Company for quotation from *The Journals of Amos Bronson Alcott* (1938), edited by Odell Shepard; from *The Poems of Emily Dickinson* (1931), edited by Martha Dickinson Bianchi and Alfred Leete Hampson.

The Macmillan Company for quotation from *Literary History of the United States* (1948), edited by Spiller, Thorp, Johnson, and Canby; from *The American Novel 1789-1913* (1940), by Carl Van Doren.

The Editors of *The New England Quarterly* for quotations from my article "The Genesis of Harriet Beecher Stowe's *The Minister's Wooing,*" Vol. XXI, No. 4, December, 1948.

Oxford University Press, Inc. for quotation from *American Renaissance: Art and Expression in the Age of Emerson and Whitman* (1941), by F. O. Matthiessen.

The Ronald Press Company for quotation from *Critiques and Essays in Criticism 1920-1948* (1949), edited by Robert Wooster Stallman.

The Scarecrow Press for quotation from *Acres of Flint: Writers of Rural New England, 1870-1900* (1951), by Perry D. Westbrook.

Scott, Foresman and Company for quotation from *The Literature of the United States* (1947), edited by Blair, Hornberger, and Stewart.

Charles Scribner's Sons for quotation from *Encyclopedia of Religion and Ethics* (1913), edited by John Hastings; from *A Small Boy and Others* (1913), by Henry James; from *The Art of the Novel: Critical Prefaces by Henry James* (1934), edited with an introduction by Richard P. Blackmur.

The Viking Press, Inc. for quotation from *The Liberal Imagination* (1950), by Lionel Trilling; from *Studies in Classic American Literature* (1924), by D. H. Lawrence, as reprinted in *The Shock of Recognition* (1943), edited by Edmund Wilson.

The Westminster Press for quotation from *Experiments of Spiritual Life & Health* by Roger Williams, edited with an historical introduction by Winthrop S. Hudson. Copyright by Walter L. Jenkins, 1951. Used by permission.

A CHRONOLOGICAL OUTLINE

1811-1832

Harriet lived in New England. From 1811 until 1824 she lived in her birthplace, Litchfield, Connecticut, where her father, Dr. Lyman Beecher, perhaps the most dynamic Puritan clergyman of the 1820's and 1830's, served as minister of the First Congregational Church. From 1824 until 1832 she lived in Hartford, Connecticut, where she was student and later teacher at Hartford Female Seminary. During the Hartford years, she made occasional visits to Boston, where in 1826 her father became minister of Hanover Street Church.

1832-1850

Harriet lived in Cincinnati, Ohio. In 1832, together with most of the Beecher clan, she moved to Cincinnati, where her father had been appointed President of Lane Theological Seminary, dedicated to saving the West for Protestantism. The Cincinnati years were crucial. It was in Cincinnati that she wrote the stories with which I begin my discussion; it was here in 1836 that she married the widower Calvin Stowe, who had taught Greek at Dartmouth before joining the faculty at Lane; it was here that she gathered the materials and experienced the trials, religious and maternal, which found expression in *Uncle Tom's Cabin.*

1850-1852

Harriet lived in Brunswick, Maine. On Calvin Stowe's appointment to the faculty of his alma mater, Bowdoin College, she returned to New England and at Brunswick wrote *Uncle Tom's Cabin.*

1852-1864

Harriet lived in Andover, Massachusetts. In 1852 Calvin Stowe was appointed to the faculty of Andover Theological Seminary. During the Andover years Harriet made her three journeys to Europe (1853, 1856, 1859) and experienced deep religious perplexity on the death of her eldest son, Henry Ellis Stowe, in July, 1857. She was a prolific writer in these years, which saw the appearance of *A Key to Uncle Tom's Cabin;* her second antislavery novel, *Dred;* two of her New England novels, *The Minister's Wooing* and *The Pearl of Orr's Island;* and her Italian novel, *Agnes of Sorrento.*

1864-1881

Harriet lived in Hartford, Connecticut, and Mandarin, Florida. On Calvin Stowe's retirement from Andover Theological Seminary, Harriet's pen was busier than ever. She now wrote her masterpieces, *Oldtown Folks* and *Oldtown Fireside Stories,* her last New England novel, *Poganuc People,* three novels dealing with life in the Gilded Age, other more ephemeral work, and her second most disturbing book in the eyes of her contemporaries, *Lady Byron Vindicated.*

1881-1896

Harriet's career drew to a close in 1881. Her remaining years are essentially insignificant; toward the last she lost contact with reality and required an attendant.

CONTENTS

Preface vii

Acknowledgments xiii

A Chronological Outline xvii

I. New England Doubleness 3

II. "That Triumphant Work" 12

III. Transition 64

IV. "The Bruised Flax-Flower" 86

V. "Fictitious Shores" 129

VI. A New England Idyl 145

VII. New England's Looking-Glass.................. 161

VIII. Holiday in Yankeedom 203

IX. Vindication of a Friend 219

X. The Last Novels 227

Notes 245

Index 269

THE RUNGLESS LADDER

It spoils the *Bow* to keep it always bent, and the *Viol* if always strain'd up. Mirth is some loose or relaxation to the labouring Mind or Body, it lifts up the hands that hang down in weariness, and strengthens the feeble knees that cou'd stand no longer to work; it renews our strength, and we resume our labours again with vigour.

> Benjamin Colman, *The Government &*
> *Improvement of Mirth,* 1707

The way in which most of the things we use are serviceable to us and answer their end is in their being strained, or hard pressed, or violently agitated. Thus the way in which the bow answers its end is in hard straining of it to shoot the arrow and do the execution; the bow that won't bear straining is good for nothing. So it is with a staff that a man walks with: it answers its end in being hard pressed. So it is with many of the members of our bodies, our teeth, our feet, etc. And so with most of the utensils of life, an ox, a saw, a flail, a rope, a chain, etc. They are usefull and answer their end by some violent straining, pressure, agitation, collision, or impulsion. And they that are so weak as not to bear the trial of such usage are good for nothing. Here is a lively representation of the way in which true and sincere saints (which are often in Scripture represented as God's instruments or utensils) answer God's end, and serve and glorify Him in it by enduring temptation, going through hard labour, suffering, or self-denial, or such service as strains hard upon nature and self.

> Jonathan Edwards, *Images or Shadows of*
> *Divine Things*

My object is to interpret to the world the New England life and character in that particular time of its history which may be called the seminal period. . . . In doing this work, I have tried to make my mind as still and passive as a looking-glass, or a mountain lake, and then to give you merely the images reflected there.

> Harriet Beecher Stowe, "Author's Preface"
> to *Oldtown Folks,* 1869

1

NEW ENGLAND DOUBLENESS

AT Litchfield Academy when she was twelve years old, Harriet Beecher wrote a composition in answer to the question "Can the immortality of the soul be proved by the light of nature?" Here certainly was an appropriate beginning for the future author of novels depicting the theological wrestlings and surgings of Puritan New England, but this composition need detain us only a moment. It was not self-assigned, neither an original question nor an original answer. It was merely surprisingly mature fulfilment of a task set by Harriet's extraordinary teacher, John Pierce Brace, who like his contemporary, Edward Tyrrell Channing at Harvard, the teacher of Emerson and Thoreau, regarded composition as the expression of truth rather than as finger exercises in rhetoric. Some faint evidence of this early training under Brace should probably be read in Harriet's skilful exposition in *Uncle Tom's Cabin* and the New England novels, but we find little of the future novelist in the thoughtful schoolgirl.

When we turn to Harriet's self-assigned tasks, the stories she wrote as a young woman in Cincinnati, we stand closer not only in time but in quality to her mature work. In her first story, "A New England Sketch," presented to the Cincinnati literary society, the Semi-Colon Club, in November, 1833, and awarded a fifty dollar prize the following year in the *Western Monthly Magazine,* we find, for example, the following conversation between a small New England boy and Uncle Lot Griswold, "a chestnut burr, abounding with briers without and with substantial goodness within":

"Uncle Lot, father wants to know if you will lend him your hoe to-day?" says a little boy, making his way across a cornfield.

"Why don't your father use his own hoe?"

"Ours is broke."

"Broke! How came it broke?"

"I broke it yesterday, trying to hit a squirrel."

"What business had you to be hittin' squirrels with a hoe? say!"

"But father wants to borrow yours."

"Why don't he have that mended? It's a great pester to have everybody usin' a body's things."

"Well, I can borrow one somewhere else, I suppose," says the suppliant. After the boy has stumbled across the ploughed ground and is fairly over the fence, Uncle Lot calls,

"Halloo, there, you little rascal! What are you goin' off without the hoe for?"

"I didn't know as you meant to lend it."

"I didn't say I wouldn't, did I? Here, come and take it—stay, I'll bring it; and do tell your father not to be lettin' you hunt squirrels with his hoes next time."

In its skilful rendering of New England character and tone of voice, in its delightfully understated humor, this little scene quite clearly anticipates Harriet's mature achievement in *Oldtown Folks* and *Oldtown Fireside Stories* written thirty years later; and if we are patient, we find yet other suggestions of her later work in the stories and sketches collected in her first book, *The Mayflower* (1843). In the first of her sketches under the heading "The Sabbath," Harriet wrote realistically and humorously of the meaning of Sunday for the Puritan child. She noted with a sure sense for detail that the tick of the mahogany clock and the buzz of blue flies up and down the windowpanes were distinct items of hearing as the well-brushed family waited for the first bell. She remembered the tedium when the whole stock of excitement was the Bible and the primer, and the joy of the child who saw the gleam of a pin and had an excuse for getting down to pick it up. In *The Mayflower,* Harriet began the genre painting of Puritan life which would give her New England novels their unmistakable authority.

Also we cannot read far in *The Mayflower* before we discover a morbid intensity, erupting into pious sentimentality that calls to mind Little Eva's death in *Uncle Tom's Cabin.* "Little Edward" has a promising beginning with its picture of a humorously methodical New England couple, Uncle Abel and Aunt Betsy, and the family dog Bose, "who always walked as if he were studying the multiplication-table." But almost immediately the tone shifts. Little Edward, the child of Uncle Abel's old age, dies in a theatrically arranged ray of the setting sun that "gleams like an angel's smile across the face of the little sufferer."

But something more than sentimental *memento mori* is clearly discernible in *The Mayflower.* In "Aunt Mary," writing in the first person, Harriet told the story of an "out-of-time, out-of-place, out-of-form sort of boy, with whom nothing prospered" until his beneficent aunt visited and brought understanding and sympathy. Though the boy was called Henry and may have been drawn in part from Harriet's younger brother, Henry Ward Beecher, quite clearly the insistent earnestness points to thinly veiled self-revelation:

I was timid, and shrinking, and proud; and I was nothing to anyone around me but an awkward, unlucky boy; nothing to my parents but one of half a dozen children, whose faces were to be washed and stockings mended on Saturday afternoon. . . . But the feelings of grown-up children exist in the mind of little ones oftener than is supposed; and I had, even at this early day, the same keen sense of all that touched the heart wrong; the same longing for something which should touch it aright; the same discontent with latent, matter-of-course affection, and the same craving for sympathy, which has been the unprofitable fashion of this world in all ages.

Harriet's sketch "Feeling" is an interesting sequel to "Aunt Mary." Here again she addressed herself to her "out-of-time, out-of-place, out-of-form sort of boy," but this time she did not resolve his difficulties with the visit of an angelic aunt. Rather she contrasted her boy with his little sister, always bright, always pleasing, always cheerful. Superficially, of course, the sister was the more fortunate being, but time made another revelation. The out-of-form boy, morose, timid, unable to communicate, eventually became an orator able to sway a crowded assembly;

"his eyes are flashing with intellect, his face fervent with emotion, his voice breathes like music, and every mind is enchained." Furthermore, he was "rapt—happy." Harriet's moral was this:

> The power of feeling is necessary for all that is noble in man, and yet it involves the greatest risks. They who catch at happiness on the bright surface of things, secure a portion, such as it is, with more certainty; those who dive for it in the waters of deep feeling, if they succeed will bring up pearls and diamonds, but if they sink they are lost forever!

In "Aunt Mary" and "Feeling" Harriet, however crudely, began to express the lonely, introspective, deeply emotional side of her nature and to discover, as she was to do again and again in her future work, advantages in her disadvantages. Quite clearly, as she here suggested, her deeper self was born from a feeling of neglect in childhood. From her last novel *Poganuc People* (1878) we get a generally idyllic report on her early years in the Litchfield parsonage, but other sources indicate that she had good reasons for being often an unhappy little girl. Her mother had died when Harriet was between five and six, leaving a gap never filled by her deeply affectionate father and her stepmother, who seems to have been little more than a conscientious, hard-working visitor in the family. Harriet was also one of ten children, caught at what we might call the dead center of the generations, young enough to be supervised by her older brothers and sisters, but too old to claim the affectionate attention which went to her younger brothers, Henry Ward and Charles, and the children by her father's second marriage, Isabella, Thomas, and James. We have the case of a little girl left much to herself and of whom much was expected. It is not surprising that she felt neglected and that in lonely introspection she developed deep, unsatisfied, emotional hungers, which left their mark in her mature character and which were important factors in developing heart and imagination and determining her on her eventful career as novelist.

But in concentration on the more sober side of *The Mayflower* we must not forget the racy humor of "A New England Sketch," and two similar pieces, "Cousin William" and "Love versus Law." The most interesting fact about Harriet's first book is its contrasting, virtually contradictory moods of Puritan earnestness and Yankee comedy. How are we to explain this duality? One way is to point to the sources of Harriet's amusing Yankeedom. In "A New England Sketch" she was developing anecdotes her father liked to tell of his surly but tenderhearted uncle, Lot Benton. In "Love versus Law" she developed similarly an anecdote supplied by her husband after a visit to his "chestnut burr" relations in Natick, Massachusetts. As a beginning writer, Harriet quite naturally used attractive materials at hand. Such an explanation, however, hardly accounts for the fact that the duality of Puritan earnestness and Yankee comedy in *The Mayflower* persists as a characteristic in her later books.

Considerable light is thrown on the matter, I believe, by two passages in Harriet's early letters. In May, 1832, writing from Cincinnati to her friend, Georgianna May, she made this interesting announcement:

> The amount of the matter has been as this inner world of mine has become worn out and untenable, I have at last concluded to come out of it and live in the external one, and, as F—— S—— once advised me, to give up the pernicious habit of meditation to the first Methodist minister that would take it, and try to mix in society somewhat as another person would. . . . I have come to a firm resolution to count no hours but unclouded ones, and to let all others slip out of my memory and reckoning as quickly as possible. . . .

The following year, again in May, Harriet made an even more surprising revelation when she wrote this extraordinary passage to Georgianna:

> Recently I have been reading the life of Madame de Staël and "Corinne." I have felt an intense sympathy with many parts of that book, with many parts of her character. But in America feelings vehement and absorbing like hers become still more deep, morbid, and impassioned by the constant habits of self-government which the rigid forms of our society demand. They are repressed, and they burn inward till they burn the very soul, leaving only dust and ashes. It seems to me the intensity with which my

mind has thought and felt on every subject presented to it has had this effect. It has withered and exhausted it, and though young I have no sympathy with the feelings of youth. All that is enthusiastic, all that is impassioned in admiration of nature, of writing, of character, in devotional thought and emotion, or in the emotions of affection, I have felt with vehement and absorbing intensity,— felt till my mind is exhausted, and seems to be sinking into deadness.

When we put these two passages together, the latter of them written in the spring before "A New England Sketch," we can see that Harriet was troubled by more than a lonely and introspective childhood and that the humor of *The Mayflower* may well have been part of an intentional program to escape those "constant habits of self-government" demanded by her father's Puritanism. This program to escape the untenable inner world and live in the external one, giving up the pernicious habit of meditation to the first Methodist clergyman that would take it, is likely to strike the modern reader as very un-Puritan. But it was not inconsistent with the practice of many dyed-in-the-wool New England Calvinists. As I have tried to suggest in the epigraph to this book in the quotations from Benjamin Colman and Jonathan Edwards, the New England mind recognized not only that the good life must be lived under tension but also that "It spoils the *Bow* to keep it always bent." Edwards himself seems to have lived consistently on the stretch, but many Puritan New Englanders lived with the bow alternately pulled tight and let loose. As in Harriet's "New England Sketch" and "Cousin William," the letting loose often took the form of playing the humorous and realistic Yankee. The authoritative biographical sketches of Congregational clergymen in William B. Sprague's *Annals of the American Pulpit* (1856) furnish fascinating evidence on this point again and again. Certainly Harriet's father and her husband illustrate the practice.

After his intense services of conversion during the war with Unitarianism in Boston in the late 1820's, Lyman Beecher used to "run down" with his children. "Lively, sparkling, jocose, full of anecdote": these are Harriet's words for him on such occasions. He would do more than talk. Tuning up his fiddle, he would break into "Auld Lang Syne," "Bonnie Doon," even "Go to the Devil and Shake Yourself"; and if the second Mrs. Beecher had gone to bed, he would perform the double shuffle he used to dance as a young man at cornhuskings. Once when he was asked why he did not reply to a theological opponent, Lyman answered that he once threw a book at a skunk and he saw no reason to repeat the experiment. Harriet's husband, Calvin Stowe, ran a similar pattern. An extraordinary scholar in many languages including Arabic, a man (as witness his account of his childhood adventures with a ghostly playmate) whose inner life would have made excellent subject matter for Hawthorne or the Henry James of *The Turn of the Screw*, Calvin Stowe was still a master-hand at playing and virtually becoming a Yankee. His anecdotes, his dryly humorous phrases, were an important resource for Harriet in her re-creation of Puritan New England, particularly in *Oldtown Folks* and *Oldtown Fireside Stories*. How amusing a Yankee Calvin Stowe could be we can sense in a passage from an early letter which inspired Harriet's "Love versus Law":

I have had some rare talks with your old Uncle "Jaw" Bacon, and other old characters, which you ought to have heard. The Curtises have been flooding Uncle "Jaw's" meadows, and he is in a great stew about it. He says: "I took and tell'd your Uncle Izic to tell them 'ere Curtises that if the Devil didn't git 'em far flowing my medder arter that sort, I didn't see no use o' havin' any Devil." "Have you talked with the Curtises yourself?" "Yes, hang the sarcy dogs! and they took and tell'd me that they'd take and flow clean up to my front door, and make me go out and in in a boat." "Why don't you go to law?" "Oh, they keep alterin' and er tinkerin'-up the laws so here in Massachusetts that a body can't git no damage fur flowing; they think cold water can't hurt nobody."

In alternating Puritan earnestness with the comic mask of the Yankee in her first book, Harriet was so much like her father and her husband that we are tempted to say that she was imitating them as well as borrowing anecdotes from them. But whether or not this was actually the case, she had begun in *The Mayflower*, because of her double mood of seeing and saying, to assume status as an indigenous expressor of matters New England. The alternating of seriousness with humor is, of course, nearly a universal human trait and may be found over and over again in literature. We find it in Shakespeare, in Scott, in Dickens, to name obvious examples, and almost always humor is associated, as it is in Harriet, her father, and her husband, with the common people. But if we cannot mark off precisely the local from the universal in this matter and declare with finality that this belongs to New England and that to the world, still there seem grounds for making local practice particular by calling it New England doubleness. Perhaps the nearest we can come to defining this concept is to suggest that in his humor the introspective, intellectual New Englander, unlike his fellow Englishman across the sea, virtually became a new person; he did not find delight so much in imitation as in identification, in the sudden revolution of temperament which brought him in emotion, in thought, in expression into the role of his usual opposite, the shrewd and dryly humorous Yankee. In notable instance after instance the thoughtful New Englander embraced and even blended sociological extremes.

In "Mr. Higginbotham's Catastrophe" and in his journal of his trip to Western Massachusetts in 1838, Hawthorne showed unmistakable relish for the earthy and humorous and a strong inclination to identify himself with the Yankee, but generally he contented himself with mere grace notes of amusement. Emerson was far more indigenous in his mood of seeing and saying. There is something highly appropriate in the supposition that Daniel Chester French's statue of Emerson splits into two faces, one that of the angelic seer, the other that of the shrewd and humorous Yankee. We read Emerson's spirit inaccurately if we suppose he was always the serious artist we find in the address to the divinity students at Cambridge or in that Neoplatonic rhapsody "The Over-Soul." Emerson was Yankee as well as seer at his most characteristic and sometimes almost exclusively Yankee as in his comic masterpiece, *English Traits*. Thoreau, of course, was a master artist in New England doubleness, saying the light thing seriously and the serious thing lightly and often assuming the role of Yankee "chestnut burr." Similarly Emily Dickinson masked serious concern with wit, and it would be hard to say where she was most herself, in such intensely introspective lyrics as "One need not be a chamber to be haunted" or in such witty poems, written with Yankee economy of phrase, as "The show is not the show,/But they that go." In our time Robert Frost impresses us as New Englander not only because he can write an almost Puritan lyric such as "Desert Places" but also, and perhaps primarily, because his characteristic practice is to fulfil his own dictum: ". . . to be at all charming or even bearable, the way is almost rigidly prescribed. If it is with outer seriousness, it must be with inner humor. If it is with outer humor, it must be with inner seriousness. Neither one alone without the other under it will do."

Doubtless Harriet recognized a congenial disposition in Emerson and Thoreau, but she stood nearer to a contemporary of whom she may never have heard. She would have understood immediately what Emily Dickinson meant when she wrote:

> Mirth is the mail of anguish,
> In which it cautious arm,
> Lest anybody spy the blood
> And "You're hurt" exclaim!

Doubleness for Harriet had usually a deeper source than play of mind and emotion; humor was usually an emotional necessity. She belonged to what we might call the primitive manifestation of New England doubleness—that is, to its intensely Puritan phase. In her work we seldom find Emerson's and Thoreau's and Frost's blending of extremes; generally she assumes her opposing roles by distinct turns. But such a practice was appropriate, of course, in an author who aspired to be New England's looking-glass, reflecting Puritan New England without distortion.

Of all this, however, we have only suggestion in her first book. *The Mayflower* is merely prelude to her Puritan drama and the expression of her culture in fiction. Act One begins with *Uncle Tom's Cabin*.

2

"THAT TRIUMPHANT WORK"

I

When in *A Small Boy and Others* (1913) Henry James referred to *Uncle Tom's Cabin* as "that triumphant work," he meant that it was triumphant in winning readers of all classes, not that it was triumphant in the sense that Harriet with fine calculation and intelligence had lifted life to form. In fact for him, her first novel was remarkable in constituting a triumph exactly opposite to that he admired in Hawthorne, Flaubert, and Turgenev and had sought to achieve in his own masterpieces. Looking back to his youth, he remembered that *Uncle Tom's Cabin* "had above all the extraordinary fortune of finding itself, for an immense number of people, much less a book than a state of vision, of feeling and of consciousness, in which they didn't sit and read and appraise and pass the time, but walked and talked and laughed and cried and, in a manner of which Mrs. Stowe was the irresistible cause, generally conducted themselves." From the point of view of James's prefaces, such literary hypnotism should have been the result of a carefully formulated strategy, beginning, let us say, with a full outline, and developed with intense concern for structure and character and the employment of *ficelles* through which we might learn necessary details without the fracturing of art. But what was the actual case? To James:

Appreciation and judgment, the whole impression, were thus an effect for which there had been no process—any process so related having in other cases *had* to be at some point or other critical; nothing in the guise of a written book, therefore, a book printed, published, sold, bought and "noticed," probably ever reached its mark, the mark of exciting interest, without having at least groped for that goal *as* a book or by the exposure of some literary side. Letters, here, languished unconscious, and Uncle Tom, instead of making even one of the cheap short cuts through the medium in which books breathe, even as fishes in water, went gaily roundabout it altogether, as if a fish, a wonderful "leaping" fish, had simply flown through the air.

With fine perception James here sums up the impression of most twentieth-century readers who have exposed themselves to *Uncle Tom's Cabin* and the conventional accounts of its creation. Emphatically, there is something perverse in the spectacle of a first novel, by a minor writer of tales and sketches, driven through the works at top speed and never revised, which becomes the most famous and immediately influential book of its century. In this aspect *Uncle Tom's Cabin* is a literary leaping fish. For anyone, however, who wishes to understand Harriet and her development into novelist of New England, her first novel cannot be written down simply as an enigma and dismissed. An attempt must be made to solve what looks so much like the insoluble.

The most obvious place to begin, of course, is the influence of Harriet's reading. Lucy Poate Stebbins and Richard Poate Stebbins find significant points of resemblance between *Uncle Tom's Cabin* and Frances Trollope's antislavery novel appearing fifteen years earlier, *The Life and Adventures of Jonathan Jefferson Whitlaw*. It is quite possible that Harriet read this book during the Cincinnati years when the problem of slavery was constantly forced on her attention, not only by Negroes escaping from the South, but by the proslavery and antislavery elements disrupting instruction at Lane Seminary. The sadistic overseer of Mrs. Trollope's novel may have contributed suggestions toward the creation of Simon Legree; and there seem to be at least faint adumbrations in Mrs. Trollope of several of Harriet's Negro characters. But it would be oversimplification to suppose that *Uncle Tom's Cabin* derived on the literary side simply from the reading of *Jonathan Jefferson Whitlaw*. As Herbert Brown has indicated in *The Sentimental Novel in*

America, there are numerous similarities between characters and situations in *Uncle Tom's Cabin* and motifs familiar in the popular sentimental novels appearing in Harriet's youth and maturity. The pious departures of Eva, Uncle Tom, and other characters were well-worn patterns. In her novel *Resignation* (1825), Sarah Evans, for example, managed (the count is Herbert Brown's) to introduce fifty-seven deaths, most of them pious.

But once we realize that *Uncle Tom's Cabin* was in some aspects a coda of themes Harriet could have encountered in easily accessible books, we still must wonder at the source of her strength in manipulating the familiar. Possibly, her superiority came in part from her knowledge of the master of sentimental novelists, Samuel Richardson, but her remark in *The Minister's Wooing* that Richardson's *Sir Charles Grandison* was a "seven-volumed, trailing, tedious, delightful old bore" principally suggests her difficulty in enduring the father of the English novel. We may, however, misread her meaning. In New England, Richardson had long held the most respected place among novelists. Very appropriately in view of the similarities between Richardsonian sentimentalism and the case histories of Abigail Hutchinson and Phebe Bartlet, converted at four, Jonathan Edwards placed *Pamela* and *Clarissa* on his list of future reading. In our awareness of Hawthorne's austere, lonely Puritans, we are likely to forget that the eighteenth century Puritan in New England, like his cousin across the sea, was usually middle-class in his sensibility. Richardson almost perfectly mirrored the middle-class tendency toward sentiment on the one hand and delight in the specific details of everyday reality on the other. Harriet Beecher Stowe, still in essentials an eighteenth-century New Englander, could have found in Richardson's mélange of sentimentalism, realism, and comedy a close parallel to what I have called New England doubleness. We should perhaps emphasize the word "delightful" in her description of Richardson and minimize the word "bore" and write down Richardson as an admiration who might have taught her much of the art of the novel.

Sunny Memories of Foreign Lands (1854), her account of her first journey to Europe, furnishes us, in any case, with grounds for supposing that she found a teacher in at least one of the early masters of English fiction. There, two years after *Uncle Tom's Cabin,* she praised Defoe as "the most suggestive writer to an artist of fiction that the English language affords" because of "that power by which he wrought fiction to produce the impression of reality." Presumably Harriet, like most New England girls of her day, read *Robinson Crusoe* in childhood, but the titles she referred to in her discussion were *A Journal of the Plague Years* and the *Memoirs of a Cavalier.* It seems possible that after the epidemic of Asiatic cholera in Cincinnati in 1849 Harriet read or reread Defoe's *Journal* as the report of a similar catastrophe and that this work, read with intense concern, made a profound impression upon her. It would be natural that she should inquire as to Defoe's sources and her discovery that he had achieved his effects through the combination of authentic records with his own visions and reminiscences may have suggested a method to her when she came to write *Uncle Tom's Cabin.*

Like *Moby-Dick* and *Huckleberry Finn, Uncle Tom's Cabin* is in structure an expanded tale of travel. Harriet may have developed this form quite naturally because she wished to give a broad view of slavery through Uncle Tom's journey south and George's, Eliza's, and little Harry's journey north. But we may be overlooking literary influences. In childhood, Harriet avidly read a battered portion of *Don Quixote* discovered in the attic of her father's parsonage. The fundamental pattern of this greatest of all expanded tales of travel may have remained in her mind and proved unconsciously suggestive when she sat down to write *Uncle Tom's Cabin.* This, however, is only in the realm of possibility. Much more likely is the influence of Scott, the favored, even the recommended novelist during her childhood. From the *Autobiography of Lyman Beecher,* we learn that Lyman once ran a contest with his son George to see who could remember the more of Scott's novels; we also learn that Harriet read *Ivanhoe* seven times in one summer. Though we are right in designating Scott as "historical romancer," we might almost as appropriately call him a writer of the expanded tale of travel. His characters are always on the move. *Kenilworth*, for example, could be represented by a series of maps tracing the various journeys of Edmund Tressilian and Amy Robsart. Maps might also serve for *The Heart of Midlothian*. In making *Uncle Tom's Cabin* a panorama of mid-America, Harriet could easily have been influenced by Scott. Not only had she known his works since childhood, but the year before beginning her novel, during pregnancy with her last child, she read his "historic novels," as she called them, "in their order." Here may be a partial explanation of the journeys in *Uncle Tom's Cabin*, which Edmund Wilson has described as revealing a whole civilization.

Possibly, Harriet was also indebted in her studies of mid-America to the almost forgotten American author James Hall, editor of the *Western Monthly Magazine* of Cincinnati, in which her first story, "A New England Sketch," was published. Hall's *Legends of the West* (1832) could have furnished a model for such scenes in *Uncle Tom's Cabin* as that at the inn in Kentucky where George found the frontiersmen, hats tipped at the angles temperament suggested. Perhaps even more important was the fact that Hall joined certain other influential Cincinnatians in trying to force a Western flowering. Harriet would certainly have heard the arguments favoring a Western-Southern literature when the Semi-Colon literary society held its meetings at the home of Dr. Daniel Drake. Harriet Martineau's *Retrospect of Western Travel* (1838) suggests in a long quotation from Drake the program which he and Hall laid down as a challenge to the East. Speaking before the Literary Convention of Kentucky, Drake let himself go in magniloquence concerning the West. The facts, geographical and cultural, invited, he said, perpetual union between the West and South, particularly between the states bordering the Ohio. In his poetical enthusiasm, he noted that the plants along the Ohio lodge their seeds indiscriminately on either shore: "Thus the very trees and flowers emigrate from one republic to another." He summarized his program: "In short, we should foster Western genius, encourage Western writers, patronize Western publishers, augment the number of Western readers, and create a Western heart."

Miss Martineau is our witness that in the 1830's Cincinnati parties were marked "by the diversity in the company, and in the manners of the natives of the East and West. The endeavor seems to be to keep up rather than to disuse distinctive observances. The effect is entertaining enough . . . but not very salutary to the temper of the residents to judge by the complaints I heard about sectional exclusiveness." In this atmosphere of aroused regionalism, we may be sure that the Beecher clan and Calvin Stowe did not hesitate to assert their New Englandness; it may even be that Harriet's "A New England Sketch" derived in part at least from the impulse to show that Yankeedom was as good a subject for literature as anything the West could offer. But when Harriet sat down in Brunswick, Maine, to write *Uncle Tom's Cabin,* she had eighteen years of Ohio behind her. In the long-familiar challenge of Hall and Drake for a Western-Southern literature, she may have found encouragement for painting slavery in the mid-America she had known at first hand and in the South which escaping Negroes had dramatized to her again and again in the pauses of domestic labor.

This brief consideration of Mrs. Trollope, of Richardson and the sentimental novel, of Defoe and a method of realism, of Scott and the expanded tale of travel, of Hall and Drake and the challenge for a Western-Southern literature, drives some shadows from the enigma of *Uncle Tom's Cabin.* We begin to sense that, like every other book, Harriet's first novel undoubtedly derived in part from the books its author read and approved. But through academic glasses we see darkly at best: no book is a mere product of its author's reading. We move nearer to understanding *Uncle Tom's Cabin* when we try, with the help of all available sources and some flights of imagination, to reconstruct Harriet's own increasing comprehension of the genesis of her famous novel.

II

At first, the explanation must have seemed easy to her. She had a knack for writing, as witness *The Mayflower; Uncle Tom's Cabin* was simply the result of her putting her talents to the use of humanity and God, as her sister-in-law, Mrs. Edward Beecher, and her brother, Henry Ward Beecher, had urged. There was, of course, more power in her novel than in her first sketches, but that was natural. For one thing, she had been thrown into despair and indignation at that vicious legislation, the Fugitive Slave Law of 1850. For another, she knew a good deal about the Negro from intimate experience and wide reading; she had lived with his problem for many years in Cincinnati. When the truth of her novel was questioned, she promptly set to work to collect, as the title page of *A Key to Uncle Tom's Cabin* (1853) reads, "the original facts and documents upon which the story is founded. Together with corroborative statements verifying the truth of the work." Uncle Tom, of course, came from acquaintance with the Reverend Josiah Henson but also from reading *The Life of Josiah Henson, Formerly A Slave, Now An Inhabitant of Canada, As Narrated by Himself* (1849). Then there was George Harris: George's being whipped by the child of his white master came from Theodore Weld's *American Slavery As It Is* (1839); other parts of his story were borrowed from the adventures of Lewis Clark and particularly from *Narrative of the Life of Frederick Douglass, An American Slave* (1845).

But *A Key* turned out to be more difficult than she had supposed. There was no lack of "corroborative statements." Calvin uncovered newspaper stories and slavery legislation that substantiated everything she had written, indeed, that went beyond her indictment in most cases. From all over the Union, men and women wrote eagerly in confirmation of her picture; often they seemed to have known her characters. The real disappointment was nearer home. Try as she would, she could not remember exactly the source of certain characters and incidents. The chapter called "Eliza" was an example. She had begun vigorously: "The writer stated in her book that Eliza was a portrait drawn from life. The incident which brought the original to her notice may be simply narrated." But actually what had she been able to recall? Only the fact that many years ago in Kentucky she had been struck by the beauty of a quadroon girl and had been chilled to discover that she was "*owned by Mr. So-and-So.*" Harriet had had to confess, "This is all that the writer knows of that girl." Then there was the scene that impressed a good many people, Eliza's crossing the ice. Where had she heard the story? It was on the edge of her mind but she could not reach it. The best she could do was to tell her readers that "last spring" a Presbyterian clergyman in New York had told her all about it; he had had the story "from the very men that helped her up the bank." *A Key to Uncle Tom's Cabin* would do great good, of course: it was proof that Harriet Beecher Stowe had told the truth about slavery; once Christians knew the facts in their awfulness, they would certainly see to it that at the very least the Negro slave was given legal status. But it was disturbing to find that she could not remember the sources for a book she had written, even when Calvin helped her.

Why was it she could not remember? Was it that she was getting old and tired or was it her usual forgetfulness? But was she forgetful? People said so, but she could remember the smallest details of a conversation or a personality longer than anyone she knew. What people did not seem to understand was that she had her own way of seeing and listening; she looked dreamy-eyed and far away, but actually she was totally absorbed; she stopped thinking and what was before her filled her so that she never forgot it. No, she was not forgetful; she should have been able to remember everything about the characters and incidents in *Uncle Tom's Cabin*. It was almost as if she had not written the book. As a matter of fact, had she written it? Of course, she had used this and that book; of course, she had held the pen, but she had not thought out what her characters would be like or what they would do. She had known what they would do, and how had she known? The visions, of course, were the answer.

Take Uncle Tom's death. She had met the Reverend Mr. Henson at the home of her brother Edward in Boston. Among other things, Mr. Henson had told her (or had she read it later?) that his arm and both his shoulder blades had been broken in a completely unprovoked attack by a man named Bryce Litton. She had been horrified to think that such brutal treatment had befallen a devout and patient servant of Christ. But she had not gone home and written out Uncle Tom's death. That chapter had been written in Andover. She could remember it all vividly. Calvin had accepted a call to Andover Theological Seminary (a far better appointment than the professorship at Bowdoin), and they had gone to see about the Stone Cabin. They had been busy all morning consulting with an architect (there had been a thousand matters to consider), and after an early lunch they had gone to their room in a boardinghouse to rest. Calvin had thrown himself on the bed and she had been about to lie down on the lounge when suddenly Uncle Tom's death arose before her. She had sat down and written nine pages of foolscap without pausing except to dip her pen. When Calvin awoke and she read him the chapter, his sobs had shaken the bed on which he lay; he had told her no revision was necessary; he had folded the pages and sent them off immediately to her publisher.

That was the way *Uncle Tom's Cabin* was written. Harriet told her friend Mrs. John T. Howard about it one night in Hartford in the 1850's. Mrs. Howard had gone to bed; Harriet sat on the floor brushing her hair. She was thinking how foolish her brother Edward was to fear that all the praise and notoriety from *Uncle Tom's Cabin* would induce pride and vanity and harm her Christian character. As she told Mrs. Howard, "Dear soul, he need not be troubled. He doesn't know that I did not write that book." Mrs. Howard was surprised to learn that the whole book had come to Harriet in a series of visions, that she had merely written down what she saw. But Harriet felt she must speak the truth about her extraordinary experience. The real author of *Uncle Tom's Cabin* was God, who had sent the visions and had given her the skill to put them in words.

As the years passed, Harriet returned again and again in her thinking to the religious sources of her book. As she searched her memory for further details of the composition, she began to remember that, contrary, to her earlier accounts, the book had actually begun at the communion table in Brunswick, Maine. In "The Author's Introduction" to the 1878 edition of *Uncle Tom's Cabin* she wrote: "The first part of the book ever committed to writing was the death of Uncle Tom. This scene presented itself almost as a tangible vision to her mind while sitting at the communion-table in the little church in Brunswick. She was perfectly overcome by it, and could scarcely restrain the convulsion of tears and sobbings that shook her frame. She hastened home and wrote it, and her husband being away she read it to her two sons of ten and twelve years of age." Mrs. Howard reminded Harriet that she had told a very different story long ago in Hartford; there was serious inconsistency. Harriet replied: "No . . . both are true, for I had entirely forgotten that I had ever written that sketch, and I suppose that I had unconsciously woven it in with the other." The explanation seems to have satisfied Mrs. Howard, but it is not clear which sketch Harriet wove with what. Worse yet, as Annie Fields pointed out, Calvin did not accept the appointment at Andover until after *Uncle Tom's Cabin* was published; none of Harriet's book was written in an Andover boarding-house, at least none under the circumstances she remembered.

It may seem that this attempt to reconstruct Harriet's increasing comprehension of the genesis of *Uncle Tom's Cabin* has turned out to be the reconstruction of her own utter incomprehension as to how it was written. It must be granted that she was confused, but certainly she was trying to explain an overwhelming experience, not to propound a hoax such as Poe's fraudulent account of writing "The Raven," and some truths start up dimly in the mist. *Uncle Tom's Cabin* was not written as a consciously calculated work of propaganda; rather it came to Harriet, as works of literature usually occur to their authors, as vision seemingly imposed from without. Harriet's insistence that God, not she, was the author we may be tempted to dismiss as mere pious declaration. Why, we may be inclined to ask, did she not simply say that she was inspired and let it go at that? Here I think we verge on a serious error. Harriet's insistence on the religious origin of her famous novel actually constitutes a major clue. This, however, we can only understand if we examine in detail her experience, particularly her religious experience, from the early years of her marriage to the writing of *Uncle Tom's Cabin* in 1851-1852.

III

Cincinnati was not a cheerful place in the 1830's and 1840's for anyone with a lively imagination. In 1836 the riffraff wrecked the press of James Birney, printer of the antislavery *The Philanthropist,* and swept on to pull down the houses of respectable Negroes. In 1840 a mob, incited by proslavery elements, attacked the Negro quarters with a cannon. Houses were set afire; Negroes killed and their bodies thrown in the street; Negro women raped; children in the confusion kidnaped and hurried off into slavery. Harriet could see the fires and hear the shouts and cries from her home on the brow of a hill. Later, Negro families beginning the long trek to Canada passed her front door. The sight must have reminded her that, the year before, Calvin and Henry Ward Beecher had rescued her colored servant from illegal capture.

Such a nightmarish world made it difficult for Harriet to keep her resolve to live a life of outward circumstances rather than inward probing. Everything drove her deeper into herself. How could she reconcile the horrors befalling the Negro with her Uncle Samuel Foote's motto for her (translated from a Venetian sundial) "I will count only sunny hours"? The assumption of the comic mask of Lyman and Calvin became more and more difficult. The depression of 1837 brought an end to the Semi-Colon Club, and Calvin's rapidly decreasing salary and rapidly increasing family made it necessary for her to grind out conventional sketches at so much per page for periodicals. Harriet began to remember the moods and problems of her adolescence.

During the summer of 1825, when she was fourteen, she had heard her father preach a "frame sermon" on the text "Behold, I call you no longer servants, but friends." She had been deeply moved. Walking home, she had felt "as if nature herself were hushing her breath to hear the music of heaven." She had gone to Lyman's study and told him: "Father, I have given myself to Jesus, and He has taken me." Lyman had looked on her with great gentleness, held her silently to his heart, wept hot tears on her childish head, and declared: "Then has a new flower blossomed in the kingdom this day." It had seemed a moment of Puritan loveliness that would expand into a life of calm faith. But Harriet's sister Catherine had had sharper eyes than their father: she had known from her own difficulties that conversion could not be so easy a matter. When Harriet began to attend the Female Seminary at Hartford, Catherine urged her to take her case to the pastor of the First Church. His investigations uncovered the depressing truth that Harriet was actually unregenerate. By 1827, when she was in Boston with her father, Harriet was crying and groaning till midnight and wishing she could die young. But she did not dare burden her father with her troubles; she knew the deep consolation he took in the erroneous conclusion that she was among the elect; then too he had passed on her case once; it would be ungracious to show him he was wrong. Harriet had gone on in her thinking until she had reached the very center of the Calvinistic web in regard to sin and free will: "The case seems to me exactly as if I had been brought into the world with such a thirst for ardent spirits that there was just a possibility, though no hope, that I should resist, and then my eternal happiness made dependent on my being temperate."

The dark inner world of such thoughts might be frightening but it was more solid, so Harriet doubtless came to feel, than the mirage of happiness that had swum before her eyes when she wrote Georgianna May in 1832 of her plan to live externally. One simply could not live deeply and miss perplexity. In the Cincinnati years Harriet's brother Charles was led into hopeless fatalism by Jonathan Edwards' *A Careful and Strict Enquiry into . . . Freedom of Will.* Harriet shared the burden of his difficulties. Then in 1843, another brother, George, met death when his double-barreled shotgun exploded as he was driving birds out of the orchard. On June 2, 1845, she wrote her brother Thomas: "The sudden death of George shook my whole soul like an earthquake; and as in an earthquake we know not where the ground may open next, so I felt an indistinct terror as if father, brothers, husband, any or all, might be just about to sink." But she knew what the trouble was; it had been clear in Hartford and Boston. She was unwilling to submit to God's will. But yet, as she asked Thomas, "When you have demonstrated that it is a deranged and unsubdued *will* that is the disease, are you any nearer the remedy?" To her, it was doubtful. She knew that she loved Christ with devotion and lived "what might in Christian courtesy be called a religious life," but the death of George had shown her that her trust was partial, superficial.

The winter after George's death she felt haunted by care that drank her life blood; she groaned in spirit, longed and prayed for the ability to submit; but her every effort seemed to break like a wave upon a rock. Her troubles were now far more agonizing than any she had known in adolescence. She concluded that circumstances were against her; the pressure of outward care stood in her way; God must remove her difficulties. But she could not satisfy herself with excuses. Again and again, she sought to make her will identical with that of God. Finally, in the winter of 1844-1845 when despair seemed final, the long-expected help arrived: "*All* changed. Whereas once my heart ran with a strong current to the world, now it runs with a current the other way. . . . The will of Christ seems to me the steady pulse of my being. . . . Skeptical doubt cannot exist. I seem to see the full blaze of the Shekinah everywhere. I am calm, but full—everywhere and in all things instructed, and I find I can do all things through Christ."

But her faith exceeded her performance. She wrote Calvin (he was frequently absent from Cincinnati during these years): "I am sick of the smell of sour milk, and sour meat, and sour everything, and then the clothes *will* not dry, and no wet thing does, and everything smells mouldy; and altogether I feel as if I never wanted to eat again. . . . As to my health . . . I am bad enough and daily growing worse. . . . I suffer with sensible distress in the brain, as I have done more or less since my sickness last winter, a distress which some days takes from me all power of planning or executing anything." Still there was a new light that permeated the darkness. She knew no real evil could befall her; she feared nothing for the future because "God, the mighty God, is mine, of that I am sure, and I know He knows that though flesh and heart fail, I am all the while desiring and trying for his will alone." In her nervous and physical exhaustion, however, she needed to get away for a rest. As for the money, God, of course, would provide that. Here Harriet's faith was not in error. The necessary funds were found and from May, 1846, to March, 1847, she lived at Brattleboro, Vermont, taking a water cure and outdoor exercise, summer and winter. Catherine accompanied her.

The interval in Vermont is best described as the moment of calm before crisis in Harriet's spiritual history. Six months after her return, her eyesight began to fail and she found herself in what she called a strange state. After the birth of her sixth child, Samuel Charles, in 1848, she experienced a temporary improvement, but soon she was so burdened with cares, so she wrote Georgianna May, as to be drained "dry of all capacity of thought, feeling, memory, or emotion." Then, in this fearfully weakened state, when her baby was only a year old, she was forced to face alone (Calvin was again in the East) the horrifying spectacle of Asiatic cholera. Americans in 1849 had little more understanding of the operations of plague than that vouchsafed the primitive Greeks in the first book of the *Iliad* as they encountered the invisible arrows of disease shot by Apollo from a hill above Troy. Fires of soft coal burned on every Cincinnati street corner to neutralize the miasma. Through the clouds of suffocating smoke rolled hearse after hearse (there were a hundred and twenty burials in one day) interrupted from time to time by bands of drunken men and women roaming the streets determined on one last fling. In the midst of these terrors, Harriet watched the cholera as it stalked her own household.

The first victim was Aunt Frankie, her colored laundress; Harriet helped make her shroud and followed her body to the grave. Then the family dog was seized with fits and died horribly in a half hour. Meanwhile little Charley Stowe had been taken ill. Dr. Pulte, to whom Harriet carried her child, thought his case might result in "dropsy on the brain." Following her doctor's advice, Harriet put Charley "into a wet sheet, and kept him there until he was in a profuse perspiration." Momentarily, he seemed to recover, but a week after Aunt Frankie's death, it was clear that Charley had contracted cholera and would die. When after watching her baby writhe in agony for four days, and after praying that he might die soon, Harriet sought to formulate advice for herself and Calvin, she wrote: "Bear up. Let us not faint when we are rebuked of Him."

To a modern mind, this may seem abysmal superstition and one more proof that Puritanism was a benighted faith. But that would be to interpret Harriet's letter and her brand of Calvinism superficially. The Puritan made a double reading of disease as of all other events. Cotton Mather urged inoculation for smallpox; Jonathan Edwards died from an unsuccessful inoculation during the smallpox epidemic of 1758. On one plane, disease was disease to the Puritan and was to be fought with whatever weapons intelligence and scientific investigation could provide. On the more profound plane, however, disease, like all other matters, was a manifestation of God's ways to men. Thus when Sarah Pierrepont Edwards learned the death of her husband, she passed over the scientific aspects and made the traditional response: "A holy and good God has covered us with a dark cloud. O that we may kiss the rod and lay our hands on our mouths! The Lord has done it."

Like Mrs. Edwards, Harriet in her reaction to her child's death was trying to kiss the rod. As a Puritan, she regarded every event as somehow a part of the divine plan, and as a Puritan, she felt the obligation insisted on in her faith that man must convert even his losses into the furthering of the Kingdom. But the obligation was an almost unbearable one for her even though she believed she had made her will identical with divine will four years earlier. Still, as she wrote Mrs. Follen in 1853: "It was at his [Charley Stowe's] dying bed and at his grave that I learned what a poor slave mother may feel when her child is torn away from her. In those depths of sorrow which seemed to me immeasurable, it was my only prayer to God that such anguish might not be suffered in vain. There were circumstances about his death of such peculiar bitterness, of what seemed almost cruel suffering, that I felt that I could never be consoled for it, unless this crushing of my own heart might enable me to work out some great good to others. . . . I allude to this here because I have often felt that much that is in that book ('Uncle Tom') had its root in the awful scenes and bitter sorrows of that summer."

Harriet's last sentence furnishes the final clue to the genesis of *Uncle Tom's Cabin* and her insistence that God wrote it. In the arch of her faith, every stone supported every other stone. If she could not transmute grief into high usefulness, Charley had died in vain, and if he had died in vain, an innocent child had been a purposeless sacrifice and, quite as awful, his mother had deluded herself in the belief that "I am calm, but full—everywhere and in all things instructed, and find I can do all things through Christ." But it must be emphasized that such a line of reasoning, if we may call it that, is only a loose approximation of what Harriet felt. If she had reasoned matters out, she never would have written *Uncle Tom's Cabin:* works of imagination do not take their rise from reasoned conclusions. It was crucial that she did not give logical formulation to her feelings concerning her son's death but allowed them to sink almost out of consciousness in the deep places of her mind and heart. There in the half-hidden, dreaming underself those feelings could begin to grow into patterns of outrage in which the Negro mother again and again was separated from her child and in which the Negro saint was forced to submit to every indignity. It is very doubtful that unconsciously Harriet was beginning to shape materials for a book. The underself is not prophetic in that fashion. Rather the patterns of nightmare and sentiment were obsessions quite naturally accompanying Harriet's frustration and fear. Those dream sequences forming in her mind might under other circumstances have led to some impulsive act of martyrdom, the half-mad hurling of herself into the cruel machinery of slavery to block its operation. The fact that the visions eventuated in a book rather than in action was an accident of history.

The storm dislodging the images rooted in the depths of her mind like sea plants in the floor of the ocean was the Fugitive Slave Law of 1850. Fearfully dismayed by this legislation, which seemed to sound the ultimate doom of the Negro in its denial of jury trial for escaping slaves and its imposition of heavy penalties for those assisting their flight, Harriet visited her brother Edward in Boston. Edward Beecher had been a friend and supporter of Elijah P. Lovejoy, the abolitionist editor of the Presbyterian *Observer,* who was murdered by a proslavery mob at Alton, Illinois, in 1837. We scarcely need consult the record to be certain that in 1850 Edward's "soul was stirred to its very depths by the iniquitous law which was at this time being debated in Congress," and to know that "The most frequent theme of conversation while Mrs. Stowe was in Boston was this proposed law." Harriet returned to Brunswick profoundly disturbed in heart and mind but as yet the idea of writing a book apparently had not occurred to her.

The suggestion for a book came from Mrs. Edward Beecher. After the passage of the Fugitive Slave Law, Mrs. Beecher wrote letter after letter to Harriet reporting on the heart-rending tragedies befalling Negroes in Boston and the vicinity. In one of the letters, she spoke of her sense of futility; there was little that a woman could do, but as she continued, "Now, Hattie, if I could use a pen as you can, I would write something that would make this whole nation feel what an accursed thing slavery is." According to Charles Edward Stowe, when Harriet read this passage to the assembled family, she "rose up from her chair, crushing the letter in her hand, and with an expression on her face that stamped itself on the mind of her child, said: 'I will write something. I will if I live.' "

The dramatic coloring in this passage seems strong: Harriet was not given to dramatic gestures, but in essentials here was the beginning of *Uncle Tom's Cabin*. Presumably, she made the usual false starts as she planned her book. Soon, however, she must have made the surprising discovery that there was little need consciously to search for pictures or incidents. It may well be, as Charles Edward Stowe wrote, that the final inspiration came to his mother during the communion service at Brunswick in February, 1851, when the scene of Uncle Tom's death passed before her mind in such vividness that she could hardly keep from weeping aloud. In any case, I think Harriet told essential truth when she wrote in "The Author's Introduction" of 1878: "From that time [the writing of Uncle Tom's death] the story can less be said to have been composed by her than imposed upon her. Scenes, incidents, conversations rushed upon her with a vividness and importunity that would not be denied. The book insisted upon getting itself into being, and would take no denial."

What happened, we might say, was that the impulse from without in her sister-in-law's letter and the impulse from within in her religious commitment had finally battered down the psychic wall separating the dreaming underself with its store of images and situations and the conscious self intent on fighting the Fugitive Slave Law. So we may try to compass the experience with the inadequacies of metaphor. Actually, of course, we can no more compass it than Harriet could with her statement, "God wrote that book." In fact, her brief sentence comes about as close to summarizing the experience as more lengthy statements in more sophisticated language. Such an inner adventure, verging closely on the trance of the mystic, the vision of the prophet, may well be interpreted as the work of the power we conveniently call God.

IV

But how are we going to reconcile the basic genesis of *Uncle Tom's Cabin* in the hidden work of the unconscious, or of God, with the conclusion already reached that the book shows in all likelihood the influence of Mrs. Trollope, Samuel Richardson, Scott, and others? The answer, I believe, lies in the fact that the unconscious can work only in terms of images and imaginative patterns made available through the conscious mind. *Kubla Khan*, for example, would appear to be a work shaped completely in the unconscious of its author; but Lowes has been able to trace down almost all its images in works of travel; and the pattern of the poem is based, of course, on Coleridge's reading and his instinctive artistic preferences. All of this is obvious in its gloss on similar relations between Harriet's inspired shaping of her book and the literary patterns it assumes. But I have suggested that probably she was indebted to Defoe, in part, for the method of her book. How is it possible to reconcile a self-conscious use of sources with a welling of images from the underself?

Again it seems to me that the answer lies in reference to what we know of another author. In writing *Moby-Dick*, Melville apparently turned over every available book on whaling. In a large sense, he too was practicing Defoe's art in using the authentic source to buttress an imaginative conception; but in chapter after chapter of his great book we see clear evidence that in the fire of creation the researcher and the poet were essentially one. The fact, we might say, only remained fact for a moment: almost immediately it sank in the depths of Melville's imagination and became scarcely distinguishable from images that had been accumulating meaning since his whaling voyage of a decade before. Though Harriet's results lack the power and the magnificence of Melville's achievement in blending the literal and what Newton Arvin has called the "oneiric," something approaching the same assimilation went on as she read antislavery pamphlets and autobiographies and wove their information and misinformation into her book.

In *To Master, A Long Goodnight: The Story of Uncle Tom, A Historical Narrative* (1946), Brion Gysin implies that Harriet's Uncle Tom was essentially the Reverend Josiah Henson under a new name. In the 1850's Harriet would have welcomed that interpretation. In the desire to authenticate Uncle Tom, she wrote an introduction to *Truth Stranger than Fiction: Father Henson's Story of his own Life* (1858). But in assuming from her religious commitment the role, as she wrote, of "one who is forced by some awful oath to disclose in court some family disgrace," Harriet stood in an isolation comparable to that forced on Hawthorne, Melville, and other American writers. Like them, she felt the psychological need to objectify her situation by projecting herself symbolically into her writing. She took, therefore, only a few hints from *The Life of Josiah Henson* . . . (1849): the Uncle Tom who came to her in visions symbolized the perfect Christian she felt she had become through conversion. Point by point Uncle Tom offers a contrast to Henson.

Tom's conversion made him willing to be sold South so that the other Shelby slaves might be spared a similar fate; his faith made him risk loss of favor in trying to convert his kind but worldly master St. Clare; as a Christian Tom found it impossible to come to terms with Legree, who planned to make him his overseer. Henson's conversion may have been genuine but he began to feel ambition when the reputation for probity had earned him the position of overseer of Isaac Riley's Maryland plantation. Soon he was willing to go almost any lengths to consolidate his new relationship with his master. Henson was candid on this point in his autobiography: "For many years I was his factotum, and supplied him with all his means for all his purposes, whether they were good or bad. I had no reason to think highly of his moral character; but it was my duty to be faithful to him in the position in which he placed me; and I can boldly declare, before God and man, that I was so. I forgave him the causeless blows and injuries he had inflicted on me in childhood and youth, and was proud of the favor he now showed me, and of the character and reputation I had earned by strenuous and persevering efforts."

One of those strenuous efforts was rescuing his master from tavern brawls; it was his possible striking of Bryce Litton in such an encounter that brought down on him the beating Harriet remembered in creating Tom's death. Henson's most persevering effort was marked by both dishonesty and inhumanity. When in 1825 Isaac Riley faced bankruptcy, Henson obligingly helped to defraud the creditors by carrying his master's slaves off to brother Amos Riley in Kentucky. There were countless opportunities along the way for Henson and the other slaves to escape; at Cincinnati white men even offered assistance; but Henson would not sacrifice his position of authority. Later when he saw these same slaves on a plantation in the Deep South, he repented—a bit too late.

Such actions would have been impossible to Uncle Tom. When Legree ordered Tom to flog the slave-girl Lucy, he refused again and again. When Legree knocked him down and asked if he did not own him body and soul, Tom indignantly replied: "No! no! no! my soul ain't yours, Mas'r! You haven't bought it,—ye can't buy it!" Tom's talking back earned him a beating at the hands of the Negro henchmen, Sambo and Quimbo. Legree then told him to get on his knees and beg forgiveness for disobeying orders; Tom remained standing: "Mas'r Legree . . . I can't do it. I did only what I thought was right. I shall do just so again, if ever the time comes. I never will do a cruel thing come what may." Later, Tom would not listen to Legree's almost friendly attempt to win him from the Bible into co-operation: "Ye'd better hold to me. I'm somebody, and can do something." Tom was always loyal to his race. He refused to escape since he believed the other slaves needed his help; he would furnish Legree no details concerning the whereabouts of the runaways Cassy and Emmeline; his devotion finally cost him his life.

Harriet probably borrowed from Henson's story Tom's temptation to murder Legree; but it was an easy matter for her pious hero to resist; the temptation was not actually his; it came from Legree's former mistress, Cassy. Henson's temptation to murder Amos Riley, who was about to sell him in New Orleans, was self-originating. I think we are entitled to wonder whether his resisting and his subsequent caring for Riley in sickness were not piety tempered by prudence. In Louisiana, a Negro unable to account for himself would not long retain his freedom. Once back North, in any case, Henson escaped with his wife and children to Canada. There he founded a community for runaway slaves, not entirely in self-interest, but not entirely in selfless piety. To the last, Henson was something of the self-seeker and a good deal of the self-publicizer.

In the other main strand of the plot, the escape of Eliza and George Harris with their boy to Canada, Harriet seems at first glance to have used the character and career of Frederick Douglass to create a countersymbol to Uncle Tom: as Tom symbolizes Christian submission, George seems to symbolize democratic revolt. George, the skilled artisan exploited and humiliated by his sadistic master, parallels Douglass hired out as day laborer in the shipyards of Baltimore. George's statement to his former employer Mr. Wilson, encountered during his escape, "I'll fight for my liberty to the last breath I breathe," might easily have been made by Douglass. After his flight North in 1838, Douglass emerged as a paid agent of the Massachusetts Anti-Slavery Society, the editor of the Negro abolitionist paper *North Star,* and a violent figure in the slavery controversy. On one occasion, he not only refused to move into the Jim Crow section of a railroad train, but forcibly resisted the brakeman and conductor who tried to put him there. In Faneuil Hall, Boston, he told his fellow Negroes and abolitionists that there was no hope save force; matters must come to blood; the Negro could redeem himself only by fighting for his liberty. Harriet seems to echo Douglass when George and other escaping Negroes are attacked by slave-catchers. George declares: ". . . we stand as free, under God's sky, as you are; and, by the great God that made us, we'll fight for our liberty till we die"; George shows his determination by shooting, though not killing, Tom Loker, who seeks to take him prisoner.

The same religious compulsion, however, which led Harriet to transform Henson into a symbol of perfect piety operated in her fictionalizing of Douglass. When he reaches Canada, George does not become a militant abolitionist. Rather, he yields to the influence of Eliza, fights down "the hot and hasty

Saxon" in his nature, and urges his fellow Negroes "to bind closer to their hearts that sublime doctrine of love and forgiveness, through which alone they are to conquer." George's dream becomes the settlement of Liberia and the Christianizing of Africa as the first step in the spiritual restoration of the white man's civilization. In these views, George was, only a little less than Uncle Tom, a Christian hero through whom Harriet could project her own ideals and beliefs.

V

Harriet's projection of herself symbolically into her novel was by no means limited to her characterization of Uncle Tom and George Harris. Her compulsions, her obsessions, shaped *Uncle Tom's Cabin* in a far more decisive fashion and are, in fact, primarily responsible for her being able to reach the minds and hearts of men and women everywhere when from the standpoint of form, superficially considered, her book should have failed and failed badly. Consider, for a moment, the structure of the novel. In the first half of *Uncle Tom's Cabin*, Harriet alternated the story of George, Eliza, and little Harry with that of Uncle Tom. She here employed the device of contrasting pictures as a double argument against the Fugitive Slave Law. But in the second half of the novel she returned in only two chapters to her Negroes escaping north. Also when we analyze the flight of Eliza and Harry, we can almost agree with George L. Aiken when he added the bloodhounds in his stage version of *Uncle Tom's Cabin*. Eliza's fear that Harry will be captured inspires her to risk her life and his in crossing the ice-choked river; but almost immediately Senator and Mrs. Bird welcome her; soon she is placed in the capable hands of the Quakers. There is, of course, the subsequent pursuit by the slave-catchers, whom George battles at the rocks, but the slave-catchers are outnumbered and quickly outmaneuvered. In isolation from the rest of the book, the flight of Eliza, Harry, and George strikes us as tepid. We tend to conclude that the escape north is so ineffective in itself and so infrequently spliced with Tom's story that *Uncle Tom's Cabin* misses its intended contrast and anything approaching truly effective structure.

But the notable fact is that *Uncle Tom's Cabin* is an effective book. When we begin to inquire critically into our reactions to it, we discover that one of our most powerful impressions is apprehension for Eliza and her child. Though we should forget them in following Uncle Tom, actually their images remain on the edge of consciousness; we fear for the Harris family until, late in the book, they board the boat for Canada at Sandusky, Ohio, and the slave-catcher Marks, who has not penetrated their disguise, walks down the plank to the shore.

When we search the text for an explanation of our apprehension, we find a possible clue in the pictures created in the talk of the slave-catchers, Marks and Loker, with the slave-trader Haley while they wait for a boat to carry them over the Ohio in pursuit of Eliza. Loker, who is dressed in a coat of buffalo skin with the hair outward, listens to Haley's recital of his difficulties with surly attention; Marks, who is lithe and catlike, pokes his sharp nose and chin almost into Haley's face. Marks starts the talk by suggesting: "If we could get a breed of gals that didn't care, now, for their young uns . . . tell ye, I think 't would be 'bout the greatest mod'rn improvement I knows on." He remembers buying a gal once, "a tight, likely wench she was, too, and quite considerable smart," but she had a sickly child: ". . . it had a crooked back, or something or other; and I just gin 't away to a man that thought he'd take his chance raising on 't, being it didn't cost nothin',—but Lord, yer oughter seen how she went on." Marks sounds like a modern salesman discussing the vicissitudes of trade; Haley might be another salesman making the expected reference to his own experience. He, it turns out, has had a similar adventure. He got a gal traded off on him with a likely enough looking child, but the child was stone blind. Haley thought there was no harm in passing the child along and saying nothing: ". . . and I'd got him nicely swapped off for a keg o' whiskey; but come to get him away from the gal, she was jest like a tiger . . . what should she do but ups on a cotton-bale, like a cat, ketches a knife from one of the deck hands, and, I tell ye, she made all fly for a minnit, till she saw 't warn't no use; and she jest turns round, and pitches head first, young un and all, into the river,—went down plump, and never ris." Loker tells Marks and Haley they are shiftless. When he has a child to be sold, he walks up to the mother, puts his fist in her face, and tells her: "Look here, now, if you give me one word out of your head, I'll smash yer face in."

Our apprehension for Eliza and Harry, suggested by the talk of Harriet's unholy three, is also fed by an incident on *La Belle Rivière,* carrying Tom down the Ohio as a member of Haley's slave gang. At a small town in Kentucky, Haley buys Lucy and her child. Lucy has understood from her master that she is being hired out to a tavern in Louisville where her husband works. When Haley's bill of sale for her and her child is read by one of the passengers, Lucy says, "Then it's no account talking." She clasps her child tightly in her arms and gazes listlessly into the river. At Louisville, however, she puts her baby down and rushes to the rail for a possible glimpse of her husband. This is Haley's chance: he has sold her baby for forty-five dollars. Without a word to Lucy, he passes it to the new owner, who is soon lost in the crowd on the wharf. When she learns the truth from Haley, Lucy does not scream; she does not even cry; hers is the utter calm of despair. Haley tries to flatter her: "You're a smart wench, Lucy. . . . I mean to do well by ye, and get ye a nice place down river; and you'll soon get another husband,—such a likely gal as you." Uncle Tom is horrified; he talks to Lucy of a pitying Jesus and an eternal home. But Lucy is as deaf to his Christian comfort as to Haley's flattery. At midnight, she hurls herself silently into the river. Next day, Haley puts her down in his little account book under the head of losses.

We may fear for Eliza and her child through the rest of the book because of these initial impressions. When we first look into Tom's idyllic existence in the St. Clare household, we feel that there is nothing there which could remind us of Eliza. But soon, however, we discover that there are several

Negro characters who may call us back to her and Harry. Marie St. Clare's maid, Mammy, has been separated from her husband and children and longs for them. The little colored boy Dodo, whipped by Eva's cousin Henrique on the slightest provocation, may suggest what could befall Harry, were he captured by Marks. Possibly, in a half-conscious fashion, we are apprehensive for Eliza when we meet the old Negress Prue, who sells rolls and rusks to the St. Clares.

Prue's life has been a long torment from violence to her maternal affections; it is small wonder that she steals her master's money and gets drunk. As a young woman, she was used to breed children for the market and they were sold as soon as they were old enough. When she was bought by her present master, who was not a speculator, she believed that at last she was to rear one of her children. But again she was trapped by circumstance. When Prue's milk dried up from fever, her mistress insisted that she feed her baby what other people ate, and when its constant crying became a nuisance, her mistress forced Prue to put it in a little garret where one night it cried itself to death. Prue believes herself destined for hell; she is uninterested in Tom's vision of a heavenly home: "I'd rather go to torment and get away from Mas'r and Missie." From the woman who takes her place with the rolls and rusks a few days later, we learn Prue's end. In a whispered conversation with the Negro cook Dinah, the woman says: "Well, you musn't tell nobody. Prue, she got drunk again,—and they had her down cellar—and thar they left her all day,—and I hearn 'em saying that the *flies had got to her,—and she's dead!*" Southern readers pointed out that there were no cellars in New Orleans; but this is carping criticism. The announcement of Prue's death is highly dramatic in the bursts of understatement and the detail of the flies. We feel the imaginative validity of the scene, whatever the facts may have been concerning cellars.

After Augustine St. Clare's death, we have further instances of maternal woe that may make us fear for Eliza and Harry. At the slave warehouse where Simon Legree buys Tom, we see the young girl Emmeline separated from her mother. On the boat carrying Legree and his slaves down the Red River to his plantation, Emmeline talks with a mulatto woman sold so abruptly she did not have time to say goodbye to her husband and four children. At Legree's plantation, his discarded mistress, Cassy, tells Tom a long story of her anguish as a mother. Her first master, whom she loved, gambled his money away and was forced to sell her and their two children to his cousin, a melodramatic villain named Butler. At first Cassy yielded to Butler because of his threat to sell her children. Later, when he had sold both of her children, he kept her submissive by telling her that whether or not she saw their faces again depended on her being agreeable. But Cassy could not remain agreeable. One day as she walked past the slave warehouse, her little boy ran to her screaming and caught hold of her dress. Cassy pleaded with the men who dragged him off to be whipped, but they only laughed at her. She then begged Butler to buy Henry back. When Butler told her that Henry was getting his deserts, Cassy could stand no more. She grabbed a bowie knife from the table, stabbed Butler, and fainted.

Butler did not die. He sold Cassy during her ensuing illness to a slave-trading establishment where, as soon as her health returned, she was forced to make herself attractive to the men who smoked their cigars and debated her price while they looked her over. Captain Stuart finally bought Cassy. Again she was a mistress, but this time she did not wait for her child to be sold away; she murdered him with laudanum when he was two weeks old. Captain Stuart did not discover the murder, but his death from cholera set her again passing from hand to hand until she was bought by Legree. After so many troubles (too many, I think, to be convincing), it is a comfort to learn at the end of the book that Cassy is Eliza's mother and that mother and daughter are finally reunited in Canada.

Cassy's story, like Prue's, probably makes its contribution to our apprehension for Eliza and Harry. But when we discover that Simon Legree's villainy is attributed to the fact that he ran away from his mother as a young man and that he is haunted by visions of her and feels the soft twining of her hair around his fingers, we see, if we have not before, that Harriet was obsessed with the separation of mother and child. Lucy, Prue, and Cassy might be the work of artistry instinctively linking the story of Uncle Tom with that of George, Eliza, and Harry. Simon Legree is one instance too many. Looking back through the book, we find that Harriet dwelt on the theme of mothers separated from children in the lives of other white characters. In an early chapter Mrs. Bird selects certain of her dead child's clothes for Eliza, and Harriet editorializes: "And, oh, mother that reads this, has there never been in your house a drawer, or a closet, the opening of which has been to you like the opening again of a little grave? Ah, happy mother that you are, if it has not been so!" Mrs. Bird suffers a temporary collapse when she glimpses her dead son's aprons, stockings, shoes, and toys. Augustine St. Clare discusses his love for his mother at great length with his cousin Miss Ophelia; he suggests that he might have been "a saint, reformer, martyr" if he had not been separated from his mother at thirteen. Eva's dying, which seems unnecessarily to occupy so many pages since it has little to do with the slavery issue, is, of course, one more instance of the child torn from its parents.

It was anguish over the loss of her son, of course, rather than art which caused Harriet to make the separation of mother and child the *leitmotif* of *Uncle Tom's Cabin,* and this anguish aroused yet another, all but hidden in the depths of her mind. In writing of her mother in *The Autobiography of Lyman Beecher,* Harriet described Roxana Foote Beecher as a saintly influence even though she died when Harriet was between five and six. In concluding, she observed: "The passage in 'Uncle Tom,' where Augustine St. Clare describes his mother's influence, is a simple reproduction of this mother's influence as it has always been in her family." Probably we are also entitled to read something of Roxana's saintliness as well as Harriet's aspiration in St. Clare's daughter Eva. When we consider *The Minister's Wooing,* we will understand how deep was the spiritual bond between Harriet and her dead mother. In any case, Harriet's anguish over Charley Stowe and her lifelong sense of deprivation at the loss of her own mother gave intensity and unity to *Uncle Tom's Cabin*. Her reiteration of a crucial human predicament may hardly be noticed by the reader but it touches off profound human responses; it is the book's working at the deep places of the human personality that makes the reader feel that slavery is a personal tragedy.

VI

Personal anguish and religious conviction were thus the passions primarily responsible for the fact that *Uncle Tom's Cabin* "insisted upon getting itself into being and would take no denial." But we miss one of the most significant aspects of Harriet's first novel if we overlook its tendency to split into two books. Not only do we have a novel of religious concern and heartbreak, but also a novel of humorous and realistic perception. In "The Author's Introduction" of 1878, Harriet wrote: "Then she was convinced that the presentation of slavery alone, in its most dreadful forms, would be a picture of such unrelieved horror and darkness as nobody could be induced to look at. Of set purpose, she sought to light up the darkness by humorous and grotesque episodes, and the presentation of the milder and more amusing phases of slavery, for which her recollection of the never-failing wit and drollery of her former colored friends in Ohio gave her abundant material." Here undoubtedly is truth, but not, I believe, all the truth.

It seems significant to me that Miss Ophelia, Augustine, Dinah, and Topsy appear just before the death of Eva and that Haley and the Shelby Negroes, Sam and Andy, carry on their comedy in the opening chapters where Harriet agonizes over Eliza and Harry. The humorous-realistic chapters, in short, seem to accompany the chapters of heartbreak rather than the chapters, such as those devoted to Tom on Legree's plantation, where we find "the presentation of slavery . . . in its most dreadful forms." My conclusion is that the key to the realistic-humorous aspects of *Uncle Tom's Cabin* is less Harriet's "set purpose" than it is her participation in what I have called New England doubleness. Just as she assumed the comic mask of her father in escaping her untenable inner world in her first story, so she sought similar relief in her first novel. Here she was not unlike Hepzibah Pyncheon in Hawthorne's *The House of the Seven Gables.* Burdened with tragic news she must convey to her brother, Hepzibah saw the old handyman Uncle Venner from the window and "wished that he would pass yet more slowly, and befriend her shivering solitude a little longer. Anything that would take her out of the grievous present, and interpose human beings betwixt herself and what was nearest to her,—whatever would defer for an instant the inevitable errand on which she was bound,—all such impediments were welcome. Next to the lightest heart, the heaviest is apt to be most playful."

Harriet was not, however, superficially playful in the humorous-realistic novel she projected from time to time to defer the inevitable errand on which she was bound. The core of her comedy as of all significant comedy was clear-eyed awareness of social fact, evidenced succinctly in Augustine St. Clare's microcosm of the Sinclair-St. Clare family of Vermont and Louisiana:

What poor mean trash this whole business of human virtue is! A mere matter, for the most part, of latitude and longitude, and geographical position, acting with natural temperament. The greater part is nothing but an accident! Your father, for example, settles in Vermont, in a town where all are, in fact, free and equal; becomes a regular church-member and deacon, and in due time joins an Abolition society, and thinks us all little better than heathens. Yet he is, for all the world, in constitution and habit, a duplicate of my father. I can see it leaking out in fifty different ways,—just that same strong, overbearing, dominant spirit. You know very well how impossible it is to persuade some of the folks in your village that Squire Sinclair does not feel above them. The fact is, though he has fallen on democratic times, and embraced a democratic theory, he is to the heart an aristocrat, as much as my father, who ruled over five or six hundred slaves. . . .

Now, I know every word you are going to say. I do not say they *were* alike, in fact. One fell into a condition where everything acted against the natural tendency, and the other where everything acted for it; and so one turned out a pretty willful, stout, overbearing old democrat, and the other a willful, stout old despot. If both had owned plantations in Louisiana, they would have been as like as two bullets cast in the same mould.

It is natural for Augustine St. Clare to pierce to the social and moral realities in this fashion, for after his mother's death when he was thirteen, he was cared for by his Vermont cousins. Miss Ophelia herself taught him his catechism, mended his clothes, combed his hair, and showed him the path of duty. In the pages devoted to Miss Ophelia's departure for New Orleans to care for Eva, Harriet reconstructed that Vermont world with a humorous insight anticipating the genre pictures of her New England novels. The Sinclair home is a large farmhouse with a clean-swept, grassy yard, shaded by sugar maples; there is an air of order and stillness over all. There are no servants, but the usual Yankee "faculty" (that is, domestic efficiency) in mother and daughters is such that nothing is ever out of place and there is plenty of time for leisurely sewing every afternoon. This has been the home of Miss Ophelia for all her forty-five years, and she is an embodiment of its punctuality and strong sense of responsibility. She is "the absolute bond-slave of the 'ought.' " If she were certain that duty called her, she would walk "straight down into a well, or up to a loaded cannon's mouth." Her religious character wears a somewhat gloomy cast, however, because her sense of right is so high and makes so few concessions to human frailty that she can never satisfy herself.

When Augustine invites Miss Ophelia to come to New Orleans, in the name of duty, to care for little Eva, the Sinclair household is thrown into perplexity, indeed the whole village. Squire Sinclair takes down Morse's *Atlas,* from the bookcase with the glass doors, to find the exact latitude and longitude of New Orleans, and reads Flint's *Travels in the South and West* to learn the nature of the country. Mrs. Sinclair wonders anxiously "if Orleans wasn't an awful wicked place . . . that it seemed to her most equal to going to the Sandwich Islands, or anywhere among the heathen." The strongly abolitionist minister fears that Miss Ophelia's visit may encourage the Southerners to hold on to their slaves; the village doctor con-

tends on the contrary that Miss Ophelia should go as an am-
bassador of good will. The public mind is divided when the
Squire makes the extraordinary outlay of fifty dollars for his
daughter's going-away clothes; some feel the money should have
been sent to missionaries. There is a rumor that Miss Ophelia
has "one pocket-handkerchief with lace all around it,—it was
even added that it was worked in the corners; but this latter
point was never satisfactorily ascertained, and remains, in fact,
unsettled to this day."

Even more refreshing than this picture of the Vermont village is Harriet's portrayal of Augustine St. Clare and his tragi-
comic household in New Orleans. Some of the scenes on the
river-boat carrying Uncle Tom, Haley, Eva, Miss Ophelia, and
Augustine south are impressive (for example the suicide of
Lucy, to which I have already called attention), but toward
the end of the voyage Harriet seems to be flogging her invention
with no great success when suddenly Augustine erupts. There
would seem no other word for his vital and energetic entrance
into a world where Eva has recently been gliding around the
boat lifting the chains of slaves and then sighing woefully as
she glides on. There is nothing spiritually diaphanous about
Augustine. In his eyes, Harriet writes, "all was clear, bold,
and bright, but with a light wholly of this world: the beautifully cut mouth had a proud and somewhat sarcastic expression."

She makes good her description in Augustine's bargaining
with Haley for Uncle Tom, who has dived overboard and saved
Eva from drowning. Augustine's first question is "Well, now,
my good fellow, what's the damage, as they say in Kentucky;
in short, what's to be paid out for this business? How much
are you going to cheat me, now? Out with it!" In the rest
of the conversation, he sustains this note of mocking banter.
When Haley points up Tom's smartness, Augustine wants him
to take off a couple of hundred for it since smart fellows are
inclined to run off. When he looks over Haley's bill of sale
from Mr. Shelby, Augustine remarks: "A gentlemanly hand
. . . and well spelt, too," and launches into ironic comments on
the probable truth that Tom has had a deeply religious master

and mistress. He then asks Haley how much value he puts on religion in the slaves he sells. Haley feels the jab but he says there is still sense in the emphasis on religion. Switching the ironic play, Augustine now wants to know if Haley can guarantee that he possesses piety in owning Uncle Tom, and he offers to pay a little extra for it. Poor Haley! His dim mind cannot keep up with the pace of such thinking: "Wal, raily, I can't do that. . . . I'm a thinkin' that every man'll have to hang on his own hook, in them ar quarters." Augustine will not give up the probing; he asks Haley how much he supposes he would bring: "Say so much for the shape of my head, so much for a high forehead, so much for arms, and hands, and legs, and then so much for education, learning, talent, honesty, religion! Bless me! there would be small charge on that last, I'm thinking."

Having given us this vivid introduction, Harriet then explains what makes Augustine Augustine. In New England, he had fallen passionately in love with and become engaged to a high-minded and beautiful woman. Through the machinations of her guardian, however, his letters were returned and he was given the impression that she was going to marry someone else. In despair, Augustine threw himself into the whirl of Southern society, and married the reigning belle, Marie Benoir, only to discover on his honeymoon the sad truth that his first fiancée still loved him, and the unpleasant truth that his wife "consisted of a fine figure, a pair of splendid eyes, and a hundred thousand dollars; and none of these items were precisely the ones to minister to a mind diseased."

In Eva's mother, Marie St. Clare, Harriet created a neurotic and hypochondriac who more often convinces us of her reality than some critics seem willing to grant. Of course, she is not brought to life with the vigor Harriet displayed in realizing Augustine; but in the complaints concerning her husband to Miss Ophelia and in her jealousy of Eva, Marie is less a conventional villainess than a surprising foreshadowing of the emotionally repressed women of modern fiction. As in the portrayal of other characters in *Uncle Tom's Cabin*, Harriet's imagination seems to have outrun her conscious understanding. According to *A Key to Uncle Tom's Cabin,* Marie was meant to illustrate the type of.woman North and South who exploited her servants; in the North, "She likes to get hold of foreign servants, who have not yet learned our ways, who are used to working for low wages, and who will be satisfied with almost anything." Undeniably, Marie does illustrate such a tendency, but she illustrates much more. The basis for her neurosis is symbolized by the fact that Augustine carries "upon his bosom a small, plain miniature-case, opening with a spring. It was the miniature of a noble and beautiful face; and on the reverse, under a crystal, a lock of dark hair." Marie's hypochondria, her petulance, are all strategies to win Augustine from the love of his first fiancée. Her keeping her Negro maid Mammy separated from her husband and children and late in the story her sending the quadroon Rosa off to receive fifteen lashes at a whipping establishment are attempts to punish life for having deprived her of the love and devotion she craves. The spring of her actions is jealousy.

We can understand Marie's jealousy when we look into the sensuous and joyous Negro world of the backhalls at the St. Clares'. St. Clare's valet, Adolph, and the quadroon maids, Rosa and Jane, open the doors on this society in their talk after old drunken Prue has left the kitchen:

"I think such low creatures ought not to be allowed to go round to genteel families," said Miss Jane. "What do you think, Mr. St. Clare?" she said, coquettishly tossing her head at Adolph.

.   .   .   .

"I'm certainly of your opinion, Miss Benoir," said Adolph.

.   .   .   .

"Pray, Miss Benoir, may I be allowed to ask if those drops are for the ball, to-morrow night? They are certainly bewitching!"

"I wonder, now, Mr. St. Clare, what the impudence of you men will come to!" said Jane, tossing her pretty head till the ear-drops twinkled again. "I shan't dance with you for a whole evening if you go to asking me any more questions."

"Oh, you couldn't be so cruel, now! I was just dying to know whether you would appear in your pink tarlatan," said Adolph.

"What is it?" said Rosa, a bright piquant little quadroon, who came skipping downstairs at this moment.

"Why, Mr. St. Clare is so impudent!"

"On my honor," said Adolph, "I'll leave it to Miss Rosa, now."

"I know he's always a saucy creature," said Rosa, poising herself on one of her little feet, and looking maliciously at Adolph. "He's always getting me so angry with him."

"Oh, ladies, ladies, you will certainly break my heart, between you," said Adolph. "I shall be found dead in my bed, some morning, and you'll have it to answer for."

"Do hear the horrid creature talk!" said both ladies, laughing immoderately.

Miss Ophelia's experience with Topsy, who is a black rascal and thief until she bleaches into a New England Calvinist under the influence of Eva, constitutes one of the most amusing aspects of *Uncle Tom's Cabin,* but Harriet spoiled the fun at moments by underlining all too heavily Miss Ophelia's racial intolerance. Most modern readers will be more entertained by Miss Ophelia's attempt to bring order into Dinah's kitchen. Dinah is a fascinating human magpie. She collects old rags, shoes, and haircombs in the kitchen drawers, keeps her hair grease in one of the best saucers, wraps the meat in a fine damask table cloth, stacks the dirty dishes for days, and likes, pipe in mouth, to prepare her excellent dinners on the floor, with help from the pickaninnies who can be drafted into service. Miss Ophelia shocks Dinah by going to work herself in the kitchen, washing, wiping, arranging dishes in order: "Lor, now! Miss Phelia; dat ar ain't no way for ladies to do. I never did see ladies doin' no sich; my old Missis nor Miss Marie never did, and I don't see no kinder need on 't." When Dinah is alone with the other Negroes, she tells them "Lor, now! if dat ar de way dem northern ladies do, dey ain't ladies, nohow. . . . I has things as straight as anybody, when my clarin' up time comes; but I don't want ladies round, a-henderin' and getting my things all where I can't find 'em."

Quite in keeping with the realistic-humorous novel dealing with the Sinclair-St. Clare family are certain characters the slave trader Haley encounters at the start of the book. Mr. Shelby's Sam, who knows, he says, which side his bread is buttered on, is a Negro as fully and humorously realized as

Dinah. His immorality and wit he has learned from watching white men at political rallies. He has concluded that the essence of political wisdom is that "It's an ill wind that blows nowhar— that's a fact." The central tragedies of the book, the selling away of Uncle Tom and the misfortunes of George and Eliza, strike him as opportunities. Tom's departure will open a place at the top for a trusted slave; Eliza's escape furnishes the chance to curry favor with Mr. Shelby by helping in the pursuit, and favor with Mrs. Shelby by making sure that Eliza is not caught. All readers of *Uncle Tom's Cabin* will recall the confusion with the horses and Sam's artful befuddling of Haley so that he takes the wrong road. Sam shows equal craft in his relations with the Negroes, approaching Aunt Chloe, Uncle Tom's wife and the Shelby cook, in a spirit of humility, and at an opposite extreme, his companion, Andy, in a spirit of vast superiority. When the Negroes accuse Sam of inconsistency in holding in the morning that he will catch Eliza for Mr. Shelby and in the evening taking credit for having prevented her capture, he lets go with this explanation:

"Dis yer matter 'bout persistence, feller niggers . . . dis yer 'sistency's a thing that ain't seed into very clar by most anybody. Now, yer see, when a feller stands up for a thing one day and night, de contrar de next, folks ses (and nat'rally enough dey ses), why he ain't persistent—Hand me dat ar bit o' corncake, Andy. But let's look inter it. I hope de gen'l'men and der fair sex will scuse my usin' an or'nary sort o' 'parison. Here, I'm a-tryin' to get top o' der hay. Wal, I puts my larder dis yer side—'t ain't no go; den, 'cause I don't try dere no more, but puts my larder right de contrar side, ain't I persistent? I'm persistent in wantin' to get up which ary side my larder is; don't you see, all on yer?"

In his brief appearance, Sam catches the modern imagination far more easily than Uncle Tom. What a book *Uncle Tom's Cabin* could have been if Harriet had skipped her pious characters, made the Shelbys cousins of the Sinclairs and St. Clares and sent Sam to Louisiana or New England in Tom's place! In either humorous-realistic world, Sam, we feel, would have prospered, but certainly on his way we would want him to meet

Marks, the slave catcher, who, in one speech at least, seems a long lost brother of the King or Duke in *Huckleberry Finn:*

"Ye see," said Marks to Haley, stirring his punch as he did so, "ye see, we has justices convenient at all p'ints along shore, that does up any little jobs in our line quite reasonable. Tom, he does the knockin' down and that ar; and I come in all dressed up,—shining boots,—everything first chop, when the swearin' 's to be done. You oughter see, now," said Marks in a glow of professional pride, "how I can tone it off. One day I'm Mr. Twickem, from New Orleans; 'nother day, I'm just come from my plantation on Pearl River, where I works seven hundred niggers; then, again, I come out a distant relation of Henry Clay, or some old cock in Kentuck. Talents is different, you know. Now, Tom's a roarer when there's any thumping or fighting to be done; but at lying he ain't good, Tom ain't,—ye see it don't come natural to him; but, Lord, if thar's a feller in the country that can swear to anything and everything, and put in all the circumstances and flourishes with a longer face, and carry 't through better'n I can, why, I'd like to see him, that's all! I b'lieve my heart, I could get along and snake through, even if justices were more particular than they is. Sometimes I rather wish they was more particular; 't would be a heap more relishin' if they was,—more fun, yer know."

With such a speech ringing in our ears, we can understand why the English novelist Charles Kingsley found *Uncle Tom's Cabin* "a really healthy indigenous growth, 'autochthones,' free from all second and third hand Germanisms and Italianisms, and all other unrealisms." But, of course, Kingsley went too far. *Uncle Tom's Cabin* is not free of "unrealisms." What we should say is that it is partly literary-sentimental-pious, partly indigenous. Sensing the contrast, we may conclude that Harriet's novel was unconsciously a battle between piety and a talent approaching Mark Twain's for humorous-realistic perception. Like critics of a generation ago, we may be tempted into pronouncements concerning the baneful influence of Puritanism on the arts in America. But when we are so tempted, we should remember that it was Puritanism primarily which generated *Uncle Tom's Cabin* and that if Harriet had felt less intensely those spiritual ardors which may weary us, she never would have sought relief in the creation of the Sinclairs-St.

Clares, Dinah, Sam, and Marks. Most of all, *Uncle Tom's Cabin* would have lacked the quality noted by Edmund Wilson: "The eruptive effect of the book, as of a throbbing and breathing creation suddenly turned loose on the world. . . ."

VII

As I have suggested, the core of Harriet's comedy was clear-eyed awareness of social fact, but we have hardly begun to appreciate the extraordinary range of her first novel if we limit ourselves to her social insights stated in terms of character and situation. Through Augustine St. Clare's conversations with Miss Ophelia and his brother Alfred, Harriet made an analysis of slavery so bold, so uncompromising, so impressive that some of her Southern contemporaries, notably William J. Grayson in *The Hireling and the Slave* (1854 and 1856), felt compelled to answer her indictment in vitriolic language. There is little in the early chapters of *Uncle Tom's Cabin* to suggest the radical analysis to follow. Until we reach the humorous-realistic novel of the Sinclairs-St. Clares, Harriet has discussed and dramatized the outrage of slavery on a plane quite in keeping with the piety and humanity of a simple New England woman. If we were asked to find her spokesman in the first part of the book, we might well select Mrs. Bird. When her senator husband argues in favor of the Fugitive Slave Law, she asserts: "Now, John, I don't know anything about politics, but I can read my Bible; and there I see that I must feed the hungry, clothe the naked, and comfort the desolate; and that Bible I mean to follow." This view, of course, is in perfect harmony with George's conversion to Christian pacificism and with Uncle Tom's triumphantly Christian death. But in terms of Augustine's insights, we are not justified simply in equating Mrs. Bird with Harriet. Again, we must resort to the concept of New England doubleness. Apparently, the same compulsion which led Harriet to escape her inwardness in the creation of a vigorously humorous and realistic world also led her to analyze slavery with sharp intelligence.

How radical and how perceptive Harriet was in this aspect of *Uncle Tom's Cabin* has usually gone unnoticed. What most critics have underlined is her lack of provincialism, her recognition that the human qualities developed by the slave system were less a matter of personal virtue than of economics and geography. But Augustine's statement that Squire Sinclair would be indistinguishable from Mr. St. Clare if both owned plantations in Louisiana is only one of her radical insights and easily explainable when we remember that as Puritan she had been trained all her life in the direction of moral realism. We begin to run into the true surprises when we listen to Augustine on the church and slavery and particularly on the place of slavery in a world-wide pattern of economic exploitation.

From Augustine's remarks, we might suppose that he was once a reader of the *Boston Quarterly Review,* edited by that New England radical of radicals, Orestes A. Brownson, and that he had been particularly impressed by the issues for July and October, 1840. Augustine, at least, is not very far from the essay Brownson contributed to those issues under the title "The Laboring Classes." Brownson's belief, for example, that "The evils of slavery do not result from the personal characters of slave masters. They are inseparable from the system, let who will be masters," is basic in Augustine's analysis. He tells Miss Ophelia: "Talk of the *abuses* of slavery! Humbug! The *thing itself* is the essence of all abuse. And the only reason why the land don't sink under it, like Sodom and Gomorrah, is because it is *used* in a way infinitely better than it is. For pity's sake, for shame's sake, because we are men born of women, and not savage beasts, many of us do not, and dare not,—we would *scorn* to use the full power which our savage laws put into our hands."

Brownson was convinced that the cause of the inequality of conditions lay in the official distortions of religion seeking to make God congruent with Mammon. In commenting on a proslavery sermon Marie has heard, Augustine comes to approximately the same conclusion. In indignation he cries, "Religion!

. . . Religion! Is what you hear at church religion? Is that which can bend and turn, and descend and ascend, to fit every crooked phase of selfish, worldly society, religion?" Later, he notes the intimate relation between the preaching of the church and economics: "Well . . . suppose that something should bring down the price of cotton once and forever, and make the whole slave property a drug in the market, don't you think we should soon have another version of the Scripture doctrine? What a flood of light would pour into the church all at once, and how immediately it would be discovered that everything in the Bible and reason went the other way!"

For Brownson, the only solution to economic exploitation was the abolishing of hereditary property, which could never be achieved by peaceful means since the status quo was maintained by armed soldiery and the conservatives would never voluntarily relinquish their exclusive privileges. A glance at Europe, Asia, Africa, and even our own country convinced him that war between the classes, between the people and their masters, on a world-wide scale was inevitable. Such an interpretation of history, so clearly anticipating by eight years the *Communist Manifesto* of Marx and Engels, we would hardly expect to find approximated in a novel by the daughter of that Federalist-Calvinist, Lyman Beecher. But in the talk of Augustine St. Clare, Harriet voiced virtually the same perception and prophecy.

Putting his head in Miss Ophelia's lap and asking her to stay him with flagons and comfort him with apples in the form of a nearby basket of oranges, Augustine begins with a mockery of the *Declaration of Independence:* "When, in the course of human events, it becomes necessary for a fellow to hold two or three dozen of his fellow-worms in captivity, a decent regard to the opinions of society requires—" But he is only teasing his Vermont cousin and collecting his thoughts. Soon he is deeply serious. There can be, he asserts, only one opinion concerning the slave system: "Planters, who have money to make by it,—clergymen, who have planters to please,—politicians, who want to rule by it,—may warp and bend language and ethics to a degree that shall astonish the world at their ingenuity . . . but, after all, neither they nor the world believe in it one particle the more. . . . Strip it of all its ornament, run it down to the root and nucleus of the whole and what is it? Why, because my brother Quashy is ignorant and weak, and I am intelligent and strong,—because I know how, and *can* do it,—therefore, I may steal all he has, keep it, and give him only such and so much as suits my fancy." Augustine is not impressed by the argument that the lot of the English laborer is a vast improvement over the lot of the American slave: "He is as much at the will of his employer as if he were sold to him. The slave-owner can whip his refractory slave to death,—the capitalist can starve him to death. As to family security, it is hard to say which is the worse,—to have one's children sold, or see them starve to death at home." Augustine is hardly an orthodox nineteenth-century capitalist. He gave up the plantation he shared with his brother Alfred, after all manner of improvements, because "The fact was, it was, after all, the THING that I hated,—the using these men and women, the perpetuation of all this ignorance, brutality, and vice,—just to make money for me!"

With such views, it is not surprising that he should sound the apocalyptic Marxian note: "One thing is certain,—that there is a mustering among the masses, the world over; and there is a *dies irae* coming on, sooner or later. The same thing is working in Europe, in England, and in this country." This *dies irae* Augustine returns to later in conversation with his feudally Southern brother, Alfred. When Alfred asserts that the lower classes will never get the upper hand, Augustine remarks ironically: "That's right . . . put on the steam, fasten down the escape-valve, and sit on it, and see where you'll land." Alfred says he is not afraid to sit on the escape valve "as long as the boilers are strong and the machinery works well." With awful earnestness, Augustine tells him: "I tell you . . . if there is anything that is revealed with the strength of divine law in our times, it is that the masses are to rise, and the under class become the upper one."

Like Brownson, Harriet, of course, was impetuous and inaccurate, immediately at least, in prophesying war between the upper and lower classes and the rule of the proletariat. But the extraordinary element in Brownson's essay and in *Uncle Tom's Cabin* is not the prophecy but the recognition of economic exploitation and class conflict and their frightening inconsistency with our officially acknowledged Christian democracy. Those who have taken their measure of Harriet and her first novel from Eva's mechanical ascension into heaven in some opera house of long ago may well find themselves rubbing their eyes. How did Harriet Beecher Stowe ever come to express such views? Had she read Brownson's essay or heard in some devious fashion of the *Communist Manifesto?* Some forgotten letter of Harriet's, reposing in an old desk, might tell us the answer; in the light of present knowledge we can only speculate.

It is not at all impossible that Harriet heard her father and husband or their friends talk of Brownson's essay in the *Boston Quarterly Review* and that she herself looked it up and pondered its radical analysis. In the 1830's and 1840's Cincinnati intellectual circles could scarcely be blind to the "newness," however much they might disagree with it. In 1835, one year after Harriet's "A New England Sketch" was published in the *Western Monthly Magazine,* another periodical with a similar name was established in Cincinnati. This was the *Western Messenger: devoted to Religion and Literature,* founded by James Freeman Clarke, William G. Eliot (grandfather of T. S. Eliot), and Ephraim Peabody, with T. H. Shreve and W. D. Gallagher as publishers. Beginning primarily as the promulgator of Unitarianism, the *Western Messenger* soon became a vehicle for Transcendentalism. The first four of Emerson's poems to be published, "Each and All," "The Humble-Bee," "Good-bye, Proud World," and "The Rhodora," appeared in the *Messenger;* William Ellery Channing was a contributor; Jones Very sent twenty-seven sonnets from Boston; at least ten of the contributors to the *Messenger* were later contributors to that primary organ of Transcendentalism, the *Dial,* edited by Emerson and Margaret Fuller. It is not difficult to imagine that all the Beechers were excited when news reached the Ohio Valley of Emerson's "An Address Delivered before the Senior Class of Divinity College." It would be very natural for Lyman and Calvin, who had long battled Unitarianism, to notice the existence of the heretical *Messenger* in the frontier town they were trying to save for Puritanism, and to read, like generals studying the strategy of the enemy, the two articles concerning Emerson's *Address,* "R. W. Emerson and the New School," by James Freeman Clarke and Christopher Pearse Cranch in the *Western Messenger* in 1838. We can be almost certain, I believe, that the "newness" was a subject for animated conversation among the faculty of Lane Seminary, and that Harriet was given a thorough, if very biased, briefing on Emerson and other radical New Englanders. This information would contribute ultimately to the surprising insight in *Oldtown Folks* that "Waldo Emerson and Theodore Parker were the last results of the current set in motion by Jonathan Edwards."

If I have correctly diagnosed the intellectual atmosphere of Cincinnati, the inevitable interest of the Beechers in the "newness" also led to the dramatizing of New England radicalism in the talk of Augustine St. Clare. Brownson's "The Laboring Classes" was a scandal in all conservative Unitarian circles, but, as Perry Miller has pointed out, "it was in Cincinnati that Brownson found his one real defender, and [William Henry] Channing's action, though it ruined the *Western Messenger,* is an unsung deed of courage in the annals of American journalism." It seems almost certain to me that here is the link between Brownson's "The Laboring Classes" and the archaeo-Marxian talk of Augustine St. Clare. What, at least, would be more likely than a full discussion by the Beechers of the collapse of the *Western Mesenger* and the cause, Brownson's "The Laboring Classes"?

Augustine St. Clare, in any case, was Harriet's spokesman in a far deeper sense than has been generally appreciated. In *A Key to Uncle Tom's Cabin,* to be sure, she tended to modify the revolutionary implications of her vision. There she argued, with Amos Lawrence as her symbol, that "the *true* socialism . . .

comes from the spirit of Christ, and, without breaking down existing orders of society, *by love* makes the property and possessions of the higher class the property of the lower. . . . Men would break up all ranks of society, and throw all property into a common stock; but Christ would inspire the higher class with that Divine Spirit by which all the wealth and means and advantages of their position are used for the good of the lower." But Harriet's verdict on the Civil War in *Men of Our Times* (1868) suggests that she retained her belief—and Augustine St. Clare's—in a world-wide proletarian revolution:

The revolution through which the American nation has been passing was not a mere local convulsion. It was a war for a principle which concerns all mankind. It was the war for the rights of the working class of society as against the usurpation of privileged aristocracies. You can make nothing else of it. That is the reason why, like a shaft of light in the judgment day, it has gone through all nations dividing the multitudes to the right and left. *For* us and our cause, all the common working classes of Europe— all that toil and sweat, and are oppressed. *Against* us, all privileged classes, nobles, princes, bankers and great manufacturers, all who live at ease. A silent instinct, piercing to the dividing of soul and spirit, joints and marrow, has gone through the earth, and sent every soul with instinctive certainty where it belongs. The poor laborers of Birmingham and Manchester, the poor silk weavers of Lyons, to whom our conflict has been present starvation and lingering death, have stood bravely *for* us. No sophistries could blind or deceive *them;* they knew that *our* cause was *their* cause, and they suffered their part heroically, as if fighting by our side, because they knew that our victory was to be their victory. On the other side, all aristocrats and holders of exclusive privileges have felt the instinct of opposition, and the sympathy with a struggling aristocracy, for they, too, felt that our victory would be their doom.

Uncle Tom's Cabin, of course, was not founded any more than Brownson's essay on dialectical materialism; like Brownson, who finally became a Roman Catholic, Harriet saw all life ultimately in religious terms. But the undeniable power of her book in moving her countrymen and indeed men and women everywhere to enlightened social action rested on the fact that she combined radical speculation with piety. Augustine St.

Clare would now strike us as another communist in capitalist clothing, but in the mid-nineteenth century, he spoke for thousands of Christians obsessed with the conflict between cruel laissez-faire capitalism and Christian democracy. Here was the masculine edge, the intellectual bite of *Uncle Tom's Cabin*. No reader, however, could put down Harriet's first novel feeling inconsistency between her social radicalism and her Christianity. Her concluding paragraph struck the same profound religious-social chord Lincoln would strike thirteen years later in his *Second Inaugural*. She wrote: "A day of grace is yet held out to us. Both North and South have been guilty before God; and the *Christian Church* has a heavy account to answer. Not by combining together, to protect injustice and cruelty, and making a common capital of sin, is this Union to be saved,— but by repentance, justice, and mercy; for, not surer is the eternal law by which the millstone sinks in the ocean, than that stronger law by which injustice and cruelty shall bring on nations the wrath of Almighty God!"

This concluding paragraph should remind us once again not only of the religious impulse behind *Uncle Tom's Cabin* but of the insistently Puritan nature of that impulse. In 1852 the last vestiges of the seventeenth-century Puritan theocracy had faded from sight; but in the heart and mind of a Puritan like Harriet, who had been nourished since childhood on Cotton Mather's *Magnalia Christi Americana*, patterns of feeling and thought fundamental to the Massachusetts Bay Colony persisted. For her, America, like seventeenth-century New England in the eyes of Cotton Mather, was a covenanted society peculiarly inviting the wrath of Almighty God for injustice and cruelty yet still able through repentance, justice, and mercy to find its place once more in God's favor. And at no place in *Uncle Tom's Cabin* was Harriet more fundamentally Puritan than in her reminder (her very phrasing suggests Mather) that "the *Christian Church* has a heavy account to answer." Of all dark omens prognosticating social woe in the mind of the seventeenth-century Puritan clergyman, the darkest was the decay of mercy and justice in those who professed to follow Christ. If Harriet looked forward to modern radicalism in certain aspects of her social theory, she also looked backward, even behind Jonathan Edwards, who had freed himself of federal theology, for essentials of her vision calling her countrymen to repentance.

VIII

We cannot fully understand, however, the power and appeal of *Uncle Tom's Cabin* unless we realize that, in addition to the matters I have already noted, Harriet's personal history had thrust upon her the role of expressing those facts of American experience and those moods of the popular mind which waited on the verge of expression. Surveying the literary possibilities of the American scene from Cincinnati, six months after Harriet had departed for Brunswick, Maine, the Swedish novelist, Fredrika Bremer, wrote this virtually prophetic passage to her sister in Europe:

I have heard histories of the flight of slaves which are full of the most intense interest, and I can not conceive why these incidents do not become the subjects of romances and novels in the literature of this country. I know no subject which could furnish opportunities for more heart-rending or more picturesque descriptions and scenes. . . . I can not understand why, in particular, noble-minded American women, American mothers who have hearts and genius, do not take up the subject, and treat it with a power which should pierce through bone and marrow, should reduce all the prudential maxims of statesmen to dust and ashes, and produce a revolution even in the old widely-praised Constitution itself. It is the privilege of the woman and the mother which suffers most severely through slavery. And if the heart of the woman, and the woman would heave warmly and strongly with maternal life's blood, I am convinced that the earth, the spiritual earth of the United States, must quake thereby and overthrow slavery!

Often when I have heard the adventures of fugitive slaves, their successful escape or their destruction, and have thought of the natural scenery of America, and of those scenes which naturally suggest themselves on "the way of the North Star," I have had a wish and a longing desire to write the history of a fugitive pair, so as it seems to me it ought to be written, and I have been inclined to collect materials for that purpose. And if I lived by this river and amid these scenes, I know for what object I should then live. But as it is, I am deficient in local knowledge. I am not sufficiently acquainted with the particular detail of circumstances, which would be indispensable for such a delineation, which ought to be true, and to take a strong hold upon the reader. That office belongs to others besides myself. I will hope for and expect—the *American mother*.

When *Uncle Tom's Cabin* appeared in Sweden, Miss Bremer wrote Harriet: "It was the work I had long wished for, that I had anticipated, that I wished while in America to be able to write, that I thought must come in America, as the uprising of the woman's and mother's heart on the question of slavery. I wondered that it had not come earlier. . . . I wondered, and God be praised! it has come."

Here through the eyes of an extraordinarily sensitive foreign observer, we see the final basis for Harriet's appeal to her contemporaries. Examining the event in retrospect, we may sense supernatural conspiracy in Miss Bremer's insight that such a book was inevitable and particularly in the suggestion that "the earth, the spiritual earth of the United States, must quake thereby and overthrow slavery!" But there is no need to retreat into critical obscurantism. As Orestes Brownson wrote thirteen years before *Uncle Tom's Cabin*, "Few things are less dependent on mere will or arbitrariness than literature. It is the expression and embodiment of the national life. Its character is not determined by this man or that, but by the national spirit. . . . So he who would move the people, influence them for good or for evil, must have like passions with them; feel as they feel; crave what they crave; and resolve what they resolve. He must be their representative, their impersonation. . . ."

Uncle Tom's Cabin became a major event in American history because it was the kind of organic expression of the national spirit for which Brownson argued. We can see more clearly than any of Harriet's contemporaries how crucial it was that she symbolized and dramatized the popular Christian-democratic indignations of the North. Brownson was nowhere more perceptive in his description of literature as organic expression than in his noting that it would influence the people "for good or for evil." In furnishing the popular mind and heart with unforgettable symbols of slavery, *Uncle Tom's Cabin* influenced the people for both good and evil. In dramatizing the obvious inconsistency between slavery and Christian democracy, it enlisted the popular will in the abolition of slavery as no other work had done; but the highly personal nature of its argument also made the Civil War virtually inevitable. After *Uncle Tom's Cabin,* objective analysis of the slavery issue was almost impossible. Abraham Lincoln was not far from the truth when he greeted Harriet as the little lady who had started the big war.

IX

Uncle Tom's Cabin remains a document no one can afford to neglect who hopes to understand the springs of our history. But for us, who read a century after the event, the crucial literary question is whether Harriet's first novel possesses more than sociological interest. It is not an easy question to answer. The overwhelming sociological significance of the book, its popular reputation as a work of propaganda pure and simple, makes an impartial reading something of a feat. Also, it is the confusing quality of *Uncle Tom's Cabin* that it possesses most of the large virtues, inaccessible to mere talent, and few of the graces accessible to any painstaking and intelligent craftsman. We must lose our modern microscopic eyes to read Harriet's novel for its virtue; we must put behind us our preference for the clearing with the single perfect shrub and learn to appreciate a forest of broken trees punctuated with magnificently vital pines and oaks. But even the sophisticated may find it worth the trouble. Henry James, the most artful of our novelists, with his characterization of *Uncle Tom's Cabin* as a literary " 'leaping' fish," a book that made its impression despite its disregard of art, warns us that in our exclusiveness we may be excluding ourselves from a memorable experience. The perceptive judgment of Edmund Wilson is a yet more modern reminder.

Uncle Tom's Cabin belongs to a lower species than the American masterworks of the 1850's: *The Scarlet Letter, Moby-*

Dick, Walden, and *Leaves of Grass.* As writer, Harriet stands
close to that other important regional novelist, James Fenimore
Cooper, who died the year before *Uncle Tom's Cabin* appeared
as a book. Like Cooper, she did not see her way to the destruction of the conventional novel and the creation of a new form
appropriate to her new subject matter. Like him, she continued in broad outlines the tradition of the sentimental novel.
George and Eliza have much of the rhetorical unreality of
similar characters in Cooper and, if we remember the incident
of the slave catchers, they are even involved in an approximation of Cooperesque flight and pursuit with the woodsman in
the form of Phineas Fletcher thrown in for good measure. But
much more significant is the similarity between *Uncle Tom's
Cabin* and *The Pioneers,* for example, in their true centers of
interest. In Natty Bumppo and Uncle Tom, Harriet and Cooper
were not seeking to create myth; they were simply projecting
against the American landscape figures larger than life who
stalked their imaginations. Something closely resembling myth
resulted, however, in both instances. As Natty Bumppo popularly became the archetypal frontiersman ever in conflict with
civilization, so Uncle Tom became the archetypal American
Negro, exploited by the white man and sold South symbolically
again and again. Uncle Tom is still a figure who can move us
as we read. In our concentration on the truly artistic myth-
maker, Melville, we are likely to underrate Harriet's achievement. Criticism must eventually recognize her, I believe, as a
major myth-maker to the populace throughout the world.

    Once we grant the importance of Uncle Tom as myth is there
any other aspect of Harriet's first novel which may hold our
attention on the literary level? Uncle Tom appears overideal-
ized when we compare him with Jim in *Huckleberry Finn,* and
Lucy and Cassy fare only slightly better when we compare them
with Roxana in *Pudd'nhead Wilson.* But, as I have indicated,
Sam, Marks, and Dinah would not be out of place in Mark
Twain's St. Petersburg and Dawson's Landing. These characters, together with Miss Ophelia and her Vermont friends and

relations, by fits and starts bring us into a vigorously conceived American world.

It is possible also that some readers of fiction will be intrigued by Harriet's anticipation of Faulkner, Caldwell, and other contemporary Southern writers. Faulkner's objective correlative to his awareness of the curse brought to the South by slavery is one of the major works of the American imagination. Harriet's St. Clare family appears paper-thin by comparison; but the Sutpens, the Sartorises, the Compsons are more clearly implied in Alfred St. Clare, his son Henrique, and Augustine's wife, Marie, than in characters of any earlier American book. Perhaps the most striking foreshadowing of Faulkner is the denouement of the novel. In terms of his legend, as it is brought down to modern times, there is something almost prophetic in the fact that Uncle Tom, the Negro, who was not freed by his noble but ineffective master, becomes the property of a man embodying the greed, the vulgarity, the lust, the inhumanity which outrage Faulkner as he broods over the South following the heroic days. In picturing Legree's plantation, Harriet anticipated the decadent, the negative elements in the Faulknerian landscape with such finality that an innocent reader might suppose he was confronted by a passage from, let us say, *Absalom, Absalom!*:

What was once a smooth-shaven lawn before the house, dotted here and there with ornamental shrubs, was now covered with frouzy tangled grass, with horse-posts set up, here and there, in it, where the turf was stamped away, and the ground littered with broken pails, cobs of corn, and other slovenly remains. Here and there, a mildewed jessamine or honeysuckle hung raggedly from some ornamental support, which had been pushed to one side by being used as a horse-post. What once was a large garden was now all grown over with weeds, through which, here and there, some solitary exotic reared its forsaken head. What had been a conservatory had now no window-sashes, and on the mouldering shelves stood some dry, forsaken flower-pots with sticks in them, whose dried leaves showed they had once been plants.

The wagon rolled up a weedy gravel walk, under a noble avenue of China-trees, whose graceful forms and ever-springing foliage seemed to be the only things there that neglect could not daunt or alter,—like noble spirits, so deeply rooted in goodness, as to flourish and grow stronger amid discouragement and decay.

The house had been large and handsome. It was built in a manner common at the south; a wide veranda of two stories running round every part of the house, into which every outer door opened, the lower tier being supported by brick pillars.

But the place looked desolate and uncomfortable; some windows stopped up with boards, some with shattered panes, and shutters hanging by a single hinge,—all telling of coarse neglect and discomfort.

Bits of board, straw, old decayed barrels and boxes, garnished the ground in all directions; and three or four ferocious-looking dogs, roused by the sound of wagon-wheels, came tearing out, and were with difficulty restrained from laying hold of Tom and his companions, by the effort of the ragged servants who came after them.

The quality in *Uncle Tom's Cabin,* however, which will probably constitute the most essential literary interest for the modern reader is its panoramic sweep of mid-America. Edmund Wilson has written that "The Negro characters, like the traveller of Gogol's 'Dead Souls,' are involved in a series of wanderings which progressively reveal a whole civilization." This is a perceptive comparison, but perhaps the book which will occur to most American readers when they seek equivalents for *Uncle Tom's Cabin* is *Huckleberry Finn.* The books have much in common once we get beyond their significant differences. In both, the cause of the journey is often forgotten in the vigorous display of character and scene shifted almost as soon as we have comprehended their dimensions. It is Harriet's distinction, ultimately, like Mark Twain's, that she can touch the man or woman, seen only momentarily, with the implication of character and a way of life. This praise applies as fully to the Kentucky frontiersmen and the Indiana Quakers whom George encounters as it does to the multitude of figures whose paths cross that of Uncle Tom.

From the standpoint of Harriet's career as novelist of New England, however, her first novel possesses a special significance beyond its importance as a national event and a book with at least some intrinsic interest for the modern reader. In genesis,

"THAT TRIUMPHANT WORK" 63

in the counterpoint of humor and realism to piety and sentimentalism, in the candor and moral fervor of its social vision,
Uncle Tom's Cabin is a vivid expression of Puritan New England sensibility in the 1850's. Feeling as she told Mrs. Follen
that she was "obliged to write, as one who is forced by some
awful oath to disclose in court some family disgrace," Harriet
reached the turning point inwardly and outwardly of her career.
Behind her now were those minor strategies of escape into the
humorous Yankee which constitute the main attraction of her
Mayflower sketches. Propelled by maternal loss, by religious
commitment, by the urgency arising from the Fugitive Slave
Law, she had assumed the role of spokesman for the New England conscience and imagination. Compared with her later
work in *The Minister's Wooing* and *Oldtown Folks,* her expression in her first novel is often crude, even naïve. But the act
of writing her book was crucial. We are not born to a culture;
we earn a culture through participation in the battle, public,
private or both, to make its values, its ideals, prevail. In her
battle to establish Christian democracy, Harriet earned her in-
heritance from the New England church and the New England
townmeeting, and in the speculations of Augustine St. Clare,
some portion of that radical tendency of the New England
mind evident as far back as Roger Williams and John Wise.
She now knew in the heart, in the mind, in the imagination, what
it meant to be a double-distilled New Englander. *Uncle Tom's
Cabin* was not simply an extraordinary first novel; it was the
fundamental act preparing Harriet for her full and informed
expression of her native region.

3

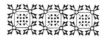

TRANSITION

I

Following the serialization of *Uncle Tom's Cabin* in the *National Era,* Harriet contributed to that periodical two letters from Maine. These letters, reprinted in 1853 in *Uncle Sam's Emancipation; Earthly Care, A Heavenly Discipline; and Other Sketches,* indicate her future plans as author. She was charmed by the Maine coast where "the sea luxuriates, swells, and falls, in the very lap of the primeval forest," and where from behind some lonely point, "swan-like, with wings all spread, glides in a ship from India or China, and wakes up the silence, by tumbling her great anchor into the water." In the Maine farmers and fishermen, she discovered frankness, freedom, and hospitality that reminded her of Kentucky, with "that stability and intelligent firmness peculiar to the atmosphere of New England." Particularly, she found life attractive a dozen miles from Brunswick on the islands of Casco Bay. She could think of no more enjoyable way to spend Sunday than to sail for some point where there was a church, spend the day there, and return at evening. Between farming and fishing, the islanders clearly made "a very respectable amphibious living." On a visit in a small cottage, she met one of the prettiest, most lady-like women, and a young girl from the neighborhood came in dressed in the latest fashion. After a time, the husband arrived from Portland with a new bonnet for his wife and gaiters for their little girl. When a member of Harriet's party suggested that it must be possible in such a retired place to lay up a good deal of money, the young man said: "Don't know about that . . . there's women and girls everywhere; and they must have their rings, and their pins, and parasols and ribbons. There's ways enough for money to go."

Readers of *The Pearl of Orr's Island* (1862) will recognize in the husband and wife possible models for James and Naomi Lincoln, and in the little girl, an original, perhaps, for Mara; the young lady dressed in the latest fashion may have suggested Sally Kittridge. Harriet began *The Pearl of Orr's Island* while Calvin was still teaching at Bowdoin. At Andover, Massachusetts, in July, 1852, to supervise repairs on the Stone Cabin, which would be her home while Calvin taught at Andover Theological Seminary, she wrote him that she was composing her Maine story every day, though she needed another trip to Orr's Island to fill out the character of " 'old Jonas,' my 'fish father' " (Captain Pennel, I think we may assume). She was also projecting an article on Maine and a letter on Hawthorne. New England life, her primary concern in her first book, *The Mayflower,* and tangentially her concern in Miss Ophelia in *Uncle Tom's Cabin,* was again exciting her imagination.

Momentarily, Harriet was released from involvement with the slavery issue. She had kept her commitment to God at Charley's grave; she felt the joy of a servant who had been faithful through a long and arduous task. She wrote Calvin that she could not describe to him the constant undercurrent of love, joy, and peace flowing through her soul. More explicitly she noted: "A day or two ago, my mind lay clear as glass, and I thought I had no will but God's, and could have none. Lo! his hand touches a spring, and I see what poor trash I am. But I am his chosen one for all that, and I shall reign with Him when all the stars have done blossoming, and if I am so poor I am betrothed to One who is Heir of all things." In her new mood, she was reading Chaucer and being "charmed at the reverential Christian spirit in which he viewed all things." Later in the year, her sense of closeness to God led her to compose the famous hymn verses, "Still, Still with Thee, When Purple Morning Breaketh."

Uncle Tom's Cabin, however, was breaking all records in its appeal to men and women of every class, not only in the United States but in Great Britain and, before the year was out, on the Continent in two French translations (eventually it would appear in over twenty-five languages). Those who had a financial stake in slavery sensed a positive danger; the New York *Journal of Commerce* led the attack; soon other newspapers were ranged for or against the book. In the South *Uncle Tom's Cabin* was regarded not only as destructive of "the peculiar institution," but as an invitation to slave rebellion. Before she left Brunswick, Harriet began to receive anonymous, obscene letters, and once a package, fortunately opened by Calvin, containing a black and bloody ear.

Harriet wished to continue *The Pearl of Orr's Island,* but a New England Puritan could not evade the call of duty. *Uncle Tom's Cabin,* it seemed, was a half-driven spike; she must send it home with a well directed blow. Late in 1852 she began *A Key to Uncle Tom's Cabin* to prove circumstantially that she had told the truth about slavery. By working herself to the edge of endurance, she finished it in April, 1853, but still she was not free to return to her Maine story. Dr. Ralph Wardlaw in the name of the Committee of the New Ladies' Anti-Slavery Society in Glasgow and the Committee of the Glasgow New Association for the Abolition of Slavery invited the Stowes to visit the British Isles, all expenses paid. Harriet found the invitation imperative, particularly in view of a letter, drawn up by the Duchess of Sutherland, and other distinguished ladies, and signed by over five hundred thousand British women. The letter pleaded with American women to raise their voices and prayers for the removal of the affliction and disgrace of slavery, and, at the close, acknowledged the "heavy share in this great sin" which Great Britain bore in introducing and compelling slavery in the colonies. Harriet felt that duty called her to Europe to strengthen this mighty feminine alliance.

The European reception accorded Harriet was without precedent; no American before had been given such grounds for vanity as she received in being acclaimed and welcomed by almost all distinguished Britons and Europeans and by the common people wherever they could catch sight of her. But in her conviction that God had written *Uncle Tom's Cabin,* and in her realization of the impermanence of reputation, she was largely a detached observer; she neither tried to impress her admirers nor was she particularly impressed by them. In *Sunny Memories of Foreign Lands* (1854), we can see that what interested her, beyond consolidating the antislavery forces, was the opportunity Europe afforded to widen her knowledge of history and the arts and particularly to measure New England against foreign backgrounds.

Such appraisal was natural. In the early weeks of her tour, she was confronted by evidence that Puritanism, which she had known only as a great constructive force in America, had been fanatically destructive in the British Isles. The altar of Aberdeen Cathedral, hacked by the Covenanters in 1649, drew from her the comment that "the good divine might better have aimed a sermon at the heart than an axe at the altar." Later, when she had seen ruin after ruin attributed to Cromwell's army, she conceded those might be pardoned "who did not look deeper than the surface, for the prejudice with which they regarded the whole movement." But she added: "a movement, however, of which we, and all which is most precious to us, are the lineal descendants and heirs." This tendency to recognize the limitations of Puritanism and at the same time to defend it characterized her response to the tombs of Allan Ramsay and other Covenanters in the churchyard of the Gray Friars, Edinburgh. Whether they were right in all respects seemed to her beside the point. They had kept liberty alive, and in so doing had made possible the literature of Scotland since "a vigorous and original literature is impossible, except to a strong, free, self-respecting people." She granted that it was a trial of spirit that the world's benefactors and reformers were "so often without form or comeliness." The criticisms leveled by descendants of the Puritans and Covenanters against their ancestors were as ill-timed, however, she wrote, as the comments a son might make on the disheveled hair and singed garments of the mother who had just borne him from a burning building.

In France, toward the end of her tour, she returned to the association of liberty with Puritanism, noting that wherever the system of that "expelled French refugee," John Calvin, had penetrated, civil liberty had entered with it. The political turmoils of French history she traced to the fact that "a Jezebel de'Medici" (this is not fair to Catherine de Médicis) had exterminated the Huguenots; the ultimate failure of the French Revolution to establish democracy she explained on the grounds that "the great unchaining of human passion had no element of religious control." Even when she divested herself of the prejudice of New England education and acknowledged "all the agreeableness, the joyousnes, and vivacity" of the French-Catholic Sabbath, she found ultimate superiority in Puritanism. It was no accident that popular freedom adhered in those countries subscribing to the Puritan Sabbath; there was an important relation between the mental discipline in the white New England meeting house and New England's traditional democracy. When the New England laborer took his wife and children to church on Sunday, he heard "two or three sermons, in each of which there are more elements of mental discipline than a French peasant gets in a whole lifetime." In consequence, the Yankee, laying his stone fence, discussed "the consistency of fore-ordination with free will," or attempted to settle some debated point in politics, while the French laborer had few thoughts beyond his daily toil.

Switzerland led Harriet to evaluate other aspects of Puritanism. Observing Mont Blanc from Geneva, she found confirmation in nature for the truth of Calvinism: "Calvinism, in its essential features, never will cease from the earth, because the great fundamental facts of nature are Calvinistic, and men with strong minds and wills always discover it. The predestination of a sovereign will is written over all things. The old Greek tragedians read it, and expressed it. All this I say, while I fully sympathize with the causes which incline many fine and beautiful minds against the system." Those fine and beautiful minds were in the ascendancy, of course, among contemporary American authors. Only Melville in *Moby-Dick,* similarly meditating on one of the white terrors of nature, fully shared Harriet's insight. Emerson in the chapter "Fate" in *The Conduct of Life* (1860) at first shattered the illusion of "Nature, kind mother of us all," but at the end he reconciled man to nature with an ease impossible to a good Greek or a Calvinist: "If Fate is ore and quarry, if evil is good in the making, if limitation is power that shall be, if calamities, oppositions, and weights are wings and means,—we are reconciled."

The beauty of Alpine flowers suggested to Harriet, however, grounds for criticizing the New England expression of the truths of nature: ". . . can we suppose that this Being can take delight in dwellings and modes of life or forms of worship where everything is reduced to cold, naked utility? I think not." Later, when she was staying in Paris with M. Belloc, Director of the Imperial School of Design, the beauty of his home, added to her many impressions from the great galleries and museums of Europe, led her to a bitter denunciation of the New England attitude toward beauty:

> But did not He who made the appetite for food make also that for beauty? and while the former will perish with the body, is not the latter immortal? With all New England's earnestness and practical efficiency, there is a long withering of the soul's more ethereal part,—a crushing out of the beautiful,—which is horrible. Children are born there with a sense of beauty equally delicate with any in the world, in whom it dies a lingering death of smothered desire and pining, weary starvation. I know, because I have felt it.

This attitude Harriet would express through Mrs. Marvyn in *The Minister's Wooing;* in fact, the maturity of Harriet's analysis of New England life in all her later books depended on her having measured New England against foreign backgrounds during her first and subsequent journeys to Europe.

Back in Andover in the fall of 1853, Harriet may have read over *The Pearl of Orr's Island* and projected future chapters, but soon she was engaged on another work dealing with New England which could not be postponed. At seventy-eight,

Lyman Beecher asked his children's help in preparing his autobiography. Charles Beecher, who served as editor, wrote that his father related his reminiscenses "in the course of 1853 and onward . . . during successive visits at Mrs. Stowe's in Andover." Harriet's major role in the *Autobiography, Correspondence, Etc., of Lyman Beecher* (1864) can be estimated from the fact that the first few chapters are largely replies to questions posed by "H.B.S." and that she contributed at least five chapters re-creating the personalities and events of her childhood. Before Lyman died in 1863, Harriet had absorbed from him a full and intimate knowledge of New England life and character; this knowledge would be fundamental in her future work.

Undoubtedly, Lyman was disturbed by his daughter's accusation, in one of the letters later printed in *Sunny Memories of Foreign Lands,* that New England life crushed the desire for the beautiful. It would have been like him to argue the matter with her. In any case, in a brief essay "The Old Oak of Andover—a Revery," printed in the 1855 edition of *The Mayflower,* Harriet reversed her earlier position. She wrote that the ancient oak across the street from her Andover home was like the Puritan settlers of the town "so gnarled and knotted were they, yet so outbursting with a green and vernal crown, yearly springing, of noble and generous thoughts, rustling with leaves which shall be for the healing of nations." The oak should be cherished for their sakes as "the broken statue of some antique wrestler, brown with time, yet glorious in its suggestion of past achievements." Of this, she was all the more convinced because of a recent attack, which she did not identify, on the Puritans as men who gored grace and beauty. If beauty was only that which appealed to the senses, there was some truth in the charge, but Plato had noted that there were two beauties, one celestial, one vulgar. The Puritans were the worshipers of celestial beauty; they broke the shrine of physical loveliness so that men might "gain access to the divine, invisible One." Remembering the artistic glories of Europe, Harriet now argued: "There were abundance of people to think of pictures, and statues, and gems, and cameos, vases and marbles, and all manner of deliciousness. The world was all drunk with the enchantments of the lower Venus, and it was needful that these men should come, Baptist-like in the wilderness, in raiment of camel's hair." Such men, she asserted, were needed in the 1850's when art, it was said, was waking in America.

II

With this rumor of the awakening of art still in our ears, we are almost certian to regret that Harriet's second novel is another contribution to the antislavery cause. We feel that a writer, even in the midst of national crisis, should continue to grow; at least he should not step backwards and repeat himself when insight and enthusiasm bid him to "fresh fields and pastures new." In short, Harriet should not have written *Dred: A Tale of the Great Dismal Swamp* (1856). In terms of her increasing interest in matters New England, one *Uncle Tom's Cabin* was enough. Her next task should have been the finishing of her "Maine story."

Generally speaking, we are entitled to these conclusions. *Dred* is by no means so memorable as Harriet's first antislavery novel. Why this should be so, it is difficult at first to understand. In particulars—the development of character and scene, insight into the complexities of the slavery problem, tight and lively exposition—*Dred* is often superior to *Uncle Tom's Cabin*. The defect would not seem to lie in the plot, an affair of three large branches, the first two concerned with Negro and partially Negro characters, and the third with the white hero and heroine, their friends and relations. Branch one deals with a huge Negro, Dred, supposedly the son of Denmark Vesey, the leader of a slave insurrection and massacre in South Carolina in 1822. Dred, a black Old Testament prophet in his deep religious fury against "the oppressors of Israel," attempts in the 1850's to follow in his father's bloody footsteps. Involved in his conspiracy is Harry Gordon, the partially Negro overseer of the Gordon plantation, and his quadroon wife, Lisette. Harry is driven to conspiracy and finally to running away North by the sadistic treatment he receives from his white half-brother, Tom Gordon, who particularly tortures him by making love to Lisette.

Dred's conspiracy comes to an end because he is Christianized by a slave woman, Milly, who in her piety, her emphasis on the Kingdom Above, might be Uncle Tom's sister. Actually, however, Milly was based on a fascinating historical character, the Negro preacher and reformer, Sojourner Truth, the major factor, it seems probable, motivating Harriet into her second antislavery novel. It is easy to see why Sojourner should have interested her from the sketch "Sojourner Truth, the Libyan Sibyl," written after the Civil War. Harriet there told of Sojourner's visit at Andover sometime between 1852 and 1856. Tall, dressed in grey, with a bright Madras handkerchief turbanfashion around her head, Sojourner had almost an air of superiority as she looked down on Harriet and exclaimed with a twinkle: "So this is *you?*" and "Well, honey, de Lord bless ye! I jes' thought I'd like to come an' have a look at ye. You's heerd o' me, I reckon?" Harriet immediately recognized Sojourner's personal magnetism; she called in her father, Calvin, and two or three other clergymen to share the experience with her. When Harriet presented her father, "Sojourner, this is Dr. Beecher. He is a very celebrated preacher," Sojourner offered her hand and said: "Ye dear lamb, I'm glad to see ye! De Lord bless ye! I loves preachers. I'm a kind o' preacher myself." When Lyman asked her if she preached from the Bible, Sojourner, calling him "honey," admitted that she could not read; the text for all her preaching was "WHEN I FOUND JESUS."

As we fill out the facts from Harriet's sketch, Sojourner must have been brought to America and sold into slavery at the end of the eighteenth century. When she found it impossible to please her hard master and mistress, she followed her mother's advice to call on God in trouble. This she did in a place she "threshed down" in the lot, having heard that God had met a man on a threshing floor. When her prayers did not soften her owners, her next move was to make a bargain with God that she would be good if he helped her escape. God told her to start off before daybreak, and showed her in vision a house where she was to ask the people to take her in. Late at night Sojourner reached the house; there she stayed two or three years with a family of Quakers. This brings us to 1799, when slaves were emancipated in New York State. Her old master now visited her and asked if she would not like to visit her former home.

Just as she was about to get into her master's wagon, Sojourner "met God" as she phrased it. She went back to the house and sat down in her room; there she could feel "it burnin', burnin', burnin', all around me, an' goin' through me." A sudden feeling of guilt laid hold of her and she called out for somebody to stand between her and God. Something she compared to an umbrella (!) came between her and the light, and finally a voice inside her said, *"This is Jesus!"* In her own words: "An' then the whole world grew bright, an' the trees they waved an' waved in glory, an' every little bit o' stone on the ground shone like glass; an' I shouted an' said, 'Praise, praise, praise to the Lord!' An' I began to feel sech a love in my soul as I never felt before,—love to all creatures." Finally, she was able to cry, "Lord, Lord, I can love *even de white folks!*"

Sojourner's love for the white folks, however, was short-lived. On her return to New York State, she learned that her mistress had given her little black son to a daughter who had married an Alabamian. In a fall from grace, Sojourner prayed God to render double misery to her mistress; she then took her case to the courts and recovered her son. But God had heeded her prayer. In a fit of drunken fury, the Alabamian knocked down her mistress's daughter and stamped her to death. When she heard the news, Sojourner cried: "O Lord, I didn't mean all that! You took me up too quick." She did her best to repair the damage by nursing her mistress in her ensuing illness and holding her in her arms, lovingly, while she died.

After that, Sojourner journeyed to camp meetings, singing hymns and preaching on "WHEN I FOUND JESUS." She also testified at abolitionist meetings, not always in accord with the party line. Once she spoke up in the hush of Faneuil Hall, Boston, following a speech in which Frederick Douglass insisted that the Negro could win freedom only by armed insurrection; she demanded in her deep voice, "Frederick, *is God dead?*" Even more than Josiah Henson, generously interpreted, Sojourner made a natural appeal to Harriet's predilections concerning the Negro. Here in one person were the Negro, the Christian, and the mother separated from her child. Harriet could not resist fictionalizing her in *Dred* and telling her story. Harriet, in fact, continued to tell Sojourner's story after she had written *Dred*. In Rome, during her third and last journey to Europe in 1859, she put such fervor in her recital that the American sculptor William Wetmore Story asked her to repeat Sojourner's history when he was working on his famous "Libyan Sibyl." Possibly Sojourner contributed minor inspiration to Story's "Cleopatra," praised at length by Hawthorne in *The Marble Faun.*

Branches two and three in the plot of *Dred* may be indicated quickly. Branch two deals with an old Negro slave, Uncle Tiff, who settles near the Gordon plantation and wins Nina Gordon's sympathy for his dying mistress, Sue Cripps, and for her children, Fanny and Teddy, after their father, a junk man, has married the second time for the worse. With the help of the hero, Uncle Tiff finally escapes north with the children. Branch three, which I shall later discuss in detail, concerns the hero and heroine, Edward Clayton and Nina Gordon. It is by no means tediously conventional.

III

Finding at least a potentially dramatic and exciting plot in *Dred,* we may wonder if it was Harriet's program which prevented her second novel from achieving the power and intensity of her first novel. In the "Author's Preface," she wrote that her reason for turning again to slavery was twofold, the extraordinary artistic possibilities of the subject and its moral bearings, by which she meant the challenge confronting the United States as it debated the extension of slavery into the new lands of the West. In theory, this was quite as promising a program as that of *Uncle Tom's Cabin,* and Harriet was often skilful in carrying it out. Even more boldly than in the creation of Alfred St. Clare, Augustine's wife, Marie, and in details of decadence on Legree's plantation, Harriet in *Dred* anticipates Faulkner in the artistic expression of her subject matter. There is much to remind us of *Absalom, Absalom!*—the great house symbolic of worldly ambition; a gentlemanly eldest son (Harry Gordon) with Negro blood, the slave overseer of the plantation; a second white son (Tom Gordon) who knows his half brother's identity; and a daughter (Nina Gordon) deeply attached to her partially Negro half brother. In one of the subplots, we even move close to Faulkner's locale: the Calvinist lawyer, Mr. Jekyl, tells an involved story of a Mississippi plantation which now legally belongs to the Gordons since their white Mississippi cousin has died and the deed emancipating his quadroon wife is so much waste paper.

Like *Uncle Tom's Cabin, Dred* again and again re-creates the American scene with that unconventional freshness and rough vigor which have been the passport in Thoreau, in Melville, in Mark Twain, in Hemingway, in Faulkner, in Robert Penn Warren, for the free passage of our literature around the world. In the 1850's Harriet Beecher Stowe quite clearly filled the role in European eyes which Faulkner and Warren fill in our own time: she was the outspoken reporter to Europe of our failures in democracy, of our crudities, our cruelties, and at the same time she was the creator of a Southern world of such vitality that the European imagination was not so much depressed as it was refreshed by her pages. Consider, for a single example, Abijah Skinflint, expatriate Yankee and owner of a log-cabin store near the Gordon plantation: "For money he would do anything; for money he would have sold his wife, his children, even his own soul, if he had happened to have one. But that article, had it ever existed, was now so small and dry, that one might have fancied it to rattle in his lean frame like a shriveled pea in a last year's peascod." Abijah's drunken wife and blowsy daughter, Polly, who delays his departure for a camp meeting, "a-plastering down her hair," point up the amusement. When Polly hoists her fat form into the wagon, the hooks on her red calico dress explode and fly off:

"Durned if I knows what to do!" said she; "this yer old durned gear coat's all off my back!"

"Gals is always fools!" said Abijah consolingly.

"Stick in a pin, Polly," said her mother in an easy, sing-song drawl.

"Durn you, old woman, every hook is off!" said the promising young lady.

"Stick in more pins, then" said the mamma; and the vehicle of Abijah passed onward.

Harriet's second official intention, to fight the extension of slavery into the new West, results in disclosures quite as interesting as the radically democratic analysis of Augustine St. Clare. Economically, slavery means a wasteful upper class (the Gordons) and an impoverished and ignorant lower class (the Cripps and other poor whites). Socially, the Southern system contradicts democracy. If all men are created equal, the partially Negro Harry Gordon, a man of marked ability, should have the same opportunities as his white half brother, Tom. Actually, though Harry is the overseer of the Gordon plantation and the ultimate source of its wealth, he has no rights at all. The black woman Milly is another victim of American democracy distorted by slavery. When a Mr. Barker, to whom she hires out, beats her and shoots at her, the hero Edward Clayton argues and wins her case in a local court with the argument: "No consideration can justify us in holding this people in slavery an hour, unless we make this slavery a guardian relation, in which our superior strength and intelligence are made the protector and educator of their simplicity and weakness." But Mr. Barker carries the case to the state supreme court. There Judge Clayton, Edward's father, reverses the decision on the principle "The slave, to remain a slave, must be made sensible that there is no appeal from his master."

Harriet was not so naïve nor so unjust as to suppose that all Southerners agreed with this dark judgment. Like Augustine St. Clare, Edward Clayton is another Christian-democrat, living proof that some portion at least of the Southern mind and heart is still committed to Jeffersonian principles. For his championing of freedom, Edward is beaten within an inch of his life, his plantation school house is burned, and he and his sister are forced to flee North. No reader could miss the point. Slavery means the gradual extinction of democracy. To extend slavery would be to extend tyranny and to sow the seeds of revolution and anarchy.

Harriet also made it clear that slavery had corrupted the Christian church. Edward's first move after his defeat in the Supreme Court is an appeal to the clergy, specifically to his Uncle Cushing, one of the most influential Presbyterians in North Carolina. Harriet's chapters "The Clerical Conference" and "The Result" are biting satire. The only redeeming clergyman in her picture is a poor, devout down-and-outer, Father Dickson, whom his colleagues endure as moral decoration to their proceedings. Edward's uncle is a "man of warm feelings, human impulses, and fine social qualities; his sermons, beautifully written, and delivered with great fervor, often drew tears from the eyes of his hearers." Unfortunately, "there was a species of moral effeminacy about him, and the very luxuriant softness and richness of his nature unfitted him to endure hardness." Dr. Shubael Packthread, a leading Northern minister, is, on the other hand, built like a steel spring. He is filled with stratagems; he always speaks so a double interpretation is possible; he is a master of compromise and slander, with a whole set of smiles at his command: "The solemn smile, the smile of inquiry, the smile affirmative, the smile suggestive, the smile of incredulity, and the smile of innocent credulity, which encouraged the simple hearted narrator to go on unfolding himself to the brother, who sat quietly behind his face, as a spider does behind his web, waiting till his unsuspecting friend had tangled himself in incautious, impulsive, and, of course, contradictory meshes of statement, which were in some future hour, in the most gentle and Christian spirit, to be tightened around the incautious captive, while as much blood was sucked as the good of the cause demanded." The Reverend Dr. Calker is vicious after another fashion: "He began with loving the church for God's sake, and ended with loving her better than God. And by the church he meant the organization of the Presbyterian Church in the United States of America."

Clayton fares as we might expect in this company. When he modestly insinuates his comments into the conversation, the clergymen listen politely; Uncle Cushing, as the Judge prophesied, shows sympathy. But first, last, and always, Doctors Cushing, Packthread, and Calker, have one and only one interest: the compromising of the slavery issue so that the Old and New School Presbyterians may present a united front against the inroads of other sects. Only that innocent and primitive Christian, Father Dickson, really an outsider, feels a genuine religious and moral commitment.

In the appendix to *Dred,* Harriet furnished impressive factual evidence supporting her indictment. In 1784 the Conference of the Methodist Church had prescribed the times at which members who were slaveholders should emancipate their slaves. But in 1836 the General Conference, meeting in Cincinnati, eager for church unity, took a very different stand: "Resolved, by the delegates of the Annual Conferences in General Conference assembled, that they are decidedly opposed to modern abolitionism, and wholly disclaim any right, wish, or intention to interfere in the civil and political relation between master and slave, as it exists in the slave-holding States of this Union." Harriet noted similar shameful compromises in the Presbyterian Church. In 1836, in a year when the Natchez *Courier* noted that Alabama, Missouri, and Arkansas had imported two hundred and fifty thousand slaves from more Northern states, the majority of the General Assembly voted that it was not "expedient" to take any action regarding slavery. In 1843 the General Assembly voted to take no action on slavery; instead, as Harriet recorded with scorn, it passed a resolution against dancing.

IV

Isolated in this fashion, Harriet's pictures of Southern life, and her social, economic, and religious arguments against the extension of slavery, are impressive. Why, then, does the whole book somehow leave us approximately where it found us? I find clarification in two observations of D. H. Lawrence: "The old American artists were hopeless liars. . . . The artist usually sets out—or used to—to point a moral and adorn a tale. The tale, however, points the other way, as a rule. Two blankly opposing morals, the artist's and the tale's." What Lawrence here noted, in extreme terms, was the fact that American writers, particularly Poe, Cooper, Hawthorne, and Melville, often wrote from only half-consciously understood impulses and their work consequently differs as read for its surface intention or for its autobiographical revelation. This insight furnishes a key to *Dred,* for when we examine Harriet's book closely we see that far more than Poe or Hawthorne she was guilty of creating "two blankly opposing morals" which confuse the reader. The exposition and much of the plot furnishes as first "moral" the necessity of a relentless battle against slavery, but the second, more private moral, suggests that such a battle is futile and, moreover, should not be our primary consideration.

It would be an error, I believe, to blame this confusion on outer events. The world of the 1850's was far darker than we are likely to remember on this side of the Civil War and the Fourteenth Amendment. Since 1854, when Stephen A. Douglas's Nebraska Bill had created two new territories, Nebraska and Kansas, with local option on slavery, Harriet must have watched the unfolding of the national tragedy with mounting concern. She would have known, of course, that in 1855 when Kansas held its election under the rule of popular sovereignty, five thousand proslavery ruffians had ridden over from Missouri, barred Free Soil men from voting, and elected a proslavery legislature, and that the next year another band of Missourians had plundered and burned the Free Soil capital of Lawrence, Kansas. Harriet's brother, Henry Ward Beecher, was deeply involved in this struggle. The antislavery settlers had given the name "Beecher's Bibles" to the barrels of Sharpe's rifles Henry encouraged the congregation of his Brooklyn church to send west. Furthermore, when she had been at work only two months on *Dred,* Representative Preston S. Brooks had beaten her friend Senator Charles Sumner of Massachusetts over the head with a gutta-percha cane in reprisal for the insulting references to Senator Butler of South Carolina in a speech "The Crime against Kansas." (Harriet fictionalized this incident in Tom Gordon's beating of Edward Clayton.)

In 1856, the tide of Southern power was rising and flooding all corners of the Union, and would continue to do so for a half-decade. No Northern idealist would be able to block the election to the presidency of the South's worldly-wise, morally obtuse candidate, James Buchanan of Pennsylvania. In 1857, the slave-holding Chief Justice of the Supreme Court would hand down the infamous Dred Scott Decision, virtually permitting the Southerner to keep his Negroes in bondage anywhere in the nation. In 1858, Abraham Lincoln, candidate for the United States Senate, would be defeated by Stephen A. Douglas, who had proposed the Kansas-Nebraska Bill. In short, Harriet's fame had risen and the antislavery cause had dropped simultaneously; it was as if the Divine Hand worked buckets over a pulley in a well. Doubtless, we have a reflection of what many New Englanders felt in the observations ascribed at the close of *Dred* to a realistic Southerner, Frank Russel:

"The mouth of the North is stuffed with cotton, and will be kept full as long as it suits us. Good, easy gentlemen, they are so satisfied with their pillows, and other accommodations inside of the car, that they don't trouble themselves to reflect that we are the engineers, nor to ask where we are going. And when anyone does wake up and pipe out a melancholy inquiry, we slam the door in his face, and tell him, 'Mind your own business, sir!' and he leans back on his cotton pillow and goes to sleep again, only whimpering a little that 'we might be more polite.'

"They have their fanatics up there. We don't trouble ourselves to put them down; we make them do it. They get mobs up on our account, to hoot troublesome ministers and editors out of their cities; and their men that they send to Congress invariably do all our dirty work. There's now and then an exception, it is true; but they only prove the rule.

"If there was any public sentiment at the North for you reformers to fall back upon, you might, in spite of your difficulties, do something; but there is not. They are all implicated with us, except the class of born fanatics, like you, who are walking in that very unfashionable narrow way we've heard of."

But as Puritan, as bride of Christ, Harriet should have been charged with new fervor by the very darkness, the very hopelessness of the situation. Spiritually, and literarily, so far as she was concerned, the worse matters were, the better they were, for disaster drew the soul close to God and religion was the source of imaginative power. What had happened? I find the clue in a Christian riddle proposed by Roger Williams in the preface to *Experiments of Spiritual Life & Health:* "First, why is the heart of a David himself (Ps. 30) more apt to decline from God upon the mountain of joy, deliverance, victory, prosperity, than in the dark vale of the shadow of death, persecution, sickness, adversity, etc.?" In writing *Uncle Tom's Cabin,* Harriet had supposed that she must do some tremendous deed to sanctify the death of Charley Stowe and to demonstrate that his mother had experienced a true conversion. Lo! (we must fall if only a little into Biblical rhetoric to catch her mood) she had succeeded. Initially, this was cause for rejoicing; there was a balance in the divine ledger. But ultimately it is more blessed to be religiously in debt than to be religiously solvent. After *Uncle Tom's Cabin,* Harriet stood on what Williams called "the mountain of joy, deliverance, victory, prosperity" where even the heart of a David is "apt to decline from God." In more modern terms, she had resolved the inner conflict which had given her first novel the power of nightmare; she was no longer the dynamic writer of 1852. The half-hidden, dreaming underself now made the dismal report that God was not in his heaven though, as usual, all was wrong with the world.

Harriet could not abide the situation. Her official intention, to portray Southern life and to fight the extension of slavery, did not call for a pious heroine like Little Eva wrung dry of most of the sentimentality. But Harriet created such a heroine, nevertheless, and furthermore she killed her half way through the novel with a complete disregard of reader interest. Her basic reason for thus flawing her novel with a competing interest was the desire to experience vicariously one more encounter with the God who used to be in his heaven but who had largely faded for her on the mountain of success. Nina's story, the expression of the half-hidden dreaming underself, was quite as important to her as the battle against slavery. Of this we can be sure when we discover that Harriet called her novel *Nina Gordon* in later editions before reverting finally to her original title. But we can only understand the importance of Nina when we lift her disguises and see that she is symbolically Harriet Beecher Stowe.

There is little in the opening chapters to remind us of the author of *Uncle Tom's Cabin*. At finishing school Nina has developed a talent for shirking lessons and spending money like water, has become engaged to three young men at the same time, and even evinced a taste for sidewalk flirtation. When, at some Northern party, talk settled on Byron's *Don Juan,* and Clayton quizzed a Miss Elliott as to whether she had read it, Nina asked him in vexation: "And, pray, what's the harm if she did read it? *I* mean to read it, the very first chance I get!" As *one* of her fiancés, Clayton warned: "Miss Nina, I *trust,* as your friend, that you will not read that book. I should lose all respect for a lady friend who had read that." Under examination, Clayton admitted he had read *Don Juan,* and there then ensued a hubbub among the gentlemen. As Nina tells Harry: "They wanted us all to be like snowflakes, and all that. And they were quite high, telling that they wouldn't marry this, and they wouldn't marry that, till at last I made them a curtsy and said, 'Gentlemen, we ladies are infinitely obliged to you, but *we* don't intend to marry people that read naughty books, either. Of course you know snowflakes don't like smut!" Everything seems to mark Nina as an illustration of devil-may-care independence in the Southern belle.

But when we are a hundred pages into *Dred,* Nina changes into a serious woman, quite obviously Harriet herself. The tragic, poverty-stricken death of old Tiff's mistress, Sue Cripps, who was also born into an aristocratic Southern family, makes Nina aware of the dark underside of reality. Later Milly tells Nina her tragic history. Here in fictional terms we have a repetition of Sojourner Truth's telling Harriet her story at Andover. Like Harriet in 1856, Nina is also as much interested in New England as she is in the problem of slavery. This interest is continually erupting in the book and competing with the official intention of dealing with slavery. For example, when Nina and Clayton ride over to the Le Clare plantation to try to buy Harry's wife, Lisette, before Tom Gordon does, Nina makes the following extended comparison of North Carolina and New Hampshire:

"What is the reason, when we get down South, here, everything seems to be going to destruction, so? I noticed it all the way down through Virginia. It seems as if everything had stopped growing, and was going backwards. Well, now, it's so different at the North! I went up, one vacation, into New Hampshire. It's a dreadfully poor, barren country; nothing but stony hills and poor soil. And yet the people there seem to be so well off! They live in such nice, tight, clean-looking white houses! Everything around them looks so careful and comfortable; and yet their land isn't half so good as ours, down here. Why, actually, some of those places seem as if there were nothing but rock! And then, they have winter about nine months in the year, I do believe! But these Yankees turn everything to account. If a man's field is covered with rock, he'll find some way to sell it, and make money out of it; and if they freeze up all winter, they sell the ice, and make money out of that. They just live by selling their disadvantages!"

Nina owes her insight to her school friend Livy Ray. We hear of Livy when, in summer talk at Canema, Uncle John argues that North Carolina slaves are far better off than the free working classes in the North. Such a view Uncle John would never hold, Nina tells him, if he had traveled as she had:

"Now, . . . Uncle John, you dear old heathen, you! do let me tell you a little how it is there. I went up into New Hampshire once, with Livy Ray, to spend a vacation. Livy's father is a farmer;

works part of every day with his own men; hoes, digs, plants; but he is governor of the state. He had a splendid farm—all in first-rate order; and his sons, with two or three hired men, keep it in better condition than our places ever saw. Mr. Ray is a man who reads a great deal; has a fine library, and he's as much of a gentleman as you'll often see. There are no high and low *classes* there. Everybody works; and everybody seems to have a good time. Livy's mother has a beautiful dairy, spring-house, and two strong women to help her; and everything in the house looks beautifully; and, for the greater part of the day, the house seems so neat and still, you wouldn't know anything had been done in it. Seems to me this is better than making slaves of all the working classes, or having any working classes at all."

Unlike the Southern revivalist, whose religion makes him "very disagreeable," Livy Ray had the kind of religion Nina can respect, for Livy was "good without being stupid." Nina tells Clayton:

"Now, Livy . . . was remarkable. She had that kind of education they give girls in New England, stronger and more like a man's than ours. She could read Greek and Latin as easily as she could French and Italian. She was keen, shrewd, and witty, and had a kind of wild grace about her, like these grapevines; yet she was so strong! Well, do you know, I almost worship Livy? And I think, the little while she was in our school, she did me more good than all the teachers and studying put together. . . . She seems to me like a mine. When I was with her the longest, I always felt as if I hadn't half seen her. She always made me hungry to know her more."

Harriet too was doubtless hungry to know Livy Ray more (Livy might have become an important character in a New England novel) but there were in her yet deeper hungers. What Harriet longed for most, as I have suggested, was the sense of closeness to God she had experienced in what Roger Williams called "the dark vale of the shadow of death, persecution, sickness, adversity." This she found by imagining that cholera swept the Gordon estate much as it swept Cincinnati in 1849. Like Harriet in the dark days preceding Charley Stowe's death, Nina has to assume all the responsibility in fighting the disaster; her only help is Milly, Harry, and other slaves. But catastrophe makes victory, ultimate victory, possible; Nina dies saying, "Good-by! I will arise and go to my Father!"

Having dismissed Nina and herself from the novel in this fashion, Harriet, we might suppose, would have been satisfied and have settled down to the business of portraying the dark realities of slavery, specifically slave insurrection and massacre, for which she had harrowing source material in Nat Turner's "Confessions" published in the appendix to *Dred*. But the "Confessions" are far more effective than anything Harriet wrote. Again her religious hunger competed with her anti-slavery impulse. Instead of insurrection and massacre, we have, as I have indicated, Milly's conversion of Dred to Christian pacifism.

There was yet one more opportunity to strike a telling blow against slavery: Edward Clayton. Had he been utterly and barbarously destroyed, we might have closed the book with indignation and determination. But if Clayton's story proves anything, it proves the futility of reform and the wisdom of coming home, that is to the North, with one's shield rather than on it. And there seems something additionally destructive of Harriet's announced intention in the fact that once Clayton has left the cause, he is apparently a happy man, even to the point of possible marriage with Livy Ray.

As we may take the death of Nina to symbolize the conclusion of Harriet's career as antislavery crusader in fiction, so we may take this possible marriage as a symbol of her future involvement with matters New England. In any case, noting the decline of her ability to deal effectively with the slavery issue and remembering Nina's and finally Clayton's hunger to know Livy Ray, we seem justified in regarding *Dred* primarily as a bridge between *Uncle Tom's Cabin* and the New England novels.

"THE BRUISED FLAX-FLOWER"

I

WITH *Dred* in print the moment had apparently arrived for Harriet to complete that "Maine story" she had begun in the summer of 1852 and had postponed for new labors in the anti-slavery cause. As one given to reading God's hand in her affairs, she might easily have sensed divine planning in the fall of 1857. In September she found herself visiting the islands of Casco Bay, refreshing her imagination on the scenes and characters of her "Maine story"; then, in October, Francis H. Underwood and James Russell Lowell visited her at Andover and asked for a serial for the magazine they were establishing, the *Atlantic Monthly*. Harriet agreed to contribute, almost certainly because, though she was passing through a period of personal anguish, she already had the "Maine story" partly written and in view of her recent experience it would require no great labor to finish it. But after working through the fall and most of the winter on what would eventually become *The Pearl of Orr's Island,* Harriet once more gave it up for another book. The novel she contributed to the *Atlantic,* beginning in December, 1858, was *The Minister's Wooing.*

In a letter to James T. Fields some years later, Harriet furnishes an explanation of what may seem her strange literary behavior: ". . . I have the offer of eight thousand dollars for the newspaper use of the story I am planning to write. . . . But I am bound by the laws of art. Sermons, essays, lives of distinguished people, I can write to order at times and seasons. A story comes, grows like a flower, sometimes will and sometimes won't, like a pretty woman. When the spirits will help, I can write. When they jeer, flout, make faces, and otherwise maltreat me, I can only wait humbly at their gates, watch at the posts of their doors." Fields, the publisher of Emerson and Thoreau, may have heard a faint echo of the transcendental organic theory of art in "a story . . . grows like a flower," but Harriet, of course, was not setting up shop as a literary theorist. She was simply stating the facts of her experience and, as we can see from her remarks about the pretty woman and the spirits who make faces, stating her experience with a smile, But her disclosure is important none the less. It tells us that she did not usually force-grow her flowers, and that her postponing of *The Pearl* and her working on *The Minister's Wooing* was something more than whim: it was the yielding once again of a novelist to those inner compulsions which had given her first novel the power of a historical event.

We may well wonder, however, whether there was not something transcendentally whimsical or simply careless in Harriet's yielding to impulse in handling fact in her first New England novel. Reading the installments in the *Atlantic,* her learned friend and neighbor, Edwards A. Park, President of Andover Theological Seminary, had good reason for being disturbed by her fictionalizing of Dr. Samuel Hopkins of Newport, Rhode Island, the famous eighteenth-century theologian, who was the minister of the story. It was quite natural for Dr. Park, as he reported later, to lend Harriet his *Memoir of the Life and Character of Samuel Hopkins, D.D.* (1852) and "to converse with her from time to time in regard to her representation of him." A multitude of details made it clear that *The Minister's Wooing* was set in the 1790's, but Harriet represented Dr. Hopkins as a man who had never married and who was, furthermore, essentially an innocent, even a naïve, bachelor. Actually (Park may have thought it strange that Professor Calvin Stowe had not set his wife right on such an obvious matter of fact) Hopkins had married young, specifically in 1748, and had fathered eight children. Possibly Harriet was thinking of Hopkins' marriage to Elizabeth West in 1794, one year after his first wife's death. Elizabeth West, an active member of Hopkins' church and an expert theologian, was something like Harriet's pious and learned heroine, Mary Scudder. But if one believed *The Minister's Wooing,* Hopkins had been unsuccessful in his courtship, being obliged to give up his fiancée to a rival who returned Enoch-Arden-like from his apparent death at sea.

But an authority on Hopkins like Dr. Park would have soon remembered a famous incident which could have suggested *The Minister's Wooing.* Harriet was not writing about Elizabeth West at all; she was simply jumbling persons and chronology. The obvious source of Hopkins' wooing Mary Scudder was an anecdote in *Reminiscences of Samuel Hopkins, D.D.* (1843), by William Patten. There one might read the Puritan romance of Hopkins' youth in Great Barrington before his marriage to Joanna Ingersoll:

> After his settlement in the ministry . . . he paid his addresses to a young woman interesting in appearance and manners, and of a bright intellect, who was also rather a belle in the place. She favored his suit, and so far as appeared there was a mutual attachment, and the time of their marriage was not far distant. But a former lover who had been absent some time, returned, with the design of renewing his attentions, and by direct or explicit manifestations of it, excited in her the expectation of an offer to be his wife. These intimations engaged her affection, and when he made known to her his disappointment and his desire, she frankly disclosed the truth to Mr. Hopkins, and assured him "that however much she respected and esteemed him, she could not fulfill her engagement to him from the heart." This, he said, was a trial, a very great trial; but, as she had not designed to deceive him in the engagements she had given him, he could part with her in friendship.

Probably Dr. Park's conversations with Harriet focused primarily on the justification, if any, for making this incident, which he had merely quoted from Patten in the *Memoir,* part of Hopkins' mature experience. There were, however, yet other matters to worry a scholar-critic. Harriet represented Dr. Ezra Stiles, Hopkins' chief clerical rival in Newport, as still living there in the 1790's, whereas he became President of Yale in 1778. And this was not all: she distorted Stiles, who, as one might see in Park's *Memoir,* had joined Hopkins in signing antislavery documents, into a comic supporter of slavery as a divine providence.

Park may also have criticized Harriet's portrayal of James Marvyn, the young man who in the conclusion returned and won Mary Scudder from Dr. Hopkins. In 1858 and 1859 Park was busy on his *Memoir of Nathanael Emmons; With Sketches of His Friends and Pupils* (1861) ; and he had written, or was just about to write, a biographical sketch of Emmons' famous friend and pupil, Alexander Metcalf Fisher, 'Catharine Beecher's fiancé, who had drowned off the coast of Ireland in 1822. Knowing the ins and outs of the whole affair, Park would have seen immediately that there were striking similarities between characters and situations in *The Minister's Wooing* and this tragedy befalling Catharine Beecher in Harriet's childhood. Like Fisher, James Marvyn apparently drowned before experiencing a conversion, and his mother's revolt against the system preached by Dr. Samuel Hopkins was the thinnest of disguises for Catharine's actual revolt against the system of Dr. Nathanael Emmons, the subject of Park's work in progress, who served as Congregational minister in Franklin, Massachusetts from 1773 to 1827. Park could certainly have found substantial grounds for criticizing Harriet's fictionalizing of Fisher. Fisher may never have had "clear evidences" but he was a remarkably acute thinker, fond of speculating on religious truth and debating close points of theology with Dr. Emmons. Harriet's James Marvyn was so unintellectual that he confessed to Mary that he could not follow the preaching of Dr. Hopkins. It was impossible to imagine that Marvyn would advance, like Fisher, to an appointment as Professor of Mathematics and Natural Philosophy at Yale.

What could Harriet say to such overwhelming scholarship as Dr. Park possessed? She could only nod assent or dissent, for the most part, at appropriate places in the conversation. Somehow Dr. Park was right in all he said and yet he was wrong. Dr. Hopkins was Dr. Hopkins—and Dr. Emmons—and then he wasn't. James, of course, was not exactly Alexander Metcalf Fisher, but then he was Catharine's fiancé, or rather Mrs. Marvyn was Catharine. It was all confused, very much like the business of *Uncle Tom's Cabin* and the attempt to trace out in *A Key* "the facts and documents upon which the story is founded." Almost certainly, Harriet was irritated by Dr. Park, but he was still the kind of man she reverenced, the ascetic, the scholar, the embodiment of New England spiritual intensities, the man of Christ. Of this we can be sure when we read Emily Dickinson's report to her brother Austin of a sermon by Park in 1851: "I never heard anything like it, and don't expect to again, till we stand at the great white throne, and 'he reads from the Book, the Lamb's Book.' The students and chapel people all came to our church, and it was very full, and still, so still the buzzing of a fly would have boomed like a cannon. And when it was all over, and that wonderful man sat down, people stared at each other, and looked as wan and wild as if they had seen a spirit, and wondered they had not died."

Harriet could not close the door on such a man and dismiss his objections. She must try to explain. Finally, she wrote Park a letter, "a very beautiful letter . . . a rare specimen of genius," as he described it, which so pleased him that he loaned it to a friend and it has been lost for almost a century. Fortunately sometime in the 1880's Park summarized Harriet's explanation for the biographer, Florine Thayer McCray: "In her letter she stated that she had planted her seed, that it had germinated and was growing rapidly; she did not think it safe to cut off the branch that was too long, nor to lengthen the branch that was too short, nor to interfere with the natural growth of the plant. She thought that facts were useful in their place, but nature should not conform to them, they were so stubborn."

II

The modern critic, Kenneth Burke, would have understood Harriet far more easily than Dr. Edwards A. Park. In *Lexicon Rhetoricae* (1931) Burke has written: "When the poet has converted his pattern of experience into a Symbolic equivalent, the Symbol becomes a guiding principle in itself." As instinctive novelist, Harriet was modifying the historical circumstances of Doctors Hopkins, Stiles, and Emmons, Alexander Metcalf Fisher, and Catharine Beecher because her Symbol had become a guiding principle in itself, or as she put it in the language of the organic theory, she had planted her seed and it had germinated and was growing rapidly. But we should not suppose *The Minister's Wooing* simply an idea on the loose, a literary Topsy that just "grow'd." Quite as relevant as the recognition that Harriet's first New England novel is not the patching of fact to fact, but fact metamorphosed into a new life, and therefore essentially a work of art, is the realization that she had planted her seed for profoundly personal reasons.

Like everyone else in Andover, Dr. Park knew that Harriet had experienced a profound sorrow in the drowning of her eldest son, Henry Ellis Stowe, in the Connecticut River, July 9, 1857. It is possible that Park was present when, late in August, Henry's body was moved from the tomb in the Old South Churchyard and buried on the sloping hillside to the east of the Stone Cabin behind the Seminary buildings in Andover. Park may have known that Harriet had planted Henry's grave with pansies, white immortelles, white petunias, and verbenas, and he may even have heard that one evening, at least, she kept vigil there in the moonlight with Calvin. It is doubtful, however, that Park made a close correlation between Harriet's grief and *The Minister's Wooing*. There were excellent reasons, at least, for Harriet to practice New England reticence in her conversations with him and to hide the fact that she was anything other than the conventionally pious mother grieving over a departed son full of promise.

Had she made in the 1850's a full disclosure of her response to Henry's death, such as she made thirty years later when she allowed her son Charles to publish her letters in his biography, she might not only have placed herself in an embarrassing position but by the dark principle of guilt through association she might have endangered Calvin Stowe's relations with Andover

Theological Seminary. Park was the last outstanding defender of "the New England theology," the aim of which, he wrote, was "to exalt God as sovereign and to glorify the eternal plan by which he governs the universe." How little Park was given to compromise on theological matters we can see from his statement of 1865 when a Council of the Congregational Church debated whether the Church should call itself Calvinist: "We are Calvinists, mainly, essentially in all the essentials of our faith. And the man who, having pursued a three-years' course of study,—having studied the Bible in the original languages,— is not a Calvinist, is not a respectable man. . . . I should alter my opinion of [this council] at once and totally, if it should discard the name of Calvinists."

Harriet's love for her eldest son Henry was peculiarly tender even when we recognize maternal affection, bordering on obsession, as one of her dominant characteristics. On her second journey to Europe in August, 1856, to secure the British copyright for *Dred* and to give her three eldest children an experience of foreign lands, she was unwilling to part with Henry until the last permitted moment. At eighteen he was entering Dartmouth, but Harriet did not allow him to return to the United States with Calvin, whose duties at Andover called him home in September. She kept Henry with her well into October. Reflecting after his death on their relationship, she employed a metaphor, half-consciously reiterated, perhaps, in her letter to Park concerning *The Minister's Wooing*. She thought of herself as a gardener who had planted the seed of some rare exotic, which she shifted from soil to soil, watered and watched through thousands of mischiefs and accidents, counting every leaf and strengthening the stem until the blossom bud was formed: "What curiosity, what eagerness, what expectation,—what longing now to see the mystery unfold in the new flower."

The mystery Harriet was eager to see unfold, of course, was Henry's personality, but for her (we must remember her own conversion a decade before) the human personality could reach full development only when, through the operation of grace, the will of Christ became the steady pulse of its existence. Henry had not yet passed that crucial stage. From Dartmouth he wrote his mother in Europe: "I may not be what the world calls a Christian, but I will live such a life as a Christian ought to live, such a life as every true man ought to live." She must have read his words with profound attention; almost certainly they were in her thoughts when she returned from Europe in June, 1857, with the expectation of conferring with him at the Stone Cabin. But Henry wrote that final examinations prevented his visiting Andover; he would not be able to see his mother for two weeks. Harriet could not wait that long. With her second son Frederick, she set off immediately for Hanover. As ill luck would have it, Frederick caught cold on the journey, and she was forced to turn back to "a water-cure establishment." There she received a telegram calling her immediately to Andover. When she arrived, she found the house filled with Henry's grief-stricken classmates: Henry had drowned in the Connecticut River and they had brought his body for burial.

At first Harriet was untroubled by doubts as to her son's eternal state. When, two days after the funeral, she went with Calvin to Hanover to learn of Henry's last days, she thought of the bend in the Connecticut where he had drowned as the place whence he had risen to heaven. In consideration of her mood and her own impressive labors for the Negro, it was appropriate that at Hanover an old, deaf slave woman, with five children still in bondage, should tell her: "Bear up, dear soul . . . you must bear it, for the Lord loves ye." The speaker and the sentiment must have been nearly irresistible, but it was only at first that she could accept the old woman's words without question. Harriet's religious struggles of the 1840's had been a long, an arduous confronting of the crucial issues of Calvinism intellectually as well as emotionally; intellectual acceptance of austere hypotheses, paralleling modern existentialism in their severity, had, in fact, been the starting place for her inner adventure. After her return to Andover, the theological implications of her son's case quite naturally confronted her. Like John Calvin, whom Lyman Beecher correctly placed among the earliest refuters of the doctrine of infant damnation, neither

the Beechers nor Calvin Stowe subscribed to the doctrine of
infant damnation. In 1849 Charley Stowe, only a year old,
had certainly been received by God without a moment's hesitation, but in 1857 Henry Ellis Stowe, a young man of nineteen,
was, by the logic of his mother's Calvinism, almost certainly
in hell.

Superficially, Harriet's psychological situation paralleled that
of her sister Catharine in 1822 after the death of Alexander
Metcalf Fisher. When Lyman Beecher heard the news in New
Haven, the best consolation he could give Catharine concerning
Fisher's "present existence in the eternal state" was this: "I
can only say that many did and will indulge the hope that he
was pious, though without such evidence as caused him to
indulge hope." At first Catharine bowed to divine edict; she
wrote her brother Edward that "the Judge of the whole earth
cannot but do right," but her subsequent difficulties led to a
lengthy epistolary debate with Edward and her father in which
she questioned the basic assumptions of Calvinism. She granted
that Fisher was guilty (that is, unregenerate), and she went so
far as to confess that in herself she could see "nothing but the
most debasing selfishness and depravity." However, since she
had not received "a nature pure and uncontaminated," she could
not reasonably acknowledge guilt in the orthodox Calvinistic
fashion: "I can not feel this; I never shall by any mental exertion
of my own; and if I ever do feel it, it will be by the interference
of divine Omnipotence, and the work would seem to me miracu-
lous."

On Lyman's study desk, Catharine left a note describing herself as a helpless being in a frail bark driven relentlessly on a
swift current toward a tremendous precipice; there was One
on the shore who might save but "He regards me not." Lyman
felt the challenge of what he described to Edward as her "aw-
fully interesting" state of mind. On the reverse of Catherine's
letter, he replied for God. As God, He had seen the frail bark
and pressed to the rescue; He had called to her; He had
stretched out His Hand; all to no avail. Finally, He had
sunk (in Fisher) the bark which contained all her earthly

treasure; still He was unheard. Speaking for God, Lyman concluded: "What shall I do? Yet a little longer will I wait, and if she accept my proffered aid, then shall her feet be planted on a rock, and a new song be put into her mouth. If she refuse, the stream will roll on, and the bark, the oar, and the voyager be seen no more."

Having meditated her father's letter, Catharine proceeded to Franklin, Massachusetts, to search for overlooked evidence that Fisher had been converted and was in heaven. There she learned more definitely that though he had sought since childhood to yield himself to God, he had been unable to do so. The local expert on the unseen only deepened her gloom, for she found unanswerable Dr. Nathanael Emmons' well-buttressed assertion that God had made us all machines with wickedness *"put into us."* Catharine wrote her father that life was a maze. Her lost friend had done all that unassisted human strength could do, yet somewhere in eternity he must be wailing that he had ever been born. Since she had not herself experiencd conversion, she was following her lover to the dark world where hope never comes. She could neither bend her knees nor open her lips in prayer. She considered rejecting religion altogether and living according to the pagan philosophy "Let us eat and drink, for tomorrow we die."

With a capricious inclination to embrace the faith that was destroying her, Catharine, however, remained loyal to Calvinism. When three years later, in 1825, Harriet experienced her "easy conversion," anticipating her "true" conversion of 1845, Catharine urged her to investigate her spiritual state carefully. As Charles Stowe phrased it (doubtless quoting Harriet in the amused detachment of her old age), "Catharine was afraid that there might be something wrong in the case of the lamb that had come into the fold without first being chased all over the lot by the shepherd." After the Beechers moved to Cincinnati, Catharine published in 1836 (the year of Emerson's *Nature*) *Letters on the Difficulties of Religion,* "respectfully dedicated to an honored and beloved Father." That dedication should have warned biographers not to make their liberal reading of her assertion "God does not require of us anything but what we have full ability to perform." Catharine's main point in her book was, in fact, that "all mankind are in danger of eternal ruin; that securing true piety is the only method of safety." The *Letters* was a warning to those, who at peril of their souls, had fallen into skepticism and Unitarianism and by-passed the essential experience of conversion.

But Catharine's orthodoxy was only temporary. In 1857, the year of Henry Ellis Stowe's death, she expressed her mature views in *Common Sense Applied to Religion; or the Bible and the People.* This book was not dedicated "respectfully to an honored and beloved Father," but to "the People, as the safest and truest interpreters of the Bible, and TO WOMAN, as the heaven-appointed educator of Mind. . . ." The "illustrative Mental History" by way of preface was Catharine's account of her opposition to her father's Calvinism from her earliest years. The period following Fisher's death now seemed to her "a constant conflict between the theories to which I had bowed my intellect, and thought I really believed, and the impulses of my moral nature and common sense." In the "Addenda," she broke with the whole Beecher clan. She attacked the Augustinian basis of Calvinism; she discovered small comfort in her brother Edward's attempt in *The Conflict of Ages* (1853) to save, with the help of Origen, some vestige of the Augustinian position; she described the writings of Jonathan Edwards as "contradictory and inconsistent," and finally, she lined herself up with Augustine's opponent, Pelagius, who denied the doctrine of Original Sin, and those modern Pelagians, the Unitarians.

During her visit at Hanover, Harriet had been certain that Henry was in heaven, but after her return to Andover, she seems to have relived in a matter of weeks this pattern of dismay and ultimate acceptance of "common sense," which for Catharine had extended over a quarter century. Like Catharine in her despair of the 1820's, Harriet apparently felt "a constant conflict between the theories to which I had bowed my intellect, and thought I really believed, and the impulses of my moral nature and common sense." As she wrote Catharine:

If ever I was conscious of an attack of the Devil trying to separate me from the love of Christ, it was for some weeks after the terrible news came. I was in a state of great physical weakness, most agonizing, and unable to control my thoughts. Distressing doubts as to Henry's spiritual state were rudely thrust upon my soul. It was as if a voice had said to me: "You trusted in God, did you? You believed that He loved you! You had perfect confidence that he would never take your child till the work of grace was mature! Now He has hurried him into eternity without a moment's warning, without preparation, and where is he?"

Since Henry had given no clear evidence that he had been saved, the answer to this awful question must be that probably he was in hell.

With her profound maternal affection, Harriet shrank from such a conclusion with a horror far greater than that of Catharine confronted by the eternal loss of Alexander Metcalf Fisher, and being primarily emotional rather than logical, Harriet bypassed that long stage of intellectual conflict signalized by Catharine's epistolary debate with Lyman Beecher. Omitting entirely the later stage, indicated by *Letters on the Difficulties of Religion,* where Catharine momentarily returned enthusiastically to the logic of Calvinism, Harriet apparently in one rush of feeling left the "attack of the Devil" behind her and moved on, doubtless inspired in part by Catharine's recent book, to the comfortable realm of "common sense":

I saw at last that these thoughts were irrational, and contradicted the calm, settled belief of my better moments, and that they were dishonorable to God, and that it was my duty to resist them, and to assume and steadily maintain that Jesus in love had taken my dear one to his bosom. Since then the Enemy has left me in peace.

It is our duty to assume that a thing which would be in its very nature unkind, ungenerous, and unfair has not been done. What should we think of the crime of that human being who should take a young mind from circumstances where it was progressing in virtue, and throw it recklessly into corrupting and depraving society? Particularly if it were the child of one who had trusted and confided in Him for years. No! no such slander as this shall the Devil ever fix in my mind against my Lord and my God!

But we should not take Harriet at her word in this letter. Her heart was badly clouding her mind. Those "distressing doubts as to Henry's spiritual state" which she called "an attack of the Devil" and "a slander . . . against my Lord and my God" may have been, from a liberal point of view, "irrational" but they did not contradict what she called "the calm, settled belief of my better moments." Since her "true" conversion a decade before, her calm, settled belief had been Edwardean Calvinism. To the Edwardeans, all human souls in maturity were so intrinsically corrupt, if they had not been redeemed by the unmerited operation of a divine and supernatural light, that God with eminent justice might cast any one of them into hell. As for the argument, if we can call it an argument, that God would hesitate in the case of a young mind progressing in virtue "Particularly if it were the child of one who had trusted and confided in Him for years," this would have impressed any well-informed Puritan clergyman as a homemade doctrine, a heretical development of New England theology. God, of course, would listen to prayer and doubtless take it into consideration in his judicial review, but the trust and confidence of mothers, sisters, brothers, husbands, and wives was essentially irrelevant. The one truly relevant consideration was the inner state of the individual before the bar of eternal justice. In her maternal anxiety to find Henry saved, Harriet had forgotten the actual basis of her own faith in Edwardean Calvinism; she had invented a homemade doctrine of cosmic special privilege; she had supposed herself safe and sound in Catharine's comfortable realm of "common sense" when in fact, as her subsequent inner history makes clear, she was still involved in the Puritan maze.

For approximately a year after Henry's death, Harriet, however, either did not recognize the true nature of her predicament or was reluctant to face it. She and Dr. Park would have been in perfect agreement as to the fashion in which a Christian (that is, a Puritan) mother should react to her son's death and probable eternal loss. It was all comprised in the word "submission." The model can be found again and again in Puritan sermons and Puritan journals, nowhere more clearly, perhaps, than in a book Harriet doubtless knew, *Memoirs of the Life of Mrs. Sarah Osborne* (1798), edited by the hero of *The Minister's Wooing*, Dr. Samuel Hopkins. There Mrs. Osborne, for Hopkins the type of the Puritan saint, recorded in her journal her experience of 1744 on the death of her twelve-year-old son, like Henry unregenerate and therefore destined almost certainly for the eternal fires:

While friends were putting on his grave clothes, I went out into the field and walked, where, with more secrecy and freedom, I could breathe out my soul to God. And the sweetness of that season I cannot express. God discovered himself to be my God, my covenant God, my Father, my Friend, my only portion and happiness, my sovereign, my all in all, my infinite fountain of all fullness. . . . O, his word comforted, his *rod* comforted me. . . . But as I followed to the grave, I pleaded thus with God, "Lord, I adore thee still as my sovereign. I do not repine at thy hand. But, dear Lord, pity me, and suffer me to weep under the smart of thy rod; it is my *only son*." Then I thought on Psalm ciii. "As a father pitieth his children, so the Lord pitieth them that fear him." This comforted me. . . . These and such like were the exercises of my mind, while following and laying my dust into the grave. And ever since I have been kept composed and cheerful.

Two months after Henry's death, believing that she had reached the cheerful composure of a Mrs. Osborne, Harriet wrote her daughters still in Paris: "I think I have felt the healing touch of Jesus of Nazareth on the deep wound in my heart, for I have golden hours of calm when I say: 'Even so, Father, for so it seemed good in thy sight.' So sure am I that the most generous love has ordered all, that I can now take pleasure to give this little proof of my unquestioning confidence in resigning one of my dearest comforts to Him." She gave this confidence semi-literary expression in a brief allegory, "The Mourning Veil," published anonymously in the first issue of the *Atlantic Monthly*, November, 1857. A mourning veil is unaccountably mixed in with a purchase of dresses brought home by a father to his superficially happy wife and children. They all regard it as ugly—all except their friend and clergyman, Father Payson, who tells them "Sorrow is God's school," and

reminds them of Jesus' words, "Blessed are they that mourn."
The truth of Father Payson's view is clear after Rose, the eldest
daughter, is killed that evening rescuing her sister from a fire
in the nursery. At first the mother can see only God's "in-
flexible severity" in her own case and in such village tragedies
as that of the blind man whose son drowned in his presence
while he could do nothing to save him. She is "only crushed
and darkened,—not amended." With the tactful help of Father
Payson and the passage of time, however, she becomes "calm
once more, and happy,—happy with a wider and steadier basis
than ever before. A new world seemed opened within her; and
with a heart raised in thankfulness she placed the veil among
her most sacred treasures."

In "The Mourning Veil," Harriet was mechanical in following the platitudes of piety. The primary reason for her con-
ventionality was doubtless her psychological need to place her
own experience in the framework of orthodoxy; she wanted to
be the mother of the story. It was only in the brief reference to
the blind man whose son drowned in his presence past his help
that she dared to recognize in imagination the tragic aspect of
her own situation. Probably, it was again the desire in part,
but certainly not entirely, to prove to herself that she had no
quarrel with the ancestral faith which lay behind her enthusiasm
for Calvinism in a review in the *Atlantic,* the following February, of William B. Sprague's *Annals of the American Pulpit.*
Harriet's special point of emphasis in "New England Ministers"
was the personalities of the Calvinistic clergy. They were not
a grim lot: "There was no such thing as a clerical mould or
pattern; but each minister, particularly in the rural districts,
grew and flourished as freely and unconventionally as the apple-
trees in his own orchard. . . . New England ministers never
held it a sin to laugh; if they did, some of them had a great deal
to answer for; for they could scarce open their mouths without
dropping some provocation to a smile." Parson Hemmenway,
for example, was completely indifferent to dress. When he
was criticized for his slovenliness by the meticulous Dr. Deane,
who said, "Now I am particular always to appear with my wig

on," Hemmenway wittily replied: "Precisely. . . . I know it
is well to bestow more abundant honor on the part that lacketh."
The ministers even showed a bright enthusiasm in their prayers.
A Whig minister of New Haven, ordered during the Revolution
to pray for the King, looked to heaven and exclaimed: "O Lord,
bless thy servant, King George, and grant unto him wisdom;
for thou knowest, O Lord, he needs it." During the embargo
on New England shipping instituted by Jefferson, Federalist
Parson Eaton of Harpswell, Maine, prayed politics in this
fashion: "Forasmuch as thou hast commanded us to pray for
our enemies, we pray for the President of these United States."

Harriet did not overlook theology in her fascination with the
Calvinistic clergy. She singled out Dr. Samuel Hopkins for
special praise on the grounds of his practical application of the
doctrine of disinterested benevolence in fighting slavery. She
also found justification for the "Doctrine of Divine Sovereignty":

Doctor Arnold says it is necessary for the highest development
of the soul that it should have somewhere an object of entire reverence enthroned above all possibility of doubt or criticism. Now a
radically democratic system, like that of New England, at once
sweeps all factitious reliances of this kind from the soul. No crown,
no court, no nobility, no ritual, no hierarchy,—the beautiful principles of reverence and loyalty might have died out of the American
heart, had not these men by their religious teachings upborne it as
on eagles' wings to the footstool of the King Eternal, Immortal,
Invisible. Hence we see why what was commonly called among
them the "Doctrine of Divine Sovereignty" acquired so prominent
a place in their preaching and their hearts.

In her essay, again arguing that Calvinism was the balance
wheel of democracy, and naming Catharine's mighty opposite,
Dr. Nathanael Emmons, Harriet even defended the doctrine of
predestination:

With them predestination must be made to harmonize with free
will; the Divine entire efficiency with human freedom; the existence
of sin with the Divine benevolence;—and at it they went with stout
hearts, as men work who are not in the habit of being balked in
their undertakings. Hence the Edwardses, the Hopkinses, the

Emmonses, with all their various schools and followers, who, leviathan-like, have made the theological deep of New England to boil like a pot, and the agitation of whose course remains to this day. It is a mark of a shallow mind to scorn these theological wrestlings and surgings; they have had in them something even sublime. They were always bounded and steadied by the most profound reverence for God and his word; and they have constituted in New England the strong mental discipline needed by a people who were an absolute democracy.

How do we reconcile this clear intellectual comprehension of the major tenets of Calvinism and obvious intellectual approval of them with the homemade doctrine of special privilege in assuming Henry saved? This was the dilemma confronting Harriet. In June, 1858, almost a year after Henry's death, she wrote Lady Byron: "I think very much on the subject on which you conversed with me once,—the future state of retribution. It is evident to me that the spirit of Christianity has produced in the human spirit a tenderness of love which wholly revolts from the old doctrine on the subject, and I observe the more Christ-like any one becomes, the more impossible it seems for him to accept it; and yet, on the contrary, it was Christ who said, 'Fear Him that is able to destroy soul and body in hell,' and the most appalling language on this subject is that of Christ himself."

By February, 1859, Harriet was using the metaphor of a growing thing far less optimistically than in her earlier image of herself as gardener, helping Henry to unfold. She wrote her sixteen-year-old daughter, Georgianna:

Why haven't I written? Because, dear Georgie, I am like the dry, dead, leafless tree, and have only cold, dead, slumbering buds of hope on the end of stiff, hard frozen twigs of thought, but no leaves, no blossoms; nothing to send to a little girl who doesn't know what to do with herself any more than a kitten. I am cold, weary, dead; everything is a burden to me.

I let my plants die by inches before my eyes, and do not water them, and I dread everything I do, and wish it was not to be done, and so when I get a letter from my little girl I smile and say, "Dear little puss, I will answer it"; and I sit hour after hour with folded hands, looking at the inkstand and dreading to begin. The fact is, pussy, mamma is tired. Life to you is gay and joyous, but to mamma it has been a battle in which the spirit is willing but the flesh weak, and she would be glad, like the woman in the St. Bernard, to lie down with her arms around the wayside cross, and sleep away into a brighter scene. Henry's fair, sweet face looks down upon me now and then from out a cloud, and I feel again all the bitterness of the eternal "No" which says I must never, never, in this life, see that face, lean on that arm, hear that voice. Not that my faith in God in the least fails, and that I do not believe that all this is for good. I do, and though not happy, I am blessed. Weak, weary as I am, I rest on Jesus in the innermost depth of my soul, and am quite sure that there is coming an inconceivable hour of beauty and glory when I shall regain Jesus, and he will give me back my beloved one, whom he is educating in a far higher sphere than I proposed. So do not mistake me,—only know that mamma is sitting weary by the wayside, feeling weak and worn, but in no sense discouraged.

This does not sound like the mood in which anyone could write a readable novel, but paradoxically it was doubtless Harriet's very frustration and weariness which propelled her into *The Minister's Wooing.* In *Beyond the Pleasure Principle* (1920), Freud, after studying cases of war neurosis, maintained that there is a repetition-compulsion in the psyche, that dreams, and often the play of children, are re-creations of frustrating experiences in the attempt unconsciously to master them. In a novelist like Harriet, whose books were largely the result of inner compulsions, dream and art are almost interchangeable terms. Certainly *Uncle Tom's Cabin,* with its leitmotif of the mother separated from her child, may be interpreted in part as the attempt to master the death of little Charley Stowe. Similarly, in re-creating Henry as James Marvyn, apparently lost in flesh and spirit, Harriet imaginatively confronted the situation which had provoked "an attack of the Devil" and, at a later stage, reduced her to a "dry, dead, leafless tree." Weak and weary by the wayside, Harriet instinctively roused herself to face images of her inner conflict.

III

Analyzing only superficially the actual nature of Harriet's spiritual history, critics and biographers have leaped to the conclusion that her way out of her dismay over Henry was to demolish Calvinism. In *Trumpets of Jubilee* (1927), Constance Rourke argued that *The Minister's Wooing* chronicled a defeat for Lyman Beecher in love and religion and constituted "a long assault on the Puritan Faith." In *Saints, Sinners and Beechers* (1934), Harriet's grandson, Lyman Beecher Stowe, wrote: *"The Minister's Wooing* was an attack on the cruelty and injustice of Calvinism just as *Uncle Tom's Cabin* was an attack on the cruelty and injustice of slavery. In *The Minister's Wooing* she attacked Calvinism without attacking Calvinists just as in *Uncle Tom's Cabin* she attacked slavery without attacking slaveholders." In her later books such as *American Humor,* Miss Rourke was an exciting and perceptive critic but she was ignorant in supposing that Harriet sought to defeat her father in the person of Dr. Hopkins. Miss Rourke did not know New England heroics when she met them; Hopkins' renunciation of Mary Scudder, after James returned, was not defeat but a victory of disinterested benevolence. Mr. Stowe seems to frame a more respectable thesis, but his grandmother would have been surprised, to say the least, at his equation of slavery and Calvinism.

What most critics have missed is the fact that, in confronting Henry's death, Harriet was frustrated not only by austere hypotheses, compounded with a deep sense of loss, but by conflicting loyalties. Later generations might find Calvinism completely unlovely; to her, as witness "New England Ministers," it was "a mark of a shallow mind to scorn these theological wrestlings and surgings"; Calvinism, with its strong mental discipline, had kept self-government from degenerating into anarchy; in itself, Calvinism was a sublime faith, and in fundamentals, true. Yet these theological wrestlings and surgings led logically to the horrible conclusion that Henry was in hell. In her letters Harriet had developed what I have called a homemade doctrine to insure Henry's salvation, but she must have known in the depths of her mind that such a doctrine was homemade and that it was actually inconsistent with the logic she herself had accepted in the intense inner struggles which culminated in her own conversion of 1845. As she was driven by a repetition-compulsion to face Henry's death and the conflict of love and theology, Harriet was thus involved in a maze: what head approved, heart insisted on avoiding, yet a separation of the interests of head and heart was virtually impossible since her faith had an intellectual basis in the logic of Calvinism.

The distinction of *The Minister's Wooing* rests on the fact that Harriet did not, in fact could not, either demolish Calvinism or accept it completely, but was forced by her circumstances and her religious history to recognize both its positive and negative aspects. We find the almost perfect epigraph for a study of *The Minister's Wooing* in a searching generalization made by Lionel Trilling in discussing V. L. Parrington's *Main Currents in American Thought:*

> Parrington's characteristic weakness as a historian is suggested by his title, for the culture of a nation is not truly figured in the image of the current. A culture is not a flow, nor even a confluence; the form of its existence is struggle, or at least debate—it is nothing if not a dialectic. And in any culture there are likely to be certain artists who contain a large part of the dialectic within themselves, their meaning and power lying in their contradictions; they contain within themselves, it may be said, the very essence of the culture, and the sign of this is that they do not submit to serve the ends of any one ideological group or tendency. It is a significant circumstance of American culture, and one which is susceptible of explanation, that an unusually large proportion of its notable writers of the nineteenth century were such repositories of the dialectic of their times—they contained both the yes and the no of their culture, and by that token they were prophetic of the future.

On the level of exposition, Harriet's chapter "Views of Divine Government" illustrates her ability to speak the yes and no of her culture and by that token to prophesy the mature understanding of Puritanism mid-twentieth century scholars like Perry Miller are beginning to furnish us. Nowhere outside of Calvinistic New England, she wrote, was there a community where the roots of common life shot down so deeply and were so intensely grappled around things sublime and eternal. In the intervals of planting and harvesting, New England ministers were busy with the toils of adjusting the laws of the universe; in their old one-horse chaises, they made long journeys to settle points of celestial jurisprudence and to compare their maps of the Infinite. Their conclusions, differing only in particulars from parish to parish, were discussed by farmers at the plow and by their wives and daughters at loom, spinning wheel, and wash tub. No greater challenge was ever posed to common men and women. The accepted assumptions were that human beings came into existence with natures so fatally distorted that, although they were perfectly free agents, they could do nothing acceptable to God until regenerated by supernatural aid. But that aid was decreed only an infinitely small number; most of the human race was damned to such awful, everlasting torments that Jonathan Edwards set apart fast days on which he walked the floor, weeping and wringing his hands. In other Christian sects, the church interposed some protecting shield: baptism, which infolded the individual, however sinful, in some vague sphere of love and protection, or prayers for the dead, which might mitigate judgment. But in Calvinism, no rite, no form, no paternal relation, no faith or prayer of church, stood between the trembling human spirit and Eternal Justice; the individual entered eternity alone. In a system like this, dealing with the infinite, there was particular danger from small admixtures of human error, for (Harriet's metaphor suggests Emily Dickinson and Melville) "The smallest speck of earth's dust, in the focus of an infinite lens, appears magnified among the heavenly orbs as a frightful monster." As we might expect, Calvinism exerted on some minds the "effect of a slow poison, producing life habits of morbid action," and for almost all, fearful shadows lay over cradle and grave. It is no wonder that the funeral bell in green hollows and lonely dells was a sound which shook the soul and made the listener search his heart with fearful questions.

No Unitarian or Transcendentalist contemporary of Harriet's stated the negative aspects of Calvinism more completely than this. In fact, she would seem to have ruled out the possibility of any redeeming feature. But in the midst of her apparent demolition, she still managed to say yes, if a somewhat reluctant yes, to her culture: "Almost all the histories of religious experience of those times relate paroxysms of opposition to God and fierce rebellion, expressed in language which appalls the very soul, followed at length by mysterious elevations of faith and reactions of confiding love, the result of Divine interposition, which carried the soul far above the region of the Intellect, into that of direct spiritual intuition." Jonathan Edwards himself, as he related in *Personal Narrative,* had experienced enmity to God, which had been overcome by "an inward and sweet sense," as he walked the fields and saw "the blending of the Divine majesty with a calm, sweet, and almost infinite meekness." Doubtless making use of her own experience, Harriet had this well-tempered praise for Puritan piety: "The piety which grew up under such a system was, of necessity, energetic; it was the uprousing of the whole energy of the human soul, pierced and wrenched and probed from her lowest depths to her topmost heights with every awful life force possible to existence. He whose faith in God came clear through these terrible tests would be sure never to know greater ones. He might certainly challenge earth or heaven, things present or things to come, to swerve him from this grand allegiance."

Harriet, however, was not so naïve, nor so unrealistic, as to suppose that all the men and women in late eighteenth-century New England truly met the challenge of this grand allegiance. She knew that in Puritan civilization, as in any other civilization, there are those who simply accept, without deep personal involvement, the ideals to which the culture officially dedicates itself. She illustrated this insight in a half dozen minor characters. Mary's mother, the Widow Scudder, for example, is very little troubled by the complexities and awful challenges of her faith: she is a matter-of-fact woman, of great domestic efficiency, who accepts Calvinism because "Mr. Scudder used to believe it,—*I* will." Somewhat of her persuasion, but less intelligent, is the earthy Mrs. Jones, who can listen to Dr. Hopkins' distinctions regarding motive without the slightest disturbance. To all he says, she expresses the same reaction: "that it was

good, and she liked it, and the Doctor was a good man. . . ."
On the humorous level, the Marvyns' Negro woman, Candace,
accepts Hopkinsian theology because the Doctor has gone from
door to door raising money to redeem her cousin from a hard
master. Before Hopkins' humane deed, Candace had great
trouble with the doctrine of Original Sin, for she could not
remember taking a single bite of the fatal apple. Once he had
demonstrated his concern for her race, however, she was willing,
if he insisted, to confess that she had eaten the whole apple tree.

This humor testifies that Harriet was still inclined to the
practice of what I have called New England doubleness, that
tendency to be by turns the sober-minded, emotionally intense
Puritan and the humorous, realistic Yankee of her father's and
her husband's anecdotes. It was this doubleness which made it
possible for her to realize concretely, as no one before her had
done, the inner and outer aspects of life lived in terms of the
Puritan ideal stated abstractly by Jonathan Edwards in *A
Treatise Concerning Religious Affections* (1746):

> As on the one hand, there must be light in the understanding,
> as well as an affected fervent heart; where there is heat without
> light, there can be nothing divine or heavenly in that heart; so on
> the other hand, where there is a kind of light without heat, a head
> stored with notions and speculations, with a cold and unaffected
> heart, there can be nothing divine in that light, that knowledge
> is no true spiritual knowledge of divine things.

Simeon Brown, wealthy shipowner and slave trader of Newport,
is an almost perfect illustration of what Edwards meant when
he warned against "a kind of light without heat, a head stored
with notions and speculations, with a cold and unaffected
heart. . . ." Brown is "one of that class of people who, of a
freezing day, will plant themselves directly between you and
the fire, and there stand and argue to prove that selfishness is
the root of all moral evil." He supposes himself submissive to
God's will because he has no nerves to feel, nor imagination to
conceive, endless happiness or suffering. Calvinistic theology
is algebra to him. As his almost equally insensitive wife remarks, "nothing pleases that man better than a hard doc-

trine . . . he just reasons it all out plain; and he says people have no need to be in the dark; and that's my opinion. 'If folks know they ought to come up to anything, why don't they?' he says; and I say so too."

In contrast, Deacon Twitchell symbolizes, in Edwards' words, the need for "light in the understanding, as well as an affected fervent heart. . . ." The Deacon is not sure that he should continue his place in the church. "Disinterested benevolence" involves him in a maze. One winter night he supposed he acted without selfishness in rising from a warm bed to carry wood to an old woman, Beulah Ward, who commonly traded his gifts for rum. But when he came down with rheumatism and was taunted by his skeptical daughter, Cerinthy Ann, he was forced to conclude that he was "jest a-makin' a righteousness of it." For him, theology possesses none of the icy delights it possesses for Simeon Brown. One day as they laid stone wall, Twichell's brother, Seth, "all for imputation of Adam's sin," and "a masterhand" at reading, confronted the Deacon with the arguments of Dr. Mayhew. The Deacon came home "quite beat out," and had to rest before supper for the first time since he fell sick with typhus. After supper, before the fire, Seth started the theological debate anew, but Mrs. Twitchell told him: "Now, Seth, these 'ere things, doesn't hurt you; but the Deacon is weakly, and if he gets his mind riled after supper, he don't sleep none all night."

Far less convincing than these minor characters, who are American originals, are those figures who range somewhere between major and minor in the space allotted them, Mme de Frontignac and Senator Aaron Burr. In Mme de Frontignac, Harriet apparently intended an exotic heroine, an embodiment of her conviction, noted in *Sunny Memories of Foreign Lands,* that the French character was not "mere outside," that it possessed "an iris-like variety and versatility of nature, a quickness in catching and reflecting the various shades of emotion or fancy, a readiness in seizing upon one's own half-expressed thoughts, and running them out in a thousand graceful little tendrils." Doubtless both Harriet and her first American readers found

Virginie a relief from Puritan intensities, but for us the Puritan intensities are a relief from her. It is no longer possible to develop excitement over such an obvious symbol of Europe, the aristocratic, the fascinating, the tenderly refined, even though Harriet tells us again and again how exciting Virginie is.

In creating Aaron Burr, Harriet's source was apparently the tainted but sainted hero of James Parton's *The Life and Times of Aaron Burr* (1858). This moral enigma, an amalgam of the Byronic hero and the Gothic monster out of Horace Walpole and Mrs. Radcliffe, illustrated for Harriet Puritanism in decay. Burr's "keenest delicacy of fibre," as she called it, his intellectual ability, his delicate perceptions, were what we might expect from the grandson of Jonathan Edwards. But Burr was Puritan intellect and will unredeemed by religious commitment or earthly love. Harriet's intention was a figure like Ethan Brand, who was guilty of the Unpardonable Sin, defined by Hawthorne as "The sin of an intellect that triumphed over the sense of brotherhood with man and reverence for God, and sacrificed everything to its own mighty claims!" Like Brand, who had made Esther, the daughter of old Humphrey, "the subject of a psychological experiment, and wasted, absorbed, and perhaps annihilated her soul, in the process," Burr in *The Minister's Wooing* seeks to awaken Mme de Frontignac "from a careless child to a deep-hearted, thinking, suffering human being" as an experiment "because he felt an artistic pleasure in the beautiful light and heat, and cared not, though it burned a soul away." In Burr, Harriet registered an insight into the degenerate Puritanism which obsessed Hawthorne, but she only registered it; she did not realize it with a figure like Brand who stalks the imagination with the elemental power of a nightmare. Carl Van Doren wittily characterized Harriet's Aaron Burr as a villain "to frighten schoolgirls with." This is not fair to her intention, but unfortunately it is dangerously near the impression even a generous reader takes from the book.

In dealing with her major characters, Mrs. Marvyn, her son James, Mary Scudder, and Dr. Hopkins, Harriet, however, so fully compensates for Burr and Mme de Frontignac that Van

Doren wrote of *The Minister's Wooing:* "no other imaginative treatment so well sets forth the strange, dusky, old Puritan world of the later eighteenth century when Newport was the center at once of the ruthless divinity of Samuel Hopkins, the minister of the novel, and of the African slave trade." It is a remarkable personal and literary achievement when we remember Harriet's description of herself as "the dry, dead, leafless tree." But it was through the creation of characters who said both yes and no to Calvinism and through the creation of a young man like Henry that she could give order to her inner conflict and to a degree rid herself of it.

Mrs. Marvyn is primarily a vehicle for expressing concretely the negative aspects of Calvinism. In creating her, Harriet combined her own "attack of the devil," when she had doubted God's goodness, with her sister Catharine's struggles of 1822 in the meshes of Calvinistic logic. Mrs. Marvyn in Dr. Hopkins' church is very much like Catharine in the presence of Nathanael Emmons. For years Mr. Marvyn had been a deacon of the church, but his wife "had sat in her pew while the sacramental elements were distributed, a mournful spectator. Punctilious in every duty, exact, reverential, she still regarded herself as a child of wrath, an enemy to God, and an heir of perdition; nor could she see any hope of remedy, except in the sovereign, mysterious decree of an Infinite and Unknown Power, a mercy for which she waited with the sickness of hope deferred. . . . No pair of eyes followed the web of his [Hopkins'] reasonings with a keener and more anxious watchfulness than those sad, deep-set, hazel ones; and as she was drawn along the train of its inevitable logic, a close observer might have seen how the shadows deepened over them."

In terms of the Puritan yardstick furnished by Jonathan Edwards, here, of course, is an illustration of "a head stored with notions and speculations, with a cold and unaffected heart." But Harriet's human sympathies, her realistic imagination, her own brief rebellion, and her comprehension of Catharine's long struggle told her such a reading was mechanical. Using hints from the character of Professor Fisher's mother, she demon-

strated that the difficulties of a Mrs. Marvyn might have nothing
in common with the inhuman coldness of a Simeon Brown.
Originally, Mrs. Marvyn possessed woman's instinctive desire
to live in a world of feeling, but she married a precise, reticent
man, who taught her early in their marriage that "Once for all,
they loved each other, and after that, the less said, the better."
Her husband has set the tone for the relations of the whole
family. Though there is great mutual love and confidence, there
is little demonstrated affection between parents and children,
brothers and sisters, and "a caressing or affectionate expression
could not have passed the lips of one to another without a painful
awkwardness." Mrs. Marvyn can conceive of a better life than
one painted in low, cool tones, but hers still seems good and
reasonable to her since she is strongly inclined toward the intellectual. Repressing emotion, she has cultivated her mind.
She never misses a day in her reading, and on the table in her
bedroom, "History, biography, mathematics, volumes of the
encyclopaedia, poetry, novels, all alike found their time and place
there; and while she pursued her household labors, the busy,
active soul within traveled cycles and cycles of thought, few of
which ever found expression in words." To her, "in the old
staring, rattle-windowed meeting house," Harriet attributed
her own recognition, noted in one of her letters from Europe,
that New England stifled the love of the beautiful: Mrs. Marvyn
longs to see the pictures of Leonardo da Vinci and to hear
the music of Mozart. For days, she is absorbed in "mathematical or metaphysical studies," and like Harriet's highly intellectual aunt, Mary Hubbard, Mrs. Marvyn once found a mistake
in a treatise on perspective and corrected it.

Harriet thus made it clear that circumstances, her husband,
and her given inclination toward the intellectual made the
"affected fervent heart" virtually an impossibility for Mrs.
Marvyn: "She delighted in the regions of mathematical knowledge, and walked them as a native home, but the commerce
with the abstract certainties fitted her mind still more to be
stiffened and enchained by glacial reasonings, in regions where
spiritual intuitions are as necessary as wings to birds." Here

was a mind for which, in its inevitable fascination with theology, Calvinism could hardly fail to be a "slow poison," and one almost fatal to life. This Harriet showed in the scenes where, like herself and like Catharine, Mrs. Marvyn had to face the frightening probability that a loved one was in hell. With only a change into the plural, Harriet had Mrs. Marvyn quote Catharine's observation in *Common Sense Applied to Religion:* "I am quite sure there must be a dreadful mistake somewhere."

But logically what was the mistake of Calvinism? Making use of her own meditation on Luther and Calvin in the shadow of Mont Blanc, to which I have already referred, Harriet represented Mrs. Marvyn as arguing that the laws of nature confirm the dark insights of Puritanism:

I have thought, in desperate moments, of giving up the Bible itself. But what do I gain? Do I not see the same difficulty in Nature? I see everywhere a Being whose main ends seem to be beneficent, but whose good purposes are worked out at terrible expense of suffering, and apparently by the total sacrifice of myriads of sensitive creatures. I see unflinching order, general good-will, but no sympathy, no mercy. Storms, earthquakes, volcanoes, sickness, death, go on without regarding us. Everywhere I see the most hopeless, unrelieved suffering,—and for aught I see, it may be eternal. Immortality is a dreadful chance, and I would rather never have been. The Doctor's dreadful system is, I confess, much like the laws of Nature,—about what one might reason out from them.

There is but just one thing remaining, and that is, as Candace said, the Cross of Christ. If God so loved us,—if He died for us,—greater love hath no man than this. It seems to me that love is shown here in the two highest forms possible to our comprehension. We see a Being who gives himself for us,—and more than that, harder than that, a Being who consents to the suffering of a dearer than self.

Such a centrally Christian vision of life, virtually a summation of Harriet's own view, may seem hopelessly to confuse Mrs. Marvyn's function as a vehicle for expressing the negative aspects of Calvinism. But this is so only if we suppose that Harriet was attempting to demolish Puritanism. Emphatically, this was not the case. Through Mrs. Marvyn she was expressing her own complex awareness that she must say both yes and no to the ancestral faith. Mainly, the report through this character is negative: there was injustice in the system that demanded as the price of salvation a "fervent heart" from a woman whom temperament and circumstances had made preponderantly intellectual; there was a dreadful mistake somewhere in the faith which demanded that such a woman love the god who had surrendered her son to hell. But (here was the awful enigma) such a system, which ran counter to all one wished, might still be the only acceptable faith in terms of scripture, logic, and even the appearance of nature. It was the "truth" of Calvinism, rather than its superstition or its narrow insistence on certain doctrines, which made it a "slow poison." How could any intelligent person combat its effects? In avoiding the easy oversimplification, Harriet gave her portrait of the Puritan intellectual the confused depth of reality.

Harriet wrote that Mrs. Marvyn's mind was like a map; Mary Scudder's, like a picture. Mary has no crucial intellectual difficulties with her faith, for the simple reason that she does not follow the Calvinistic chain of logic to its end: "In all the system which had been explained to her, her mind selected points on which it seized with intense sympathy, which it dwelt upon and expanded till all else fell away. The sublimity of disinterested benevolence, the harmony and order of a system tending in its final results to infinite happiness, the goodness of God, the love of a self-sacrificing Redeemer, were all so many glorious pictures, which she revolved in her mind with small care for their logical relations." Mary sounds like a Puritan escapist, but Harriet intended nothing of the kind. Unlike Dr. Hopkins, Mary has never questioned her "evidences," that is, her right to citizenship in the celestial kingdom. Her certainty is the certainty of the elect. After discussing the matter with her pastor, she writes him a letter which reads in part:

To love God because He is good to me you seem to think is not a right kind of love; and yet every moment of my life I have experienced His goodness . . . . I am not sensible that I ever in my life imagined anything but good could come from the hand of God.

From a Being infinite in goodness everything must be good, though we do not always comprehend how it is so. Are not afflictions good? Does He not even in judgment remember mercy? Sensible that "afflictions are but blessings in disguise," I would bless the hand that with infinite kindness wounds only to heal, and love and adore the goodness of God equally in suffering as in rejoicing.

We can be certain we are to interpret Mary as Puritan saint when we discover that in writing this letter Harriet merely looked in her father's *Autobiography,* on which she had done so much work, and copied out large sections of a letter her mother, Roxana Foote, wrote to Lyman Beecher September 1, 1798. (All the sentences I have quoted appear word for word, with only minor changes in punctuation, in both the *Autobiography* and *The Minister's Wooing.*) The first Mrs. Beecher, who died when Harriet was between five and six, was the shrine at which all the Beechers worshiped—literally. When sixty years after her death Henry Ward Beecher said, "My mother is to me what the Virgin Mary is to a devout Catholic," he employed only a slight touch of hyperbole. In the *Autobiography* Harriet herself recalled that during a siege of scarlet fever in her childhood her father in prayer had reminded God "of her blessed mother who is now a saint in heaven." What Harriet wrote of Roxana's influence on her brothers is also significant: "I think it will be the testimony of all her sons that her image stood between them and the temptations of youth as a sacred shield; that the hope of meeting her in heaven has sometimes been the last strand which did not part in hours of fierce temptation; and that the remembrance of her holy life and death was a solemn witness of the truth of religion, which repelled every assault of scepticism, and drew back the soul from every wandering to the faith in which she lived and died."

Catharine's ultimate apostasy may seem to prove Roxana less influential on her daughters than her sons; but Catharine's long faithfulness to Calvinism, as witness *Letters on the Difficulties of Religion* written fourteen years after Fisher's death, seems, in the light of her own intense chapter on her mother in the *Autobiography,* another proof of Roxana's power from beyond the grave. As I have pointed out, in writing of *Uncle Tom's Cabin,* Harriet fictionalized this saintly figure as Augustine St. Clare's mother and probably attempted her portrait in the triumphant piety of Little Eva. Also, Roxana was almost certainly an influence making the separation of mother and child the leitmotif of Harriet's first novel. In view of her quoting large sections of Roxana's letter, we must conclude, I believe, that her mother was a crucial fact in Harriet's religious struggles after Henry's death and their expression in *The Minister's Wooing.* It seems likely that Roxana was in Harriet's case also: "a sacred shield . . . the last strand which did not part in hours of fierce temptation . . . a solemn witness to the truth of religion, which repelled every assault of scepticism, and drew back the soul from every wandering to the faith in which she lived and died." Here was an image profoundly rooted in her heart which was undoubtedly far more powerful in causing Harriet to say yes to the ancestral faith than any mere intellectual admiration.

Saints are notably difficult, if not impossible, in fiction, for there is little conflict, little drama, in achieved perfection. Once we get past the clichés of sentimental fiction, here is the explanation for the failure of Little Eva. Mary Scudder might have been a similar failure had she been simply the fictionalizing of Roxana, the saint in heaven, but she was something more. She was also, under idealized conditions, Harriet Beecher Stowe confronting the death of her eldest son. Critics oversusceptible to Freud may wish to read something pathological in Harriet's assuming the role of James's (or Henry Stowe's) fiancée; but this does not seem to me necessary. Mary's love for James is earthly affection almost completely refined into spirituality. She is deceiving herself only a little when she tells her mother that, though she would give her soul to save James, she does not intend to marry him or anyone else. As Harriet made clear, "In a refined and exalted nature, it is very seldom that the feeling of love, when once thoroughly aroused, bears any sort of relation to the reality of the object. It is commonly an enkindling of the whole power of the soul's love for whatever she considers highest and fairest; it is, in fact, the love of something divine and unearthly, which, by a sort of illusion, connects itself with a personality. Properly speaking, there is but One, true, eternal Object of all that the mind conceives, in the trance of its exaltation."

This would have to be the case in Mary's love for James, for there are almost unbridgeable differences between them. As we learn in the second chapter, James has had worldly motives in calling Mary's attention to his spiritual state: "Now, I confess I never did care much about religion, but I thought, without being really a hypocrite, I'd just let you try to save my soul for the sake of getting you; for there's nothing surer to hook a woman than trying to save a fellow's soul. It's a dead-shot, generally, that." Remembering Harriet's profound concern for Henry, and her sentimental report that his "fair, sweet face looks down upon me now and then from out a cloud," we could hardly ask a clearer instance of her ability to mask her feelings and speak as realist. This realism is also evident when she writes that what Mary loves in James is not "the gay, young, dashing sailor,—sudden in anger, imprudent of speech, and, though generous in heart, yet worldly in plans and schemings, but her own ideal of a grand and noble man, such a man as she thought he might become."

This love Harriet justified in terms of the metaphor she had used two years before when she pictured herself as gardener and Henry as rare exotic: "Nor was she [Mary Scudder] wrong; for as to every leaf and every flower there is an ideal to which the growth of the plant is constantly urging, so is there an ideal to every human being,—a perfect form in which it might appear, were every defect removed and every characteristic excellence stimulated to the highest point." Again, we find her employing the dominant image of the plant when she deals with Mary's response to the news that James has drowned at sea, presumably unregenerate. Harriet titled her chapter, "The Bruised Flax-Flower," and explained her meaning in these words: "Mary never thought of such a thing as self-indulgence; this daughter of the Puritans had her seed within her.

Aerial in her delicacy, as the blue-eyed flax-flower with which they sowed their fields, she had yet its strong fibre, which no stroke of the flail could break; bruising and hackling only made it fitter for uses of homely utility."

This, of course, is the way Harriet wanted to view herself in her inner struggles after Henry's death. Mary's spiritual bruising, therefore, is essentially an idealization of Harriet's own experience, so that it accords with the spiritual trials a saint like Roxana Foote would have known had she suffered a wound from God. Harriet's analysis of this spiritual bruising is a beautiful and authoritative statement of the Puritan inner adventure. The psychological pressure under which she wrote produced a clarity of perception, a concentration of phrase, a freshness and boldness of image, the uninitiated might suppose completely beyond the author of *Uncle Tom's Cabin,* and in fact, we have here left far behind us Harriet's powerful, but crude, simplicities in her first novel. It was her distinction now, as Samuel G. Ward wrote of the poems of Emily Dickinson, to be "the articulate inarticulate," to express those patterns of New England sensibility, so private and so subtle that they were seldom given full expression. Consider, for example, Harriet's description of the "landscape of the soul" in Mary Scudder as she faces the virtual certainty that James Marvyn suffers eternal torment:

> The soul seems to itself to widen and deepen; it trembles at its own dreadful forces; it gathers up in waves that break with wailing only to flow back into the everlasting void. The calmest and most centred natures are sometimes thrown by the shock of a great sorrow into a tumultuous amazement. All things are changed. The earth no longer seems solid, the skies no longer secure; a deep abyss seems underlying every joyous scene of life. The soul, struck with this awful inspiration, is a mournful Cassandra; she sees blood on every threshold, and shudders in the midst of mirth and festival with the weight of a terrible wisdom.

Quite as extraordinary as this description of the experience of "Ourself, behind ourself concealed," as Emily Dickinson phrased it, is the account of Mary's subsequent spiritual illumination. In "Give All to Love," Emerson, as perhaps was fitting in a gnomic poem, merely suggested this experience with his aphoristic hint, "When half-gods go,/The gods arrive." But in "Compensation," where surely he might have gone into detail, he was only a little more explicit concerning "the deep remedial force that underlies all facts." On close examination, there is a transcendental blur to his final image: ". . . the man or woman who would have remained a sunny garden-flower, with no room for its roots and too much sunshine for its head, by the falling of the walls and the neglect of the gardener is made the banian of the forest, yielding shade and fruit to wide neighborhoods of men." Garden flowers under careless husbandry do not change into East Indian trees with aerial roots, and we have been illuminated, if at all, only concerning the results of compensation. We know no more than we did before concerning the operation of the remedial force, an old fact of New England experience in the enshrining of renunciation. But with her image of a rose that remains a rose and her supplemental images of ocean and light, Harriet vividly re-creates the inner life of Puritanism:

It is said that gardeners, sometimes, when they would bring a rose to richer flowering, deprive it for a season of light and moisture. Silent and dark it stands, dropping one fading leaf after another, and seeming to go down patiently to death. But when every leaf is dropped, and the plant stands stripped to the uttermost, a new life is even then working in the buds, from which shall spring a tender foliage and a brighter wealth of flowers. So, often in celestial gardening, every leaf of earthly joy must drop, before a new and divine bloom visits the soul.

Gradually, as months passed away, the floods grew still; the mighty rushes of the inner tides ceased to dash. There came first a delicious calmness, and then a celestial inner clearness, in which the soul seemed to lie quiet as an untroubled ocean, reflecting heaven. Then came the fullness of mysterious communion, given to the pure in heart,—that advent of the Comforter in the soul, teaching all things and bringing all things to remembrance; and Mary moved in a world transfigured by a celestial radiance.

Seeking to evoke Mary in her inner clearness, Harriet applied to her John Donne's lines from "The Second Anniversary," elegizing Elizabeth Drury:

> . . . her pure and eloquent blood
> Spoke in her cheeks, and so distinctly wrought
> That you might almost say her body thought.

In *Oldtown Folks,* she again quoted the last line, this time writing the "you" correctly as "one," as a comment on Esther Avery, "one of those intense, silent, repressed women that have been a frequent outgrowth of New England society." For Harriet, the line of "old Dr. Donne," as she called him in the benighted days before Herbert J. C. Grierson and T. S. Eliot, implied an inner state which was admirable and at the same time morbid. Through a hyperbole, which for Donne was pure praise, Harriet in short was saying yes and no to the Puritan saint. This she made specific when she wrote of Mary that "the thousand fibres that bind youth and womanhood to earthly love and life were all in her as still as the grave, and only the spiritual and divine part of her being was active." With what is surprising self-knowledge and self-criticism, Harriet wrote further of Mary: "Through the sudden crush of a great affliction, she was in that state of self-abnegation to which the mystics brought themselves by fastings and self-imposed penances,—a state not purely healthy, nor realizing the divine idea of a perfect human being made to exist in the relations of human life,— but one of those exceptional conditions which, like the hours that often precede dissolution, seem to impart to the subject of them a peculiar aptitude for delicate and refined spiritual impressions."

Harriet's no here was, however, only a grace note, not a somber chord as in the case of Mrs. Marvyn, for she did not allow her Puritan saint to atrophy as New England saints were currently doing in lonely old houses even before the Civil War and Western migration carried off the young men. With James gone to sea, Harriet in the matter of a few chapters gave Mary a new lover in the person of Dr. Samuel Hopkins. Actually, we should say an unconscious lover, for she supposed that Hopkins for a long period attributed the "air of strange and subtile sweetness" coming from his love of Mary as a new freshness the Lord had given him: "he thought of that fair and mystical bride, the Lamb's wife, whose union with her Divine Redeemer in a future millennial age was a frequent and favorite subject of his musings; yet he knew not that this celestial bride, clothed in fine linen, clean and white, veiled in humility and meekness, bore in his mind those earthly features. No, he never had dreamed of that! But only after she had passed by, that mystical vision seemed to him more radiant, more easy to be conceived." Harriet teased her readers with the possibility that Mary might forget James and fall seriously in love with the good Doctor since women are born worshipers and a truly great man like Hopkins was an idol ready made. Mary was particularly susceptible after Hopkins showed his commitment to the doctrine of disinterested benevolence and his complete unworldliness by demanding that his wealthiest parishioner, Simeon Brown, renounce the traffic in Negroes.

Harriet did not exaggerate. Historically, Hopkins was a nobly imprudent opponent of the wealthy slave-trading interests of Newport. In representing him as confronting Mr. Marvyn with the religious obligation to free Candace, if she wanted her liberty, Harriet simply adapted an incident from Dr. Park's *Memoir.* There Park related how Hopkins had confronted his friend and fellow disciple of Edwards, Joseph Bellamy, with a similar challenge and had similarly induced that consistent divine to free his Negro farm manager. But Harriet knew, of course, that not all Calvinists were abolitionists, and here is the explanation for her making the historically liberal Dr. Stiles into a reactionary who believes slavery is a divine ordinance. She needed a symbol of the negative side of Calvinism on the social plane; and it made for artistic neatness to find this symbol, with the softening touch of humor, in the man who was Hopkins' chief clerical rival in Newport. In the balancing of Hopkins and Stiles, Harriet, of course, was again appraising Calvinism.

But because of her favorable verdict on Hopkins the abolitionist, we should not suppose that she overlooked in him any more than she did in other characters the negative as well as the positive aspects of Puritanism. In fact, Hopkins, since he

was a virtual embodiment of Calvinism, stands at the very center
of her criticism. Early in the book, she made clear the fundamental grounds of her discontent by describing his mutilation
of the ladder leading to the Good, the True, and the Beautiful:

There is a ladder to heaven, whose base God has placed in
human affections, tender instincts, symbolic feelings, sacraments of
love, through which the soul rises, higher and higher, refining as
she goes, till she outgrows the human, and changes, as she rises, into
the image of the divine. At the very top of this ladder, at the
threshold of Paradise, blazes dazzling and crystalline that celestial
grade where the soul knows self no more, having learned through
a long experience of devotion, how blest it is to lose herself in that
eternal Love and Beauty of which all earthly fairness and grandeur
are but the dim type, the distant shadow. This highest step, this
saintly elevation, which but few selectest spirits ever on earth
attain, to raise the soul to which the Eternal Father organized every
relation of human existence and strung every cord of human love;
for which this world is one long discipline, for which the soul's
human education is constantly varied, for which it is now torn by
sorrow, now flooded by joy; to which all its multiplied powers tend
with upward hands of dumb and ignorant aspiration, this Ultima
Thule of virtue had been seized upon by our sage as the all of
religion. He knocked out every round of the ladder but the highest, and then, pointing to its hopeless splendor, said to the world,
"Go up thither and be saved!"

It is not surprising that James Russell Lowell selected this
passage for special praise in his comment on *The Minister's
Wooing*. Harriet here found a brilliant metaphor for her insight into New England Puritanism. She knew far too much
of Hopkins and his master, Jonathan Edwards, to deny them,
as later critics did, their vision of spirit as beauty which "blazes
dazzling and crystalline." Like Mary Scudder, Harriet too
had felt the subtle poetry in Edwards' *The Nature of True
Virtue*. But she had also known through the agony of her own
religious experience the frustration resulting from a vision of
life which on the one hand presented almost unutterable beauty
and on the other a doctrine which held that no man or woman
could climb toward that beauty but must be lifted to it by the
extraordinary and unmerited operation of Divine Grace. Lost

in the brightness of deity there was one round, one highest step; but so far as common men and women were concerned the ladder between earth and heaven was rungless.

This Harriet with her recent experience of the art of Europe could no longer believe to be true. Dr. Hopkins' brow, she wrote, had "the squareness of ideality," but as yet his ideality "dealt only with the intellectual and invisible, leading to subtile refinements of argument and exalted ideas of morals . . . . there was lying in him, crude and unworked, a whole mine of those artistic feelings and perceptions which are awakened and developed only by the touch of beauty." The flaw in New England Puritanism was its neglect of earthly beauty as a means of salvation; this meant a warped humanity even in a great man like Dr. Hopkins. Catholic civilization, with its aesthetic emphasis, would have developed his full human potentialities and given life to his abstractions: "Had he been born beneath the shadow of the great Duomo of Florence, where Giotto's Campanile rises like the slender stalk of a celestial lily, where varied marbles and rainbow-glass and gorgeous paintings and lofty statuary call forth, even from childhood, the soul's reminiscences of the bygone glories of its pristine state, his would have been a soul as rounded and full in its sphere of faculties as that of Da Vinci or Michelangelo."

Harriet's reference to "the soul's reminiscences . . . of its pristine state" is, of course, like her sustained image of the ladder, Platonic; and Platonic-Puritan is the phrase for Dr. Hopkins' wooing of Mary. Later on in the book, Harriet quoted Plato's *Phaedrus:* "Man's soul, in a former state, was winged and soared among the gods; and so it comes to pass that, in this life, when the soul, by the power of music or poetry, or the sight of beauty, hath her remembrance quickened, forthwith there is a struggling and a pricking pain as of wings trying to come forth,—even as children in teething." For Hopkins, denied the rich aesthetic experience of an older civilization, "the first revelation of his dormant nature was to come to him through the face of woman, that work of the Mighty Master which is to be found in all lands and ages." Plato would have insisted that the wakening must come through a young man, but in Puritan New England terms, Harriet was still able to keep remarkably close to the Platonic program. The ethical idealism of New England had made a dichotomy of the carnal and the spiritual which was very un-Greek, but in this dichotomy, men and women frequently joined like Platonic master and disciple in a mutual aspiration toward high things. We can read such a relation in the case of Margaret Fuller and Emerson, and in the case of Emily Dickinson and her various "tutors," Benjamin Franklin Newton, Thomas Wentworth Higginson, and most of all, that "dusk gem, born of troubled waters," her "dearest earthly friend," the Reverend Charles Wadsworth.

Harriet knew the unavoidable ambiguities of such relations. She noted that "Even in cases where the strongest ruling force of the two sexes seems out of the question, there is still something peculiar and insidious in their relationship. . . . Grave professors and teachers cannot give lessons to their female pupils just as they give them to the coarser sex, and more than once has the fable of 'Cadenus and Vanessa' been acted over by the most unlikely performers." Mary Scudder, of course, was not unlike Vanessa in Jonathan Swift's poem, for in her case also one might suppose that Pallas Athene

> Mistakes Vanessa for a boy;
> Then sows within her tender mind
> Seeds long unknown to woman-kind;
> For manly bosoms chiefly fit,
> The seeds of knowledge, judgment, wit.
> Her soul was suddenly endued
> With justice, truth, and fortitude;
> With honor, which no breath can stain,
> Which malice must attack in vain. . . .

Dr. Hopkins was also something like Cadenus, Swift's name for himself, as Cupid describes him:

> "I find," said he, "she wants a doctor
> Both to adore her, and instruct her:
> I'll give her what she most admires
> Among those venerable sires,
> Cadenus is a subject fit,

Grown old in politics and wit,
Caress'd by ministers of state,
Of half mankind the dread and hate."

But Harriet's Puritan saint, in her "understanding" with
James Marvyn, could not be the pursuer like Swift's Vanessa,
and Dr. Hopkins, as I have noted, was an unconscious lover.
The relations of this New England Cadenus and Vanessa move,
therefore, on the conscious level toward a completely Platonic
affair of master and disciple. But the Yankee realist in Harriet
suggested through the tender ambiguities of their conversations
on theology the affection they failed to recognize:

"But, my dear sir, you are my best friend. I trust you will be
faithful to me. If I am deceiving myself, undeceive me; you cannot
be too severe with me."

"Alas!" said the Doctor, "I fear that I may be only a blind
leader of the blind. What, after all, if I be only a miserable self-
deceiver? What, if some thought of self has come in to poison
all my prayers and strivings? . . . Say, my dear friend, are you
sure, that should you discover yourself to be forever condemned
by His justice, you would not find your heart rising up against
Him?"

"Against *Him*?" said Mary, with a tremulous, sorrowful expression on her face, "against my Heavenly Father?"

Her face flushed, and faded; her eyes kindled eagerly, as if
she had something to say, and then grew misty with tears. At last
she said,—

"Thank you, my dear, faithful friend! I will think about this;
perhaps I may have been deceived. How very difficult it must be
to know one's self perfectly!"

When, shortly after this conversation, Dr. Hopkins received
Mary's letter, actually written by Roxana Foote, he escaped
Platonism, for he "felt as if he could have kissed the hem of her
garment who wrote it," and in his journal he recorded that
desire with these significant verses from Canticles: "I charge
you, O ye daughters of Jerusalem, by the roes, and by the
hinds of the field, that ye stir not up nor awake my love till
she pleases."

After James is reported drowned, the Doctor no longer
needs the assistance of the daughters of Jerusalem, and in the

accepted fashion, he asks the Widow Scudder if he may marry her daughter. Mary is dismayed by the proposal: there is no one she admires more than Dr. Hopkins (" 'he is the best, the noblest, and yet the humblest man in the world' ") and there is no doubt of her affection (" 'You love him very much, do you not?' said her mother. 'Very dearly,' said Mary.") Her difficulty is that she is still hopelessly in love with James. When her mother has left her, after she has agreed to marry the Doctor, Mary, like a Hawthorne character, contemplates her reflection in the mirror: "Nothing is capable of more ghostly effect than such a silent, lonely contemplation of that mysterious image of ourselves which seems to look out of an infinite depth in the mirror, as if it were our own soul beckoning to us visibly from unknown regions. Those eyes look into our own with an expression sometimes vaguely sad and inquiring. . . . They seemed to say to her, 'Fulfill thy mission; life is made for sacrifice; the flower must fall before fruit can perfect itself.' A vague shuddering of mystery gave intensity to her reverie. It seemed as if those mirror-depths were another world; she heard the far-off dashing of sea-green waves; she felt a yearning impulse towards that dear soul gone out into the infinite unknown."

It is only in the superficial outlines of plot that we can make *The Minister's Wooing* accord with the thousand and one nineteenth-century novels in which the young lady's lover is apparently lost at sea and in which she marries, or almost marries, as in Mary's case, his honorable rival. In Harriet's imagination, the familiar pattern was a symbolic situation in which she herself was wooed by Calvinism, embodied in Dr. Hopkins, while she still "felt a yearning impulse towards that dear soul [Henry] gone out into the infinite unknown." To Mary, the betrothed of Dr. Hopkins, she attributed "the golden hours of calm" of which she had written her daughters two months after Henry's death. Mary has been awakened by the singing of a robin between three and four o'clock in the morning: "Scarcely conscious, she lay in that dim clairvoyant state, when the half-sleep of the outward senses permits a delicious dewy clearness of soul, that perfect ethereal rest and freshness of faculties, comparable only to what we imagine of the spiritual state,—season of celestial enchantment, in which the heavy weight 'of all this unintelligible world' drops off, and the soul, divinely charmed, nestles like a wind-tossed bird in the protecting bosom of the One All-Perfect, All-Beautiful."

But Harriet did not permit Mary to persist, if we note the source of the quotation, in the mystically exalted mood of Wordsworth's "Tintern Abbey." By bringing James home, saved in the flesh and the spirit, with the beginnings of a fortune from the Canton trade, Harriet confronted her heroine with the choice between her lover and her fiancé and symbolically herself with the choice between Henry and Calvinism. But the qualities of character developed by Puritan New England saved Harriet from a real decision. Mary could not break her engagement with Dr. Hopkins. Self-denial had been her daily bread; her promise was a sacred matter, particularly since it involved the happiness of a dear friend; as for her feelings, "Every prayer, hymn, and sermon, from her childhood, had warned her to distrust her inclinations, and regard her feelings as traitors." But New England also fortunately produced busybodies and matchmakers like the quaint dressmaker, Miss Prissy, who blurted out Mary's situation to Dr. Hopkins. The champion of disinterested benevolence in a more than theoretical sense, as shown by his opposition to slavery, had virtually no choice but renunciation. Harriet was realist enough to note that the Doctor could triumph over his feelings only after an "ocean tempest of passion," but to her his renunciation, like Mary's keeping her pledge, was heroic and inevitable. Thus, James's return solved everything: Henry was resurrected regenerate and returned to his loved ones, and a final yes could be said to Calvinism for its sense of honor in Mary and its noble sacrifice in Dr. Hopkins. In view of her conclusion, it is not surprising that Harriet wrote this preface for the British edition of *The Minister's Wooing*:

The author has endeavored in this story to paint a style of life and manners which existed in New England in the earlier days of her national existence.

Some of the principal characters are historic: the leading events of the story are founded on actual facts, although the author has taken the liberty to arrange and vary them for the purposes of the story.

The author has executed the work with a reverential tenderness for those great religious minds who laid in New England the foundations of many generations, and for those institutions and habits of life from which, as from a fruitful germ, sprang all the present prosperity of America.

Such as it is, it is commended to the kindly thoughts of that British fireside from which the fathers and mothers of America first went out to give to English ideas and institutions a new growth in a new world.

This interpretation should not be accepted, of course, at face value. It is almost as misleading as the assumption of Constance Rourke and Lyman Beecher Stowe that *The Minister's Wooing* is a long attack on Calvinism. When she had expressed her inner contradition in Mrs. Marvyn, had dramatized herself as Mary Scudder, and had run the whole gamut of Puritan experience in imagination, Harriet undoubtedly did feel "a reverential tenderness for those great religious minds who laid in New England the foundations of many generations." For her, *The Minister's Wooing* had constituted what Kenneth Burke calls "symbolic action," the strategy for imaginatively encompassing a situation. But "reverential tenderness" was only part of her mood as she wrote; the preface to the British edition does not even remotely suggest the inner struggle, the tension between head and heart, which gave her first New England novel breadth and depth.

FICTITIOUS SHORES

I

THE preface to the British edition of *The Minister's Wooing* unmistakably indicates Harriet's feeling of reconciliation with her ancestral Calvinism. But her mood of 1859 was actually one of those "fictitious shores" described by Emily Dickinson:

> I many times thought peace had come,
> When peace was far away;
> As wrecked men deem they sight the land
> At centre of the sea,
>
> And struggle slacker, but to prove,
> As hopelessly as I,
> How many the fictitious shores
> Before the harbor lie.

In September, 1857, two months after Henry Stowe's death, Harriet had contributed to the *Independent* a brief article, "Who Shall Roll Away the Stone?," in which she had stated if raps, squeaks, and tricks with tables are the means of communicating with the dead, "sadly and soberly we say we had rather be without it." Here was the orthodox response to the modern cult of spiritualism, more exactly "spiritism," inaugurated in 1848 at Hydesville, New York, when the daughters of John D. Fox, puzzled by mysterious knockings, had worked out a code with the other world, three raps for yes, one rap for no, two raps for doubtful. But by 1860 Harriet had changed her mind. At Florence, on her third and last journey to Europe, she found "very pleasant" Calvin's report from Andover of his "spiritual experiences in feeling the presence of dear Henry" with him "and, above all, the vibration of that mysterious guitar." But she doubted the guitar had been struck by Henry. It seemed more likely it was the work of Eliza, Calvin's first wife, who had died in 1834, since "her spirit has ever seemed to cling to that mode of manifestation, and if you would keep it in your sleeping-room, no doubt you would hear from it oftener." Having settled the matter of Calvin's guitar in a manner that would have been acceptable to the hero of Poe's "Ligeia," Harriet went on to report her more trustworthy adventure with its Florentine equivalent. She had been reading in Revelation with a Mrs. E. of Boston, a powerful medium but an "earnest Christian . . . afraid of getting led astray," when the bass string of a little Florentine guitar was struck loudly and distinctly. Mrs. E. said: "Now, that is strange! I asked last night that if any spirit was present with us after you came to-day, that it would try to touch that guitar." Harriet asked Calvin: "What think you? Have you had any more manifestations, any truths from the spirit world?"

Inescapably we smile at this account of vibrating guitars in Andover and Florence and incline toward meteorological rather than metaphysical explanations. But smiling is not understanding. Many years later in a letter to her good friend Oliver Wendell Holmes, Harriet supplied an important illumination of the matter: "I remember a remark you once made on spiritualism. I cannot recall the words, but you spoke of it as modifying the sharp angles of Calvinistic belief, as a fog does those of a landscape." This is the clue to her exaggerated confidence. Neither the writing of *The Minister's Wooing* nor the passage of time had actually blunted the sharp edges of her creed; when she confronted it, it still told her that at best Henry's situation in eternity was uncertain. In the letter dealing with the guitars, she wrote of her inexpressible yearnings and outreachings after Henry and her "sense of utter darkness and separation, not only from him but from all spiritual communion with my God." Five months later, attempting to console Mrs. Howard on the death of her daughter Annie, Harriet confessed that submission to God was as painful as ever, that "Time but the impression stronger makes/As streams their channels deeper wear." She knew "all the strange ways in which this anguish will reveal itself,—the prick, the thrust, the stab, the wearing pain, the poison that is mingled with every bright remembrance of the past." In this predicament she needed a comforting fog to soften the theological landscape. By hiding her creed from herself in the supposition that Henry was a free agent in eternity, able and anxious to communicate with his parents, she could endure the fact of his death.

The metaphysical fog thickened once a month when Harriet read in the *Atlantic* the installments of Oliver Wendell Holmes's novel *Elsie Venner,* that strange story of a girl who was snake-like because her mother had been bitten by a rattler. Like "The Deacon's Masterpiece" of a few years before, *Elsie Venner* was a theological fable for Yankees. In his poem Holmes had announced that the wonderful "one-hoss shay" of Calvinism had gone "to pieces all at once,—/All at once, and nothing first,—" at exactly half-past nine, November 1, 1855. This was rather precise dating for the final collapse of the system developed by Jonathan Edwards and overdeveloped by Bellamy, Hopkins, and Emmons. In fact, it was too precise, as Holmes discovered when he sat down to write *Elsie Venner,* for when he looked around, there in the road was at least the shay's linch-pin, the Edwardean doctrine of Original Sin. It was to hammer this doctrine into dust that Dr. Holmes wrote his novel.

His argument is clearly indicated by the rhetorical questions in his preface to the second edition of *Elsie Venner:*

Was Elsie Venner, poisoned by the venom of a crotalus before she was born, morally responsible for the "volitional aberrations" which translated into acts become what is known as sin, and, it may be, what is punished as crime? If, on presentation of the evidence, she becomes by the verdict of the human conscience a proper object of divine pity and not of divine wrath, as a subject of moral poisoning, wherein lies the difference between her position at the bar of judgment, human or divine, and that of the unfortunate victim who received a moral poison from a remote ancestor before he drew his first breath?

In his novel Holmes wrote that the limitations of human responsibility had never been properly studied except in the pseudo-science of phrenology, which "has brought out that great doctrine of moral insanity, which has done more to make men charitable and soften legal and theological barbarism than any one doctrine that I can think of since the message of peace and good-will to men." In this great doctrine, "nine tenths" of the perversity of bad men came from "outside influences, drunken ancestors, abuse in childhood, bad company, from which you have happily been preserved, and for some of which you, as a member of society, may be fractionally responsible."

Initially it is surprising to find Harriet writing Holmes that *Elsie Venner* is "an artistic creation, original and beautiful," and even more surprising to discover that Professor Calvin Stowe of Andover Theological Seminary wrote a "remonstrance" to some paper which attacked Holmes. It hardly seems sufficient reason, as Harriet wrote the Doctor, that Calvin "was well acquainted with your father and feels the impropriety of the thing." That Connecticut-born Calvinist, the Reverend Abiel Holmes, who at Cambridge in the late 1820's had insisted on exchanging pulpits only with the staunchly orthodox such as Lyman Beecher, could have taken little paternal pride in that quip, "theological barbarism," and he could have found only danger in the doctrine of "moral insanity." The Reverend Mr. Holmes would have seen at a glance where his son had gone wrong.

Oliver Wendell Holmes had made the error of reading the famous "Sinners in the Hands of an Angry God" as Edwards' complete statement on the corrupt human heart. In his last word on the subject, *The Great Christian Doctrine of Original Sin Defended* (1758), Edwards had made it clear that man was not (like Elsie Venner) prenatally poisoned. He saw not "the least need of supposing any evil quality, *infused, implanted,* or *wrought* into the nature of man, by any *positive* cause, or influence whatsoever, either from God, or the creature; or of supposing, that man is conceived and born with a *fountain of evil* in his heart, such as anything properly *positive.*" For Edwards the obvious evil of mankind could be explained quite easily by recognizing that before the Fall man had been endowed with superior and inferior principles and that the Fall meant the subtraction of the superior principles. In his fallen state, "Man did immediately set up *himself,* and the objects of his private affections and appetites, as supreme; and so they took the place of *God.* These inferior principles are like *fire* in a house; which we say is a good servant, but a bad master; very useful while kept in its place, but if left to take possession of the whole house, soon brings all to destruction."

The Reverend Mr. Holmes would have insisted that the doctrine of "moral insanity" did not call in question that "destruction," which for Edwards extended, of course, into eternity. As Mr. Holmes would have seen the matter, Edwards had been quite right in refusing on the one hand to lift man out of the sequence of cause and effect and on the other in insisting that man is still responsible for being what he is. How else could one do justice to the inescapable influences of heredity and environment and to the inner life of man where he *knows* he is responsible? As for the belief that man would be eternally punished for possessing "the mere principles of human nature" unsupplemented by supernatural light, that was the only logical conclusion to be drawn from reading the Bible. Also, long before Oliver Wendell Holmes was born, Edwards had seen the implications of the doctrine of "moral insanity," wherein all was the fault of "inherited congenital tendencies,—some good, some bad,—for which the subject of them is in no way responsible." In 1754, confronted by a similar doctrine, Edwards had written: "Then wickedness always carries that in it which excuses it," and the stronger an evil inclination, the less blameworthy.

When we realize what the Reverend Abiel Holmes would certainly have thought of the doctrine in *Elsie Venner,* what, in short, any fully aware, traditional New England Puritan would have been obliged to think, we see that logically Harriet could not have become a Holmesian and remained an Edwardean Calvinist. For a New England Puritan, Holmes's theory closely examined could never have proved solid ground; even more than spiritism it was a fictitious shore. But quite clearly Harriet supposed herself a Holmesian not only in 1860-1861 but thenceforward; in 1878 she wrote Holmes that she had been rereading *Elsie Venner* and "all your theology in that book I subscribe to with both hands."

With this last statement staring us in the face, it seems unmistakable that the reading of *Elsie Venner* marks a major turning point in Harriet's inner history, that after 1861 she was no longer the Edwardean Calvinist of *Uncle Tom's Cabin* and *The Minister's Wooing*. But we miss the full significance of this change if we suppose that matters stood as clear in her mind as I have tried to make them stand in the reader's. In 1861 Harriet did not recognize that (from the Puritan standpoint) she had dropped anchor at "centre of the sea" for the simple reason that she did not want to recognize it. She preferred to suppose that the metaphysical fog of "moral insanity" was a perfect harbor, that Professor Oliver Wendell Holmes of Harvard Medical School by means of logic and science had *proved* Henry essentially guiltless for not having experienced regeneration and that somehow or other this comforting doctrine could be reconciled with the ancestral faith, or if not with that, at least with some form of traditional Christianity.

II

On her voyage home from Europe in June, 1860, Harriet's fellow passenger was Nathaniel Hawthorne, whose recent novel *The Marble Faun*, published in London as *Transfiguration,* had been out long enough for her to have read it. Though we have no evidence that she did more than entertain Hawthorne with stories of New England, she may well have discussed his new novel with him. Earlier in the year when she and her friends were weatherbound on the way to Rome, she too had embarked on an Italian novel, and she and Hawthorne had a common concern in the issue of Puritanism versus Catholicism. In part Harriet may have been led to consider that issue by *Elsie Venner,* for in the March, 1860, *Atlantic* Holmes's Unitarian minister, Chauncy Fairweather, had already expressed his long-ing for the luxury of devotional contact in the Roman Catholic Church. But it seems likely that *The Marble Faun* brought the issue home to Harriet even more directly, and helped give a new turn to *Agnes of Sorrento* (1862), which had begun merely as an entertainment and "a spontaneous tribute to the exceeding loveliness of all things" at Sorrento.

In *The Marble Faun,* a New England girl, Hilda, profound-ly disturbed by her secret knowledge that Donatello has hurled the villain of the book from the Tarpeian Rock, goes ("and it was a dangerous errand") to various Catholic churches to ob-serve the ways the "Popish faith" applies itself to all human needs. Inspired by the beauty of St. Peter's, Hilda dips her fingers in holy water and "had almost signed the cross upon her breast, but forbore, and trembled, while shaking the water from her finger-tips. She felt as if her mother's spirit, some-where within the dome, were looking down upon her child, the daughter of Puritan forefathers, and weeping to behold her en-snared by these gaudy superstitions." A little later Hilda again stumbles theologically, this time kneeling at the altar and sobbing out a prayer before she can snatch herself away. Final-ly she succumbs when she stands before the confessional in-scribed *Pro Anglica Lingua.*

After Hilda has poured out the dark story, all save Dona-tello's name, the kindly priest, born in New England, steps from the confessional and asks what more she has to say. When she tells him she is unreconciled with the Church, he inquires "on what ground, my daughter, have you sought to avail your-self of these blessed privileges, confined exclusively to members of the one true Church, of confession and absolution?" The word "absolution" profoundly shocks Hilda. "Absolution, father?" she cries shrinking back. "O no, no! I never dreamed of that! Only our Heavenly Father can forgive my sins. . . . God forbid that I should ask absolution from mortal man!" Hilda has simply stolen relief where relief was possible; but her act has potentially dark consequences. What Haw-thorne called those "eager propagandists who prowl about for souls, as cats to catch a mouse" imprison her in a convent where she is fully exposed to "the scarlet superstitions." Only the great strength of her inherited Puritanism brings her safely through the experience.

Here Hawthorne rather obviously expressed popular New England prejudices concerning Catholicism. But Harriet had good reasons for not following him. She could remember that at the time of Henry's death, Father James O'Donnell, the Catholic pastor at Lawrence, four miles from Andover, had written her this gracious letter:

> Dear Madame: In the deep affliction that has apparently visited you, I implore you to remember well that there is a communion of spirits of the departed just, which death cannot prevent, and which with prayer, can impart much consolation. This, with the condolence of every parent and child in my flock, I beg leave to offer you, wishing, in the mean time, to assure you of my heartfelt regret and sympathy.

Clearly there was something ungenerous in Hawthorne's notion of "eager propagandists who prowl about for souls, as cats to catch a mouse."

The most telling reason of all, however, for Harriet's reluctance to follow Hawthorne, and for her probably being stimulated into an opposing view by *The Marble Faun,* was her spiritual predicament, in broad terms duplicated in other instances. Hawthorne's daughter Rose would eventually become a convert to Catholicism and, after her husband's death, a nun under the name Sister Alphonsa. Mrs. George Ripley, wife of the founder of Brook Farm, became a Catholic before her death in 1861. In his autobiography, *The Convert; or, Leaves from My Experience* (1857), Orestes A. Brownson, a convert of 1844, furnishes the key to this apparently eccentric behavior on the part of double-distilled New Englanders: "Unitarianism has demolished Calvinism, made an end in all thinking minds of everything like dogmatic Protestantism, and Unitarianism itself satisfies nobody. It is negative, cold, lifeless, and all advanced minds among Unitarians . . . are weary of doubt, uncertainty, disunion, individualism, and crying out from the bottom of their hearts for faith, for love, for union."

In her inability to accept the Calvinistic reading of Henry's case, Harriet had so far separated herself from her ancestral faith that she stood almost in the Unitarian predicament. This we can see from the fact that she virtually echoes Brownson in her comment on her fifteenth-century Catholic heroine, Agnes: "Whatever may be thought of the actual truth of this belief, it certainly was far more consoling than that intense individualism of modern philosophy, which places every soul alone in its life-battle, scarce even giving it a God to lean on."

Harriet, of course, differed from the Unitarian converts to Rome in that she embraced fifteenth-century rather than nineteenth-century Catholicism. As she reminded her readers from time to time, Agnes was not confronted by the choice between Protestantism and Catholicism; she was only saintly by the light available. At first glance this looks like a formula for theological ambivalence, a method by which Harriet could be as Catholic as she wished in her sentiments and admirations without actually going over to the mighty opposite of New England Puritanism. But Harriet was not alone among her contemporaries in harkening back to fifteenth-century Italy and Savonarola. During the summer of 1860, George Eliot, as she later wrote, "was rather fired with the idea of writing an historical romance—scene, Florence; period, the close of the fifteenth century, which was marked by Savonarola's career and martyrdom." Like George Eliot in *Romola* (1863), Harriet in *Agnes of Sorrento* (1862) was undoubtedly led to reflect on Savonarola because as Italian champion of republican government, he was often a point of reference in discussions of Italian unification, rapidly being completed in 1860 by Cavour.

We must be careful also not to misread the fact that Harriet's judgment of Savonarola was more favorable than George Eliot's. Harriet's more favorable attitude has little to do with her larger sympathy for Catholicism; it was almost the inevitable response of a New England Puritan. In Savonarola, a champion of republican government, a severe theologian, a denunciator of Renaissance worldliness (to the point of publicly burning the *Decameron* and other "bad" books), Harriet had found a hero in the past almost as congruent with her Puritan ideals as Dr. Samuel Hopkins.

But when we have explained away all that can be explained away, Harriet's *Agnes of Sorrento* still indicates something approaching what Robert Frost has wittily defined as the revolt from Puritanism "sideways into the Catholic Church." This we recognize immediately when we see that in a broad sense *Agnes of Sorrento* is *The Minister's Wooing* retold in Catholic terms. In *Agnes* there is no shipwreck, no report of a doubly lost lover, but Agnes, who successfully restores the "believing heart" in her lover Agostino Sarelli, is Mary Scudder saving James Marvyn. After a fashion there is even a "minister's wooing." Il Padre Francesco, Agnes's confessor, longs for her with a fierce desire and does his best to send her to a convent where no other man may have her. At the end, with some small anticipation of Hopkinsian "disinterested benevolence," Francesco renounces his desire and fades out of the story, permitting Agnes to marry Agostino.

It is not difficult to understand why Harriet repeated herself in this fashion and why she wrote James Fields of the *Atlantic* that *Agnes* "must be written" when he suggested she write another New England novel in its place. In reliving Mary Scudder's story in the Catholic Agnes, Harriet could make a trial run of Catholicism in her imagination and, like Hilda of *The Marble Faun* in her confession, she could find relief for her spiritual difficulties. That relief was based primarily on her observation early in *Agnes* that in Catholicism "The holy dead were not gone from earth; the Church visible and invisible were in close, loving, and constant sympathy,—still loving, praying, and watching together, though with a veil between."

As we might expect from Harriet's observation in *The Minister's Wooing* that Dr. Hopkins would have possessed a fully rounded soul had he grown up in the presence of Florentine art, one of the main points in *Agnes* is the rich aesthetic advantages of Catholic culture. It is Agnes's good fortune to hear hymns "strong with the nerve of the old Latin" (Harriet quoted them in the original again and again in her enthusiasm). Unlike Mrs. Marvyn (and Harriet Beecher Stowe), in whom the desire for beauty was crushed by Puritan New England circumstances, Agnes is surrounded by beauty, defined by her uncle, a disciple of Fra Angelico, as "the Lord's arrow, wherewith he pierceth to the inmost soul, with a divine longing and languishment which finds rest only in him." Harriet stated the contrast between Renaissance Italy and Puritan New England in this fashion: "What the Puritans of New England wrought out with severest earnestness in their reasonings and their lives, these early Puritans of Italy embodied in poetry, sculpture, and painting. They built their Cathedral and their Campanile, as the Jews of old built their Temple, with awe and religious fear, that they might thus express by costly and imperishable monuments their sense of God's majesty and beauty."

Harriet held very different convictions concerning Catholic cathedrals and churches from those Hawthorne attributed to Kenyon in *The Marble Faun;* Kenyon favored the conversion of St. Peter's into a hospital. Harriet also differed radically with Hawthorne's Hilda on the forms of Catholic worship. Concerning Agnes's "somewhat mechanical" repetition of "Hail, Mary!" Harriet wrote:

However foreign to the habits of a Northern mind or education such a mode of prayer may be, these forms to her were all helpful and significant, her soul was borne by them Godward,—and often, as she prayed, it seemed to her that she could feel the dissolving of all earthly things, and the pressing nearer and nearer of the great cloud of witnesses who ever surround the humblest member of Christ's mystical body.

On the matter of confession, however, Harriet was at least in partial agreement with Hawthorne. There were, she wrote, "advantages attending this species of intimate direction, when wisely and skillfully managed. . . . Grovelling and imperfect natures have often thus been lifted up and carried in the arms of superior wisdom and purity. The confession administered by a Fénelon or a Francis de Sales was doubtless a beautiful and most invigorating ordinance; but the difficulty in its actual working is the rarity of such superior natures. . . ." Like Hawthorne, Harriet felt the New England reluctance to accept any form in which, as she wrote, there was "no soul-privacy, no retirement, nothing too sacred to be expressed, too delicate to be handled and analyzed."

As Harriet advanced in her novel, it was not only the ordinance of confession that she found wanting among the promised reliefs of Catholicism. More compelling than any of her other impulses in writing her novel was the longing to live in a faith where the living and the "holy dead" were in "close, loving, and constant sympathy," where, in short, Henry was not lost in the lonely reaches of eternity. Like Mary Scudder, Agnes dwells "only on the cheering and the joyous features of her faith" but early in the novel her eyes slowly dilate "with a sad, mysterious expression" as she wonders how the saints can be happy when some are damned. At this point in the novel, Harriet reported that

. . . singular to tell, the religion which brought with it all human tenderness and pities,—the hospital for the sick, the refuge for the orphan, the enfranchisement of the slave,—this religion brought also the news of the eternal, hopeless, living torture of the great majority of mankind, past and present. Tender spirits, like those of Dante, carried this awful mystery as a secret and unexplained anguish, saints wrestled with God and wept over it; but still the awful fact remained, spite of Church and sacrament, that the gospel was in effect, to the majority of the human race, not the glad tidings of salvation, but the sentence of unmitigable doom.

Agnes's recognition that Catholicism still postulated hell (an almost inevitable recognition when we remember that Calvin Stowe carried Dante's *Divina Commedia* in his pocket and read in it daily) made Harriet's Italian story follow the pattern of *The Minister's Wooing* in a fashion she doubtless wished she could avoid. Confronted with the possible "unmitigable doom" of her lover because of his "unbelieving heart," Agnes, despite the forms of Catholicism and the art of Catholic Italy, is actually in more difficult spiritual circumstances than Mary Scudder in anguish over James Marvyn. Il Padre Francesco's insistence that if she turns back from heavenly marriage in entering a convent, she will accomplish her own damnation as well as Agostino's, leads her to wear "a cross with seven steel points for the seven sorrows of Mary," and to fast severely. Toward the close of the book, her affairs reach a fearful predicament, which leads to a surprising resolution:

Was she, indeed, the cause of such awful danger to his soul? Might a false step now, a faltering human weakness, indeed plunge that soul, so dear, into a fiery abyss without bottom or shore? Should she forever hear his shrieks of torture and despair, his curses on the hour he had first known her? Her very blood curdled, her nerves froze, as she thought of it, and she threw herself on her knees and prayed with an anguish that brought the sweat in beaded drops to her forehead,—strange dew for so frail a lily!—and her prayer rose above all intercession of saints, above the seat even of the Virgin Mary herself, to the heart of her Redeemer, to Him who some divine instinct told her was alone mighty to save. . . . She had that vivid sense of the sustaining presence and sympathy of an Almighty Saviour which is the substance of which all religious forms and appliances are the shadows; her soul was stayed on God, and was at peace, as truly as if she had been the veriest Puritan maiden that ever worshipped in a New England meeting-house. She felt a calm superiority to all things earthly,—a profound reliance on that invisible aid which comes from God alone.

A few pages farther on we learn that Agostino has found a leader in Savonarola, that he has taken the sacrament from Agnes's uncle, Father Antonio, and that all is eternally well. But this passage in which Agnes finally by-passes the saints and the Virgin Mary and presents her petition like "the veriest Puritan maid" to the Redeemer, "to Him who some divine instinct told her was alone mighty to save," is the real conclusion of the book. Confronting herself in the person of Agnes with the issue of probable eternal damnation of a loved one, Harriet realized that for her as New England Puritan only God, directly petitioned, could save.

This Puritan New England denouement is supported by the most dramatic element in the novel, the inner struggle of Il Padre Francesco. In this once dissipated and still restless and intense Italian nobleman, converted by the hell-fire preaching of "Jerome" Savonarola, Harriet found another character, the study of whom drew her irresistibly back to Puritanism. Like Dr. Hopkins under the influence of Mary Scudder, Francesco's life begins to blossom when he discovers in Agnes a soul capable of understanding his inner life; but he lacks Hopkins' simplicity of soul. Gradually he makes the discovery that he did not bury his old self when as Lorenzo Sforza, to the accompaniment of mournful chants and lighted candles, he was symbolically carried in his coffin to the ancestral tomb.

In an image that carries us back to the Puritan-Platonic, rungless ladder of *The Minister's Wooing,* Harriet asked how Francesco could forget Agnes when "every sacred round of the ladder by which he must climb, was so full of memorials of her." Because of his love, he finds his "whole inner nature boiling in furious rebellion against the dictates of his conscience, —self against self." How could it be otherwise when, as Harriet perceived:

> . . . no passions are deeper in their hold, more pervading and more vital to the whole human being, than those that make their first entrance through the higher nature, and beginning with a religious and poetic ideality, gradually work their way through the whole fabric of the human existence. From grosser passions, whose roots lie in the senses, there is always a refuge in man's loftier nature. . . . But to love that is born of ideality, of intellectual sympathy, of harmonies of the spiritual and immortal natures, of the very poetry and purity of the soul, if it be placed where reason and religion forbid its exercise and expression, what refuge but the grave,—what hope but that wide eternity where all human barriers fall, all human relations end, and love ceases to be a crime?

Here Harriet supposed she wrote about the inner trials of an Italian monk. Actually she did something else and something far more significant, for this passage is an important clarification of New England sensibility and a valuable supplement to her dramatization of Puritan-Platonic love in the friendship of Mary Scudder and Dr. Samuel Hopkins. When we understand that in the imagination of a New England Puritan like Harriet, love born of "intellectual sympathy" might gradually work its way "through the whole fabric of the human existence," that from this love there would be no escape as from "grosser passions," and that the only refuge, the only hope would be "that wide eternity where all human barriers fall, all human relations end, and love ceases to be a crime"—when we understand all this, we have a new appreciation of the New England, even the Puritan, qualities in Emily Dickinson's relations with the Reverend Charles Wadsworth. It seems clear from her poems that Emily Dickinson's love also began in "intellectual sympathy," then spread through her whole being with a passionate, quite human intensity, that she concluded her love for a married man was "placed where reason and religion forbid its exercise," and that she found her hope in "the wide eternity," where, as she wrote again and again, she was to be bride and wife.

There are other New England overtones to the trials of Il Padre Francesco. Much as Roger Chillingworth probes the guilty depths of the Reverend Arthur Dimmesdale in *The Scarlet Letter,* a conscienceless monk, Father Johannes, probes Il Padre Francesco, proposing for his verdict the case of a brother who has confessed in secret that he still loves a woman. Believing that he must subdue himself before he can master his love for Agnes, Francesco retires to do penance on Vesuvius. Harriet's matching of the inner and the outer in describing this experience in the chapter "The Penance" again suggests Hawthorne. We are in the world of Young Goodman Brown and Ethan Brand when, staring into the crater of his own heart and of Vesuvius, Francesco fancies he hears "behind and around the mocking laugh of fiends, and that confused clamor of mingled shrieks and lamentations which Dante describes as filling the dusky approaches to that forlorn realm where hope never enters."

But here Harriet was doing a good deal more than to echo the masterly symbolic art of Hawthorne, for in her imagery and her psychological observations she was also remembering Jonathan Edwards' "Sinners in the Hands of an Angry God." Edwards' statement that "Unconverted men walk over the pit of hell on a rotten covering, and there are innumerable places in this covering so weak that they will not bear their weight," Harriet reiterated in describing Francesco's slow progress across the crater: "Now and then his foot would crush in, where the lava had hardened in a thinner crust, and he would draw it suddenly back from the lurid red-hot metal beneath." Even closer to Edwards' terrible pronouncements are Francesco's reflections after he has seen the cone, that "condensed, intensified essence and expression of eternal fire, rising and still rising from some inexhaustible fountain of burning":

"Ah, God . . . for this vain life of man! They eat, they drink, they dance, they sing, they marry and are given in marriage, they have castles and gardens and villas, and yet how close by burns and roars the eternal fire! Fools that we are, to clamor for indulgence and happiness in this life, when the question is, to escape everlasting burnings! If I tremble at this outer court of God's wrath and justice, what must be the fires of hell? These are but earthly fires; they can burn the body: those are made to burn the soul; they are undying as the soul is. What would it be to be dragged down, down, down, into an abyss of soul-fire hotter than this for ages on ages? This might bring merciful death in time: that will have no end."

Harriet, of course, did not distort fact in attributing these Edwardean sentiments to her Catholic priest: meditations quite as dark may be found in Augustine, Dante, and Il Francesco's contemporary, Savonarola. But a well-informed Catholic will still have difficulty with her analysis. Where in *Agnes of Sorrento,* for example, do we find recognition of the fact that Roman Catholicism regards human nature as imperfect rather than totally depraved? Where do we find recognition of the Catholic emphasis on good works rather than on faith as the primary condition of salvation? Where, most importantly of all, is recognition of the existence of Purgatory? From the Catholic viewpoint, Harriet badly needed instruction in The Faith: Catholicism was not necessarily a fictitious shore for a Puritan mother in anguish over her son's eternal welfare. But the important fact is that Harriet found it a fictitious shore.

6

A NEW ENGLAND IDYL

IF WE turn from *Agnes of Sorrento* to Harriet's long-delayed "Maine story," *The Pearl of Orr's Island,* also published in 1862 by Ticknor and Fields, with the expectation that we shall find further clarification of her struggle with Catholicism, we shall certainly be disappointed. It is only, in fact, through the most careful reading that we can find anything of her inner history reflected in her second New England novel. *The Pearl* is a very different kind of book not only from *Agnes* but from *The Minister's Wooing* and her later New England novels, *Oldtown Folks* and *Poganuc People,* where we can feel the pressure of circumstance and discover rather easily the practice of "symbolic action." But this does not mean that *The Pearl* was a mere potboiler. Like *Oldtown Fireside Stories* (1872), which also stands on the periphery of Harriet's primary concern with matters New England, *The Pearl* is a beautiful and occasionally subtle evocation of New England life; the first half at least (we shall have to wonder about it as whole book) demonstrates something approaching genius in the achievement of tone and atmosphere in bringing out the possibilities of the exquisitely slight. Other New England writers have testified enthusiastically concerning it. John Greenleaf Whittier wrote: "When I am in the mood for thinking deeply I read 'The Minister's Wooing.' But 'The Pearl of Orr's Island' is my favorite. It is the most charming New England idyl ever written." Sarah Orne Jewett wrote that she read *The Pearl of Orr's Island* when she was thirteen or fourteen and could never forget "the exquisite flavor and reality of delight" which the beginning (she meant the first seventeen chapters) gave her; she described it as "classical—historical—anything you like to say, if you can give it high praise enough."

Harriet's characters who erupt realistically, humorously, and vigorously furnish ample justification for such praise. When, for example, in the second chapter of *The Pearl,* we meet Aunt Roxy and Aunt Ruey, we have no introduction and we need none. They are perfectly in character when Roxy says, observing Mrs. James Lincoln, who has just died in childbirth, "She'll make a pretty corpse," and Ruey remarks, "She was a pretty girl." Equally appropriate when we next meet them is their complete indifference to the dreamy look of the sea and the warm, balmy day while they concentrate, Roxy on catnip tea for the new baby and Ruey on a mourning bonnet while she sings a funeral psalm in her high cracked voice. Ruey and Roxy Toothacre, whose fame has even reached the town of Brunswick eighteen miles away, are too much brisk New England to sit and look at the sea.

They are what the Old Testament calls "cunning women," nobody's aunts in particular but aunts to human nature generally, with an infinite "faculty" in practical matters from dressmaking and upholstering to nursing and doctoring. Having struck their roots deep, they seem never to grow older and are always found like last year's mullein stalks, upright, dry, and seedy. But Roxy under her black mohair frizette is very different from Ruey under her carroty companion piece.

Miss Roxy, being vigorous, spicy, and decided, a kind of priestess and sibyl, is the planet around which plump, cushiony, and elegiac Miss Ruey revolves like a satellite. Since they have talked over everything in nature and said everything they can think of to each other, their opinions incline to be alike, not because they themselves are similar but because Miss Roxy for years has come down like the coining machine in a mint on every opinion her sister puts out. For example in the matter of this baby born of a dying mother, Ruey thinks it ought to be enough for them that the name "Mara" is a "Scriptur' name," but Roxy promptly sets her right: "Now there was Miss Jones

down on Mure P'int called her twins Tig-lath-Pileser and
Shalmaneser,—Scriptur' names both, but I never liked 'em.
The boys used to call 'em, Tiggy and Shally, so no mortal could
guess they was Scriptur'." Ruey returns to the sisterly fold by
remarking with a sigh, ". . . 't ain't much matter, after all, *what*
they call the little thing, for 't ain't 't all likely it's goin' to
live. . . . This 'ere 's a baby that won't get along without its
mother. . . . If it's goin' to be called home, it's a pity, as I
said, it didn't go with its mother—" Aunt Roxy interrupts
her: "And save the expense of another funeral."

The most delicious moments furnished by these two weird
sisters occur when they find appropriate victims for their old
women's lore. Miss Ruey's opportunity comes when she is
left alone with timid Mrs. Pennel while Captain Pennel stares
through the rain and blowing surf for some glimpse of a ship
in distress. The pathetic circumstances lead Miss Ruey to
reminisce on what she calls the "sperit world." Mrs. Pennel
is nervous at Miss Ruey's report that her Aunt Lois once heard
a baby crying out in a storm; she tells her, "Laws a-mercy
. . . it was nothing but the wind,—it always screeches like a
child crying; or maybe it was the seals; seals will cry just like
babes." That's what they told Aunt Lois, Ruey says, but after
the storm, they found a baby's cradle washed ashore "sure
enough," and it turned out to be a rather peculiar cradle: "Aunt
Lois took it in—it was a very good cradle, and she took it to
use, but every time there came up a gale, that ar cradle would
rock, rock, jist as if somebody was a-sittin' by it; and you could
stand across the room and see there wa'n't nobody there." Presumably in a practical New England household, things might
have gone on in this fashion for years, or at least until all the
children were out of diapers. But Aunt Lois had a sister
Cerinthy, who was "a weakly girl, and had the janders":

"Cerinthy was one of the sort that's born with veils over their
faces, and can see sperits; and one time Cerinthy was a-visitin'
Lois after her second baby was born, and there came up a blow,
and Cerinthy comes out of the keepin'-room, where the cradle was
a-standin', and says, 'Sister,' says she, 'who's that woman sittin'
rockin' the cradle?' and Aunt Lois says she, 'Why, there ain't

nobody. That ar cradle always will rock in a gale, but I've got used to it, and don't mind it." 'Well,' says Cerinthy, 'jist as true as you live, I just saw a woman with a silk gown on, and long black hair a-hangin' down, and her face was pale as a sheet, sittin' rockin' that ar cradle, and she looked round at me with her great black eyes kind o' mournful and wishful, and then she stooped down over the cradle.' 'Well,' says Lois, 'I ain't goin' to have no such doin's in my house,' and she went right in and took up the baby, and the very next day she jist had the cradle split up for kindlin'; and that night, if you'll believe, when they was a-burnin' of it, they heard, jist as plain as could be, a baby scream, scream, scream-in' round the house; but after that they never heard it no more."

Mrs. Pennel says she doesn't like such stories " 'specially to-night," and a little later quite understandably she screams at her own anxious, excited face reflected in the pitchy black window. This is a delightful American folk tale, almost as delightful as the yarn of Dick Allbright and the "bar'l" Harriet's eventual Hartford neighbor and acquaintance, Mark Twain, would tell in the celebrated third chapter of *Life on the Mississippi*. But Harriet's, of course, is not a Western tall tale with its long rhythms and recurring patterns finally exploding into the outrageously unbelievable, but the concentrated New England blend of the macabre and the humorous Robert Frost would later dramatize in his masterly "The Witch of Coös."

Miss Roxy, being matter-of-fact and positive, cannot be expected to let herself go in the manner of Miss Ruey, particularly when she finds herself discussing the dead with a hardheaded, practical woman like Mrs. Kittridge. When the Captain has gone to bed and Mrs. Kittridge remarks, apropos of the corpse of the beautiful woman washed ashore in the storm, and now laid out decently in the keeping-room, that it's a pity she can't see all that's being done for her, Miss Roxy remarks brusquely, "How do you know she don't?" Mrs. Kittridge's authority for believing the dead stay dead is the hymn verse:

> The living know that they must die,
> But all the dead forgotten lie—
> *Their memory and their senses gone,*
> *Alike unknowing and unknown.*

Miss Roxy points out that "hymn-book ain't Scriptur'" and nods her head as if she could say more if she chose. But clearly she has to be coaxed into the macabre. When Mrs. Kittridge moves her chair nearer and asks if she has anything particular on her mind, Miss Roxy says, "I ain't one of the sort as likes to make a talk of what I've seen, but mebbe if I was, I've seen some things *as* remarkable as anybody. I tell you, Mis' Kittridge, folks don't tend the sick and dyin' bed year in and year out, at all hours, day and night, and not see some remarkable things; that's my opinion." As to whether or not she has ever seen a "sperit," she tells Mrs. Kittridge, "I won't say as I have, and I won't say as I haven't . . . only as I have seen some remarkable things."

But, of course, as she tells Mrs. Kittridge, she has had "opportunities to observe that most haven't" and she doesn't care if she does say she's "pretty sure spirits that has left the body do come to their friends sometimes." For instance, there was Mrs. Titcomb, whose "evidences" satisfied the minister, but who was still afraid of the dark valley, all the darker because she was dying with her husband and her son John off on a voyage to Archangel. The minister told her on his last visit, "Mis' Titcomb, the Lord will find ways to bring you thro' the dark valley." As she sank away at three o'clock in the morning, she looked anxious and distressed and asked, "Oh, Aunt Roxy . . . it's so dark, who will go with me?" But her face suddenly brightened and she said, "John is going with me," and "she jist died as easy as a bird." Next morning the minister was pleased to find Roxy had noted the exact hour by the Captain's chronometer. Later it turned out that John had died the very same day and the very same hour as his mother.

Then there was "that ar Mr. Wadkins that come to Brunswick twenty years ago, in President Averill's [Roxy must have meant President Appleton's] days." When Mr. Wadkins came to die, he tossed and threw off the clothes and Roxy found on his pillow a beautiful woman's "likeness" that he wore by a ribbon around his neck. Miss Roxy doesn't like to speak about these things but at the moment of death she saw that woman "at the back of the bed, right in the partin' of the curtains, jist as she looked in the pictur'—blue eyes and curly hair and pearls on her neck, and black dress." Miss Roxy doesn't know what it was, but she knows what she thinks, and she doesn't think it best to tell. Listening to Miss Roxy and Miss Ruey, we can appreciate the justice of Perry D. Westbrook's comment in *Acres of Flint* (1951) on Harriet in *The Pearl,* that "no writer except Sarah Orne Jewett has so successfully caught the rhythms of Down-East; and in reproducing the continuous scriptural allusion that flowed through such speech in the days when people still went to meeting twice every Sabbath day, Sarah Orne Jewett has not approached her predecessor."

Captain Kittridge, who discovered that beautiful corpse which starts Miss Roxy on her reminiscences, has a "rude poetic faculty." In other words, he is a somewhat artistic liar, much to his wife's distress, with stories of an anchor dropped in front of a merman meetinghouse in the sea, life among the Esquimaux, fabulous jewels, and a brief report on Polly Twitchell over at Mure P'int, who used to brew storms and go to sea in a sieve to show how great a witch she was. But his stories can only take in Mara, Moses, and Sally, the children in the book; he is no major artist in folklore like Miss Roxy and Miss Ruey, who are "always chippering and chatting to each other, like a pair of antiquated house-sparrows." Miss Roxy, Miss Ruey, and Captain Kittridge are the literary prototypes of countless New England old maids and ship captains in American fiction, and there is a freshness of original vision about all of them, but Captain Kittridge already shows signs of that quaintness without edge, which all too often would be the stock-in-trade of the local colorists of the 1880's and 1890's.

There is nothing soft, however, about Mrs. Kittridge. She regards the beautiful corpse washed ashore as "an opportunity we ought to improve to learn children what death is. I think we can't begin to solemnize their minds too young." She takes her own daughter Sally and little Mara Lincoln to inspect the lonely and cold form lighted by rays falling through the closed shutters. Sally evinces merely childish curiosity at something new, but Mara hangs back, whereupon Mrs. Kittridge places her little hand on the icy forehead. Mara gives a piercing scream and hides her face in Aunt Roxy's dress, sobbing bitterly at the distressful chill that has passed up her arm and through her brain, but Mrs. Kittridge is without sympathy: "That child'll grow up to follow vanity . . . her little head is full of dress now, and she hates anything serious,—it's easy to see that."

II

For Harriet, as for us, this scene symbolizes that callousness toward children, that tendency prematurely to push them toward the darkest realities, which was one of the unloveliest features of Puritanism. But Harriet herself seems a severe Puritan placing the reader's hand again and again on icy brows. In the first chapter, the brig *Flying Scud* is forced into the wrong channel of the Kennebec, bearing James Lincoln to a watery death in his holiday clothes. In the second chapter, his dying wife becomes the mother of little Mara while in the best room the sea water drips in a sullen pool from her husband's corpse. In the third, Mara is baptized from the silver baptismal vase on her mother's coffin. When Mara is only a few years old, the second wreck casts the beautiful stranger ashore in a shroud of kelp, with the living baby in her arms, who is adopted by Mara's grandparents, the Pennels, and becomes her childhood playmate, Moses.

But Harriet was no Mrs. Kittridge merely "solemnizing" her readers. As we reflect, we see Harriet's instinctive rightness in having Mara find *The Tempest* in her grandparents' attic, and ponder, with the ocean before and the pines behind, "Full fathom five thy father lies;/Of his bones are coral made." It is not simply that Mara's own father has drowned or that Moses' father presumably may lie quite literally "full fathom five" off Orr's Island, somewhere in Casco Bay, or that Moses and Mara are a Yankee Ferdinand and Miranda. As in Shakespeare's drama, so in *The Pearl of Orr's Island,* the guiding principle is "sea-change," the transformation of death and the mystery of death, of all tragedy, into comedy and beauty.

This, of course, explains Aunt Ruey's function in her wonderful folk tale of the rocking cradle and similarly Aunt Roxy's in her comforting reports that John accompanied his mother through the dark valley and that Mr. Wadkins' beautiful friend stood by in the hour of his parting. We can also see this guiding principle of metamorphosis at work in the funeral of Moses' mother.

Mrs. Kittridge, Harriet noted, would not for the world have had a ship wrecked on her particular account, but since a ship had been wrecked and the funeral was to take place in her own parlor, she could hardly be expected to regard it without satisfaction. It would be a matter of talk for years, there were no mourners to spoil the occasion, and glory of glories, the minister was coming to tea. The Reverend Theophilus Sewall of Harpswell, Harvard graduate, lawyer, and medical authority rivaled only by Miss Roxy, is indeed a splendid sight as he arrives tall and majestic in powdered wig, three-cornered hat, broad-skirted coat, knee-breeches, and high shoes with plated buckles. As Mrs Kittridge can see at a glance, this eligible bachelor has graced the occasion with his best things (the second best stockings, as she knows from Miss Emily, Mr. Sewall's maiden sister and housekeeper, are to be distinguished by "a certain skillful darn").

There is nothing of the dour Calvinist about the Reverend Mr. Sewall. All the springs of his life are kept oiled by a quiet sense of humor, and he is an amused spectator of life, who likes to play with and on his parishioners, as for example, at the tea following the funeral. Mrs. Kittridge has recommended blackberry-root tea as a gargle for Mary Jane Simpkins. Is it good? Yes, Mr. Sewall thinks it's a good gargle. Miss Roxy says, "Ma'sh rosemary is the gargle that I always use . . . it cleans out your throat so." Yes, marsh rosemary is a very excellent gargle in Mr. Sewall's opinion. His sister, Miss Emily, wonders if rose leaves and vitriol are not a good gargle; she always thought he liked that. Well, he does. Captain Kittridge says Mr. Sewall had better make up his mind which is most likely to cure Mary Jane Simpkins's throat. "There

won't any of them cure Mary Jane's throat," says Mr. Sewall.
All the ladies are aghast and remind him that he has praised
this and that and suggested they do good. "No, they don't,"
says Mr. Sewall, "not the least in the world . . . but they are
all excellent gargles, and as long as people must have gargles,
I think one is about as good as another."

Mr. Sewall's quip concerning gargles is not the only amusement springing from the funeral, transforming tragedy into
comedy. Miss Emily saw a look of startled recognition on her
brother's face as he examined the bracelet of the dead woman.
As she and her brother sail home to Harpswell with Captain
Kittridge, she breaks into observations concerning its singular
workmanship, but Mr. Sewall is interested only in a ship to be
launched next Wednesday. As soon as they arrive home, however, Miss Emily goes to work in earnest, laying a seducing
little fire, taking Theophilus' wig and dress-coat, and getting
him into the ease, and she hopes the confidence, of his study
gown, his black cap, and his slippers; as a final inducement
to talk she makes him a square of toast and warms his cider
before the fire in a quaintly shaped silver cup. Mr. Sewall
delightfully parries all her questions and tells her she sees
everything and everybody through a prism with a bordering
of rainbow.

There is unmistakable charm in this Puritan brother and
sister. Harriet found the perfect symbols for them. Miss
Emily is a New England brook chattering in the "back lot";
Mr. Sewall is "like one of those wells you shall sometimes see
by a deserted homestead, so long unused that ferns and lichens
feather every stone down to the dark, cool water. Dear to him
was the stillness and coolness of inner thoughts with which no
stranger intermeddles; dear to him every pendent fern-leaf of
memory, every dripping moss of old recollection; and though
the waters of his soul came up healthy and refreshing enough
when one really must have them, yet one had to go armed
with bucket and line and draw them up,—they never flowed."

Here, as in her obvious delight in such New England eccen-
trics as Miss Roxy and Miss Ruey, Harriet suggests that

Yankee Theocritus, Henry Thoreau. But Harriet differed markedly from Thoreau; she had none of his genius for savoring nature for itself. She most effectively evoked outer New England when she saw it as symbol for inner New England, as in the above passage, and in her description in the first chapter of Naomi's mother: "On the whole, she impressed one like those fragile wild-flowers which in April cast their fluttering shadows from the mossy crevices of the old New England granite,—an existence in which colorless delicacy is united to a sort of elastic hardihood of life, fit for the rocky soil and harsh winds it is born to encounter." It is such passages as these, and Harriet's appropriate quotations on the majesty of nature from the Bible, that give *The Pearl of Orr's Island* that joy in the external world without which it could hardly be called a New England idyl, and without which she could not have transformed death and the mystery of death into beauty.

Harriet may have known Theocritus, but his Amaryllis, even in homespun, would have been out of place under the hemlocks or wandering the rocky shore of Orr's Island. A better model for a New England idyl was *The Tempest* with its innocent lovers. Jonathan Edwards had held that all visions and dreams, even of Christ crucified, were merely natural occurrences in the susceptible, and had nothing spiritual in them; but Harriet was willing to suppose that on Orr's Island, as on Prospero's, visions and dreams might possess true spiritual significance. Like Miranda, who sleeps during the storm in *The Tempest,* Mara rests as quietly during the hurricane casting Moses ashore, "as if the cruel sea, that had made her an orphan from her birth, were her kind-tempered old grandfather singing her to sleep." Toward dawn, she dreams of a woman in a long white garment who puts the hand of a little black-eyed boy in her own, saying, "Take him, Mara, he is a playmate for you." When Mara sees Moses, she immediately identifies him with the child of her dream, and Harriet asks concerning the vision:

Whence it came,—whence come multitudes like it, which spring up as strange, enchanted flowers, every now and then in the dull, material pathway of life,—who knows? It may be that our present faculties have among them a rudimentary one, like the germs of wings in the chrysalis, by which the spiritual world becomes sometimes an object of perception; there may be natures in which the walls of the material are so fine and translucent that the spiritual is seen through them as through a glass darkly. It may be, too, that the love which is stronger than death has a power sometimes to make itself heard and felt through the walls of our mortality, when it would plead for the defenseless ones it has left behind. All these things *may* be,—who knows?

This love of Mara for Moses was Harriet's final means for transforming tragedy into idyl. It would be foolish to claim it is a great love story, but it carries the mark of the genuine. Harriet did not spoil its colorless beauty by having Mara tell Moses of her dream or play the role of a passionately talking, vainly loving Simaetha to a generally indifferent and lyric Delphis. Moses is Mara's hero, the other half of her soul; for Moses, Mara is only a girl, but these are children and this is the coast of Maine, not the volcanic soil of Sicily. Moses is a healthy boy, whose life is in the outward and present. When he returns at seven from a summer voyage to the fishing grounds, Mara is hurt, of course, at his naturally boyish disparagement of girls and women. But like a truly Puritan New England girl she keeps her unhappiness to herself and argues, from Goldsmith's *History of Greece and Rome,* that the nymph Egeria, who instructed Numa Pompilius in religion, is quite as heroic as Moses' ideal, Romulus. Mara does not pour out her soul; rather she asks Mr. Sewall if there aren't lives of women in Plutarch.

Mara is quite convincingly one of those bright little New England girls like Harriet Beecher in Litchfield, Connecticut. Mr. Sewall decides to teach Moses Latin, and Moses announces: "I mean to take all the declensions to begin with; there's five of 'em, and I shall learn them for the first lesson; then I shall take the adjectives next, and next the verbs, and so in a fortnight get into reading." But as Miss Roxy says to him: "I tell ye Latin ain't just what you think 't is, steppin' round so crank; you must remember what the king of Israel said to Benhadad, king of Syria." Moses doesn't remember what that was, but Mara repeats softly, "Let not him that putteth on the harness boast as him that putteth it off." And Mara and Miss Roxy are right. In hearing Moses, Mara learns the lesson perfectly, and at Mr. Sewall's when Moses fumbles, she blurts out the right answer before she knows what she has done. As a reward she is spared Miss Emily's lessons in embroidery and becomes Moses' fellow student in the classics.

Our last glimpse of these two in part one of *The Pearl* is Mara reading Moses *The Tempest,* in which he finds nothing of interest beyond the sound of her voice; he even interrupts her in the midst of "Full fathom five" to ask her help with the mast of a tiny ship he is building. This is certainly not a great scene, but in realistic terms appropriate to a childhood New England idyl, the bones of tragedy have undergone a "sea-change" into coral, and as Alcott observed of Thoreau's *A Week,* New England has found "a clear relation to the literature of other and classic lands."

III

At work on the first part of *The Pearl,* Harriet wrote Annie Fields in January, 1861: "I write my Maine story with a shiver, and come back to this [that is, to *Agnes of Sorrento*] as to a flowery home where I love to rest." Remembering Miss Roxy and Miss Ruey, the Reverend Theophilus Sewall, the racy humor, and pale, authentic beauty of *The Pearl,* we are likely to be completely baffled, even if we recall that at first Harriet had supposed Catholicism her "flowery home." Why should she shiver? It seems clear from what we know of *The Pearl,* its being begun in 1852 and its being resumed in 1857, that in the winter and the spring of 1861 Harriet wrote very little on her Maine story. Miss Roxy and Miss Ruey bear a striking resemblance to similarly vital characters in *Uncle Tom's Cabin;* it seems likely that they belong to the summer of 1852. The Reverend Theophilus Sewall almost certainly belongs to 1857-1858; with only a few changes here and there, he is the Reverend Samuel Eaton of Harpswell, whom Harriet discovered in Sprague's *Annals of the American Pulpit* shortly before starting *The Minister's Wooing.* By reference to my suggestion that Harriet was given to the practice of New England doubleness, we have no trouble in explaining why she wrote with Yankee humor in creating Miss Roxy, Miss Ruey, and Mr. Sewall in 1852 and 1857. Here she was escaping Puritan obsessions concerning the deaths of her two sons.

But why, we must ask again, when she had so much already written, should the transformation of tragedy make Harriet shiver in 1861? The shiver, I believe, came from the fact that for her *The Pearl* was no longer a genuine expression; it was a dead book, which she resurrected only because she had promised her brother Henry's friend, Theodore Tilton, the Maine story for the *Independent.* Revising *The Pearl,* linking incident to incident, and writing only a few new pages, she was engaged in a task deeply uncongenial to a novelist for whom fiction was primarily significant as it was imposed on her by inner problems rather than composed by her as a mere story.

All of this, of course, Theodore Tilton would not have even faintly suspected. He must have supposed Harriet's excuse a complete explanation when after the April, 1861, installment of seventeen chapters, she pleaded the war and her son Frederick's enlistment in Company A, First Massachusetts Volunteers, for delaying the continuation of *The Pearl* until December. Quite naturally on the basis of the first seventeen chapters, the portion of Harriet's Maine story I have just discussed, Tilton expected fine things of Harriet. He was willing to wait; and he was not particularly overyouthful or uncritical when he announced the resumption of *The Pearl,* calling it "MRS. STOWE'S GREAT STORY, said to be the best which this renowned author has ever written."

For Harriet, weary from the labor of finishing *Agnes* and even further out of touch with *The Pearl,* this was a good deal more than truth. Yielding to her New England conscience, she sent this notice to Tilton, which must have puzzled him but which he dutifully published in the next issue of the *Independent*:

That a story so rustic, so woodland, so pale and colorless, so destitute of all that is ordinarily expected in a work of fiction, should be advertised in the columns of *The Independent*, as this was last week, as "Mrs. So-and-So's *great* romance," or with words to that effect, produces an impression both appalling and ludicrous.

It is as if some golden-haired baby who had touched her mother's heart by singing:

"Jesus, tender shepherd, hear us!"

should forthwith be announced with flaming playbills, to sing in the Boston Theatre as the celebrated Prima Donna, Madame Trottietoes!

We beg our readers to know that no great romance is coming,—only a story pale and colorless as real life, and sad as truth.

You will not be interested as you have been, kind friends,—we cannot hope it; your expectations are raised only to be dashed; for our characters have no strange and wonderful adventures of outward life, and the changes that occur to them and the history they make is that of the inner life, that "cometh not with observation."

Long before Sarah Orne Jewett wrote of *The Pearl* (in the same letter with the praise for the beginning) "Alas, that she couldn't finish it in the same noble key of simplicity and harmony," Harriet recognized that the conclusion of her Maine story is a disappointment. Miss Jewett put her critical finger exactly on the cause when she continued, "but a poor writer is at the mercy of much unconscious opposition. You must throw everything and everybody aside at times, but a woman made like Mrs. Stowe cannot bring herself to that cold selfishness of the moment for one's work's sake, and the recompense for her loss is a divine touch here and there in an incomplete piece of work."

The conclusion to *The Pearl* demanded by "that cold selfishness of the moment for one's work's sake" would have been a happy resolution, a further transformation of tragedy into idyl, more "divine" touches, such as Harriet caught momentarily in describing the arrival in Maine waters of a ship from China:

There comes a ship from China, drifting in like a white cloud,—the gallant creature! how the waters hiss and foam before her! with what a great free, generous plash she throws out her anchors, as if she said a cheerful "Well done!" to some glorious work accomplished! The very life and spirit of strange romantic lands come with her; suggestions of sandalwood and spice breathe through the pine-woods; she is an oriental queen, with hands full of mystical gifts; "all her garments smell of myrrh and cassia, out of the ivory palaces, whereby they have made her glad." No wonder men have loved ships like birds, and that there have been found brave, rough hearts that in fatal wrecks chose rather to go down with their ocean love than to leave her in the last throes of her death-agony.

A ship-building, a ship-sailing community has an unconscious poetry ever underlying its existence. Exotic ideas from foreign lands relieve the trite monotony of life; the ship-owner lives in communion with the whole world, and is less likely to fall into the petty commonplaces that infest the routine of inland life.

Here Harriet stood on the verge of realizing that vibrant Maine world to which Sarah Orne Jewett's characters would look back nostalgically in *The Country of the Pointed Firs* (1896). But the second part of *The Pearl* contains only patches of "unconscious poetry," and there are no "exotic ideas from foreign lands" to relieve the monotony of life. Except for that amusing coquette, Sally Kittridge, the book tends to fall almost completely into "petty commonplaces." At twenty, Moses half-accepts a smuggler's suggestion that he rob his kindly foster father, Zephaniah Pennel, and embark on a career of piracy. Saved from a life of crime by Mara, who overhears his plotting and informs Captain Kittridge, who promptly sends him off on a long voyage, Moses is still a trial. He is in love with Mara, but he wants her to commit herself first; he tries to force her into confession by pretending to be in love with Sally Kittridge. As the story draws to a close, Mara wears more and more an omniously spiritual look. As we might guess, she is dying, like countless sentimental heroines, of consumption compounded with piety. Needless to say, Moses (after inheriting a fortune through the identification of his parents by Mr. Sewall) is converted by Mara's pious and timely death and after a decent interval marries Sally Kittridge.

When we ask how the author of *The Minister's Wooing* could so mangle her New England idyl, we have the answer in Sarah Orne Jewett's observation that "a poor writer is at the mercy of much unconscious opposition." After finishing *Agnes* in the autumn of 1861, Harriet had no desire to go on with *The Pearl*. Momentarily, she was not only written out but almost certainly she had a profound impulse to put down her pen, close her desk, and wait for the return of vitality. But twice before she had started *The Pearl* only to postpone it, and she had made a definite commitment to Tilton. With a resolution that had nothing to do with art, she therefore rushed *The Pearl* to a conclusion in which from time to time she could find herself half-heartedly at home (Moses is almost Henry, and Mara, almost Harriet). The result is that *The Pearl of Orr's Island* is an impressive half-book.

7

NEW ENGLAND'S LOOKING-GLASS

I

IN THE second chapter of his *Autobiography,* Lyman Beecher sketched the Fall of the House of Beecher. His great-grandfather, Joseph, had been able to lift a barrel of cider and drink out of the bung-hole; his grandfather, Nathaniel, a blacksmith, had been able to lift a barrel of cider into a cart; his father, David Beecher, another blacksmith, had only been able to lift a barrel of cider and carry it into the cellar. But Lyman was simply relishing Yankee anecdote. He did not for a moment suppose Beecher vigor actually in decline. So great were his own energies that during his battle with Unitarianism in the 1820's he had found it necessary to let off steam by sawing wood and shoveling sand from one end of the cellar to the other. The old vigor lived on in most of his ten children. Henry Ward Beecher, slowly walking the streets of Brooklyn, eating peanuts out of a bag and scattering the shells in his wake, may have looked like the end of a family, but Henry was then retreating into the sleepy beast. At the call of piety or humanitarianism, with the help of the precious stones he carried for their intoxicating properties, some of which he reported produced much the same results as champagne, he could rouse himself, become the poet of the populace, and lift a whole congregation or a mass meeting like a wave before the wind.

We must remember Joseph, Nathaniel, David, Lyman, and Henry Ward Beecher as we try to account for Harriet's surprising recovery from her years of weakness, signalized by *Agnes* and the second part of *The Pearl,* and her emergence into the author of *Oldtown Folks* and *Oldtown Fireside Stories*. In 1853 she described herself to Mrs. Follen as "a little bit of a woman,—somewhat more than forty, about as thin and dry as a pinch of snuff; never very much to look at in my best days, and looking like a used-up article now." She was, if we can believe her, usually "tired far into the future." But I do not think we can believe her. She had not only what runners call second wind; as a Beecher, she had third, fourth, and fifth wind. Having faced poverty, household chores, childbirth seven times, religious perplexities, a cholera epidemic, vicious attacks from half a nation, agony over the possible eternal loss of her eldest son, and the ordeal of almost daily writing for a decade, Harriet went on after 1862 to produce books which rival *Uncle Tom's Cabin* and *The Minister's Wooing* in their creative power and as art and comment surpass them. She would still be lively and perceptive in the late 1870's in *Poganuc People* and though she became decidedly vague in her last years (she lived until eighty-five), she retained even then the Beecher vigor. Mark Twain remembered that in her mental decay "as she was always softly slippered and generally full of animal spirits, she was able to deal in surprises, and she liked to do it. She would slip up behind a person who was deep in dreams and musings and fetch a war whoop that would jump that person out of his clothes."

Harriet was vital and resilient but her ability to come speedily into new life was undoubtedly assisted by events befalling her in the early 1860's. Lyman Beecher died in 1863, aged eighty-seven, and her son Frederick was wounded at Gettysburg. For the most part, however, we find the epigraph for this period of her history in Emerson's observation that "Novelty, surprise, change of scene, refresh the artist,—'break up the tiresome old roof of heaven into new forms,' as Hafiz said." In November, 1862, she visited Lincoln at the White House and inspired, and perhaps advised by him, wrote a letter to British women criticizing their stand on slavery and the union so strategically that it apparently wrought a change in British foreign policy; Hawthorne wrote Harriet that "If anything

could make John Bull blush, I should think it might be that."
The following January she experienced another surprise,
another victory. At a Boston concert she was cheered to her
feet in the presence of Emerson when news came over the wires
that Lincoln had signed the Emancipation Proclamation. Most
significant of all was the close of the Andover period in August,
1863, when Calvin retired from the Seminary. Soon Harriet
was busy with a new home near Hartford, and she was barely
settled there in 1864 when she was involved with the rush
of preparations for her daughter Georgianna's wedding, two
months ahead of the original schedule, to an Episcopal clergyman, the Reverend Henry Allen. Everything apparently con-
spired to refresh her and to "break up the tiresome old roof
of heaven into new forms."

Emerson's phrase recalled from Hafiz seems particularly
appropriate when we learn that after moving to Hartford, Harriet entered the Episcopal Church.   Here apparently was the
solution to all those difficulties besetting her after Henry
Stowe's death in 1857.   In one step, it would seem, she had
repudiated the Calvinism which had obsessed her and had
found the exact church for a protestant with the Catholic lean-
ings indicated by *Agnes of Sorrento*.   We can even supply an
immediate cause for her "signing off" to Anglicanism.   In
1863 her brother Charles was convicted of heresy by the
Essex North Conference for his belief in pre-existence of souls,
borrowed from his brother Edward's *The Conflict of Ages*.
To Harriet the conviction was outrageous.   She had seen
Charles develop from the dark fatalist of the 1840's, who had
lost practically all faith in Christian doctrines, into a deeply
persuaded clergyman, sharing her own hatred of slavery and
anticipating her in the belief in spiritism.   She wrote letters
in Charles's behalf to various New England clergymen, such
as Dr. Bacon of Yale, to whom she made this indignant pro-
nouncement :

The persecution against my brother Charles conducted by an
unscrupulous minority in his church, who used for their purposes the
various passions and prejudices of his ministerial brethren, has at

last proceeded to a length that flesh and heart can endure no longer, and he has resigned his parish—as I view it, to save his life.

Harriet, it turned out, viewed the matter too darkly: Charles's Georgetown, Massachusetts, church sustained its pastor and the Conference finally rescinded its action. But that there was a connection between Harriet's new alliance with Anglicanism and her brother Charles we seem justified in concluding from the fact that in 1867 she tried to persuade him to become an Episcopal clergyman.

When we turn to her biography by another Charles, this time her son, Charles Edward Stowe, we find, however, this brief and tame report: "Mrs. Stowe had some years before this joined the Episcopal Church, for the sake of attending the same communion as her daughters, who were Episcopalians." In the light of this statement, Harriet bears a strong resemblance to Hawthorne's Wakefield, who had hidden from his wife for twenty years in the next street and though he had every good reason for returning to her, returned only because he was caught in a rainstorm outside his own door and concluded that it was good sense to get in out of the wet. Apparently she too did for the most superficial of reasons what was demanded by the whole logic of the situation, that is, if we can believe Charles Edward Stowe. But can we believe him? Harriet wrote that his *Life* has "all the force of an autobiography" and "is perhaps much more accurate as to detail & impression than is possible with any autobiography, written late in life." But we should also remember that Charles Edward Stowe was a Congregational clergyman and that his mother's "signing off" may have been an embarrassment. In *Poganuc People* (1878) she wrote of "gentle spirits" who came to the Episcopal Church, "cut and bleeding by the sharp crystals of doctrinal statement, and courting the balm of devotional liturgy and the cool shadowy indefiniteness of more aesthetic forms of worship." This sounds like autobiography. Is it not possible that, to a degree her son did not care to recognize, her entering the Episcopal Church was a crisis in her inner drama, a true breaking up of the "tiresome old roof of heaven into new forms"?

II

Almost exactly half way through *Oldtown Folks* (1869), in a central position illuminating what has come before and what follows, Harriet made her most extended comment on the Episcopal Church and Episcopalians. At first we are likely to be baffled, for there is nothing here suggesting the fresh enthusiasm of the new convert and much that looks like mockery of Anglicanism. When her narrator, Horace Holyoke, is invited to Boston for the Easter services at Christ Church (Old North), Grandmother Badger, whom we have been taught to admire for her good sense, says, "Good Friday!—Easter!—pish, Lois!—don't tell me!—old cast-off rags of the scarlet woman,— nothing else.

> 'Abhor the arrant whore of Rome,
> And all her blasphemies;
> Drink not of her accursed cup,
> Obey not her decrees.' "

Horace explains to his friend, Harry Percival, that in the New England Primer the "whore of Rome" burned John Rogers and added (so the rough woodcut seem to indicate) the unnecessary cruelty of weighing down the heads of his nine children with heavy stones.

This, of course, is the amusing prejudice of late eighteenth-century Oldtown, Massachusetts, but it suggests the un-New Englandness of the Episcopal Church, and this un-New-Englandness is the central theme in Harriet's description of the Kittery household where Horace visits in Boston. Soon after his arrival there, Miss Deborah Kittery hands Lady Widgery a cup of tea made from cargo saved at the time of "the disgraceful Boston riot." This noble, faded, and foolish old lady stirs her tea pensively and remarks that not only did the Boston Tea Party carry Sir Thomas Widgery to unprecedented heights of indignation but that it gave her a sick headache for three days so that she had to stay in a dark room and couldn't keep the least thing on her stomach. Sententiously she observes: "What a mysterious providence it is that such conduct should be suffered to lead to success"

Miss Debby declares that "Thomas Jefferson is a scoffing infidel, and he drafted their old Declaration of Independence, which, I will say, is the most abominable and blasphemous document that ever sinners dared to sign." Lady Widgery reminds her that George Washington was a Churchman, but Miss Debby thinks that makes his case all the worse: "There is some excuse for men of Puritan families, because their ancestors were schismatics and disorganizers to begin with, and came over here because they didn't like to submit to lawful government. For my part I have always been ashamed of having been born here. If I'd been consulted, I should have given my voice against it." To Miss Debby American democracy should be equated with the French "infidelity" of Voltaire, Rousseau, and "other French heathen names." "All men created equal" is clearly against the church catechism. As the evening draws to a close, Madame Kittery, Miss Debby's mother, reads the psalm, the epistle, and the gospel for Easter eve, and concludes with prayers for the royal family.

In view of her new alliance, we might suppose that Harriet would balance these negative aspects of Anglicanism with enthusiasm for the Easter service, but Horace reports:

It yet remains a mystery to my mind, how a church which retains such a stimulating and inspiring liturgy *could* have such drowsy preaching,—how men could go through with the "Te Deum," and the "Gloria in Excelsis," without one thrill of inspiration, or one lift above the dust of earth, and, after uttering words which one would think might warm the frozen heart of the very dead, settle sleepily down into the quietest commonplace. Such, however, has been the sin of ritualism in all days, principally because human nature is, above all things, lazy, and needs to be thorned and goaded up those heights where it ought to fly.

The case against the Episcopal Church is worsened by the witty and intelligent remarks of Ellery Davenport, grandson of Jonathan Edwards, and cousin of the Kitterys, who has been sitting in on the sedition and reaction. After Madame Kittery reads the prayers for the royal family, Ellery remarks that no one needs prayer more than the King of England, but prayer doesn't seem to have helped him much since he lost his American colonies. Even more telling are Ellery's quips the next evening before the fire. When Miss Debby and Lady Widgery express fear that no one can get to heaven now that there is no bishop in America, Ellery, who knows all the ins and outs of theology, observes that "it would take two in order to start the succession in America. The apostolic electricity cannot come down through one," and he tells them, much to their dismay, Benjamin Franklin's reply when he had failed to interest the Archbishop of Canterbury in bishops for the United States:

"Well, you see, he found Canterbury & Co. rather huffy, and somewhat on the high-and-mighty order with him, and, being a democratic American, he didn't like it. So he wrote over that he didn't see, for his part, why anybody that wanted to preach the Gospel couldn't preach it, without sending a thousand miles across the water to ask leave of a cross old gentlemen at Canterbury."

Miss Debby says, "That's what I call a profane remark, Ellery Davenport." The score at this point is impressive: Episcopalians are blind to the democratic idealism of Jefferson, the unselfish patriotism of Washington, and the good sense of Benjamin Franklin.

We become even more uncertain of any claims for the Episcopal Church when Ellery confesses that he likes "the idea of a nice old motherly Church, that sings to us, and talks to us, and prays with us, and takes us in her lap and coddles us when we are sick. . . . Nothing would suit me better, if I could get my reason to sleep; but the mischief of a Calvinistic education is, it wakes up your reason, and it never will go to sleep again, and you can't take a pleasant humbug if you would." We begin to suspect that, facts to the contrary, Harriet was actually anti-Episcopalian; and there would seem to be no good reason for her having entered the Episcopal Church, when Ellery reminds us that the Calvinistic doctrines, against which she was apparently protesting in her new alliance, "are all in the Thirty-nine Articles as strong as in the Cambridge platform. . ." and "what is worse, there is an abominable sight of truth in them. Nature herself is a high Calvinist, old jade; and there never was a man of energy enough to feel the force of the world he deals with that wasn't a predestinarian, from the time of the Greek Tragedians down to the time of Oliver Cromwell, and ever since."

But we must not rush to conclusions. It is possible that the Kittery household and Ellery's comments comprise difficulties in terms of Anglicanism comparable to the negative aspects of Calvinism in *The Minister's Wooing* and that Harriet was engaged, not so much in mocking the Episcopal Church, as in stating limitations which she felt compelled to face. This, in fact, would seem to be the situation. Among her earliest recollections, as she noted in a chapter of her father's autobiography, was her being taken immediately after her mother's death for a long visit at her Grandmother Foote's at Nutplains, near Guilford, Connecticut. There Aunt Harriet, re-created as Miss Debby, and Grandmother Foote, recreated as Madame Kittery, taught her the catechism of the Episcopal Church. At the time Harriet was most impressed by the portion of the catechism which told all servants "to order themselves lowly and reverently before their betters," for this insured that at age six she would be called "Miss Harriet." But she also pondered her aunt's remark, not meant for childish ears, that "many persons out of the Episcopal Church would be saved at last, but that they were resting entirely on *uncovenanted mercy*."

On later visits to Nutplains, Harriet experienced much of what she dramatized in the Kitterys. Once when some patriotic American attacked King George, Grandmother Foote revealed in private that the King was not to blame for the Revolution and with much emotion read her little granddaughter the prayers for the King, the Queen, and all the royal family. Grandmother Foote also reported her controversy with Edward Beecher. He had told her that Jonathan Edwards was a better Christian than Dr. Samuel Johnson and had sent her a life of Edwards for proof. Grandmother admitted that the Northampton divine was a very good Christian but she doubted that he could write better prayers than Dr. Johnson, and again she read to Harriet.

The Dr. Johnson here referred to may have been Boswell's favorite subject, who was the author of some remarkable prayers, but it seems more likely that Grandmother Foote was reading from *A Short Catechism for Young Children* (1765) or *A Form of Morning and Evening Worship, and Two Collects* (1766), by the Dr. Samuel Johnson born in nearby Guilford, who had set in motion the forces carrying the Foote family into the Episcopal Church. After graduation from Yale, Johnson read widely in theology and church history and became increasingly doubtful of the validity of the "Congregational Way" and increasingly convinced of the claims of Episcopacy. At the Yale commencement of 1722, Johnson, four other Congregational clergymen, all the faculty (that is, all two members), President Cutler, and Daniel Brown, tutor, presented the Trustees with their doubts of "Presbyterian ordination in opposition to Episcopal" and expressed willingness "to embrace your good counsels and instructions in relation to this important affair as far as God shall direct and dispose us to do." As President Woolsey of Yale remarked a century and a quarter later: "I suppose that greater alarm would scarcely be awakened now if the theological faculty were to declare for the Church of Rome, avow their belief in transubstantiation, and pray to the Virgin Mary."

After receiving holy orders in England, Johnson returned to Connecticut as missionary of the Society for the Propagation of the Gospel, and until his resignation in 1753, when he became President of King's College, later Columbia University, he waged a surprisingly successful battle against New England Puritanism. We misunderstand American intellectual history badly when we overlook the significance of the Anglican Church in Colonial New England. After Johnson, Episcopalians constituted a party of vigorous dissent winning more and more converts away from Puritanism. They even tempted Ezra Stiles, whom Harriet caricatured in *The Minister's Wooing*. In his reminiscences, Stiles wrote:

> I early determined that, in whatever I trifled, I would not trifle on the subject of religion; or, however, if I sold my faith, it would be dearly bought. Hence when, in January, 1755, I had a formal invitation from the Episcopal church in Stratford, to conform, and succeed Doctor Johnson, with at least £100 sterling a year; and, before that, in October, 1752, when I sustained a vigorous application to take orders, and become a minister in the Episcopal church in Newport, then represented as a living of £200 sterling a year;—I thank God, none of these things moved me, nor addressed me with the least charm or temptation.

But many were charmed by Episcopacy. Through the labors of Johnson and his fellow apostates at the Yale commencement of 1722, and the additional temptation afforded by the fact that Anglicanism was a road to preferment in royal appointments, many of the most influential American families were insulated against the ardours of the Great Awakening of the 1740's, inspired by Jonathan Edwards. A generation later these Episcopal families constituted the powerful minority who remained loyal to the Crown and thereby created difficulties for those who sought through revolution to realize the Puritan dream of independence from England; and even after the Revolution, Episcopalians continued to run counter to what had originally been the "New England Way." In 1783, James Freeman, rector of King's Chapel, Boston, with his simplification of the Book of Common Prayer, took an important step toward Unitarianism. For many Boston and Cambridge Brahmins of the following generations, Unitarianism was not only a point of departure to transcendental radicalism; it also served as the half-way house on the way back to Canterbury. We have a significant symbol of the course of the American mind in the fact that in 1860 Frederick D. Huntington, Harvard's Professor of Divinity and Preacher of the University, resigned his Unitarian appointments and entered the Episcopal Church.

For Huntington and those New Englanders who followed him, such a step was a step forward out of spiritual loneliness.

For Harriet, entering the Anglican fold was all too much like a step backwards into the twilight world of her grandparents, the Footes. Her mother had renounced their ways in marrying Lyman Beecher; Edward and the other Beecher children had grown up arguing the "true faith" with their grandmother and their aunt; Harriet herself had repudiated Anglicanism in her own religious history and Church of England conservatism in her social radicalism in *Uncle Tom's Cabin* and *Dred*. Her grandparents and their Tory Anglicanism must have made her feel herself an inconsistent New Englander, even something of an apostate, in her new alliance. She had to describe the Footes, have the whole matter out in the open, grant like a shrewd debater the worst that could be granted, if she was to make a truly convincing case for the Episcopal Church in her imagination.

Harriet's predicament in writing *Oldtown Folks* was far more complicated than her earlier predicament in writing *The Minister's Wooing*. In her first New England novel, her intimate acquaintance with Puritanism, negatively and positively, had permitted her to say both yes and no to the ancestral faith and through "symbolic action" to effect a reconciliation, a temporary reconciliation, with the ancestral faith. But now her very knowledge was an embarrassment to her. If she had been conveniently ignorant, she could have vindicated Anglicanism, or at least furnished good reasons for making an alliance with its gentle and humane practices, by painting Calvinism in unrelieved black. But she knew too much, she had been too long, too intimately associated with Puritans and Puritanism, to make a simple and superficial indictment. It is no surprise that, though she was an extremely facile writer, she spent four years laboring on *Oldtown Folks*, that she felt compelled again and again to turn back and write over with care, and that she reported to Annie Fields, "I never put so much work into anything before." Her attempt to explain herself to herself and to the reader involved her in a résumé of the whole spirit and body of New England, a résumé in which she had to mediate between the way of life which had shaped her, and which she understood as no one before her, and a faith, to which she had committed herself, which called that whole way of life in question.

What gives particular significance to her predicament is the fact that in *Oldtown Folks* the New England mind was symbolically engaged in a review under pressure of its experience of two centuries. Like John Winthrop, John Davenport, under whose leadership the Beechers had come to Boston and moved to New Haven early in the seventeenth century, had insisted that neither he nor his flock were actually Separatists from the Church of England. As Perry Miller has demonstrated in *Orthodoxy in Massachusetts 1630-1650,* the Puritans, unlike the Pilgrims, were Non-Separatist Congregationalists; in fact, the whole authority of the Puritan experiment at Boston Bay rested on the assumption that the Church-State in the New World was an extension of the Church-State in England. In practice, however, the Congregational elements rapidly triumphed over the Non-Separatist elements and New Englanders were launched on an experiment in intense and lonely individualism. It was not an experiment destined to endure. After Dr. Samuel Johnson in the mid eighteenth century, descendants of Puritans in increasing numbers made their way back to Canterbury and even further back to Rome. By the early twentieth century even an Adams would be worshiping the Virgin, and in our day we see Anglican Eliots and Catholic Lowells. In her experience of a half century, Harriet to a remarkable degree recapitulated the experience of her region and anticipated its further developments. In childhood, at Grandmother Foote's, she was almost a Non-Separatist Congregationalist as she halfheartedly repeated the catechism and the prayers of the Church of England; in maturity, she experienced the fire and ice of Edwardean Calvinism; verging on old age, she became a member of the Episcopal Church.

As she projected *Oldtown Folks,* Harriet stood in almost the perfect situation for writing intimate history of the New England mind. But her book might have been a dismal failure, rather than an extraordinary success, had she not discovered a form through which with freedom and candor she could say all that she had on·her heart and mind to say.

III

By popular reputation, *Oldtown Folks* is less a novel than a book of sketches of New England life, and it must be admitted that its sketch aspect, evident in such chapters as "The Old Meeting-House," is perhaps its chief delight, its primary claim on our attention. These chapters, consideration of which I postpone for the moment, amply fulfil the ambition Harriet voiced in the preface to make her mind "as still and passive as a looking-glass" and to reflect without distortion or prejudice the images of New England life and culture. The preface has often been referred to as evidence of Harriet's intention, and I see no reason to question that assumption; indeed I have made a portion of the preface one of my epigraphs for this book. But it is crucial in understanding *Oldtown Folks* to notice that the preface is signed "Horace Holyoke" and to weigh carefully the following paragraph:

Though Calvinist, Arminian, High-Church Episcopalian, skeptic, and simple believer all speak in their turn, I merely listen, and endeavor to understand and faithfully represent the inner life of each. I myself am but the observer and reporter, seeing much, doubting much, questioning much, and believing with all my heart in only a very few things.

This is neither Harriet herself nor Calvin Stowe, whose childhood visions and Yankee anecdotes she admitted using in Horace's history.

Horace Holyoke originated, I believe, as Christopher Crowfield, Harriet's monologist in her *House and Home Papers* appearing in the *Atlantic* from 1864 until 1866. In these papers Harriet derided the tasteless, undemocratic extravagance of Victorian America, its tendency to overdress, its cluttered parlors clearly not made for living, its exhausting and pointless parties, its aping of the worst rather than the best in aristocratic Europe. Quite appropriately toward the last of the papers, she introduced a spokesman named Theophilus Thoro, for like

Henry Thoreau, Harriet was a critic of materialism and an advocate of simplicity and Puritan inwardness. The important matter for our discussion, however, is the dramatic quality in these papers: Harriet's creation in Christopher and Thoro of male spokesmen through whom she could speak her opinions without assuming immediate responsibility for them.

The device of an assumed personality was exactly what she needed for the writing of *Oldtown Folks*. It permitted, for example, the comment I have quoted on Easter at Old North, that the service settled down into "the quietest commonplace" and illustrated the "sin of ritualism." As one who believed in only a very few things, Horace could here make a criticism Harriet felt compelled to make but which, as a new convert to Anglicanism, she would certainly have been reluctant to express in her own person as omniscient author. Again and again in *Oldtown Folks* we can see signs of her freedom through theater, nowhere more impressively perhaps than in the letter written early in the story by Jonathan Rossiter. That Horace quotes this letter removes it doubly from Harriet herself.

Anyone acquainted with Lyman Beecher's *Autobiography* will immediately realize that the Calvinist minister, Mr. Avery, in Jonathan's letter is Lyman Beecher. Mr. Avery is neither sentimental, plaintive, nor theocratic, but "a lively, acute, full-blooded *man*," shrewd in things temporal and spiritual, who loves his work, gives no one a chance to sleep in meeting, and makes conversion of sinners an immediate practical business. So far we have the tribute of an affectionate daughter to a father recently dead; but as Jonathan, Harriet went on to make a completely uninhibited judgment of Lyman Beecher and his theology. Mr. Avery preaches New Divinity, that is, the Old Calvinism in "the commencing process of disintegration." It is his conviction that

the system, as far as Edwards and Hopkins have got it, is almost absolute truth; but, for all that, [he] is cheerfully busy in making some little emendations and corrections, upon which he values himself, and which he thinks of the greatest consequence. What is to the credit of his heart is, that these emendations are generally in favor of some original-minded sheep who can't be got into the sheep-fold without some alteration in the paling. In these cases I have generally noticed that he will loosen a rail or tear off a picket, and let the sheep in, it being his impression, after all, that the sheep are worth more than the sheep-fold.

Mr. Avery's forte is logic, and like a true New Englander he burns incense before this golden calf "with a most sacred innocence of intention." He has caught many of the shrewdest infidel foxes in the neighborhood, there being no trap for the Yankee like the logic-trap. But he is not always successful. Ezekiel Scranton, a rich farmer-atheist, who gives himself out "as a plucky dog, and able to hold the parson at bay," spoils one of Mr. Avery's stratagems by refusing to say he believes in his own existence: "Tell you what, Parson, ain't a-going to be twitched up by none o' your syllogisms." Jonathan is another who is not going to be caught; he avoids every trap Mr. Avery sets. He regards New Divinity as a "bitter pill in a chestnut-burr; the pill is bad,—there is no help for that,—but the chestnut-burr is impossible." Jonathan believes it incredible that with not so much experience of suffering as a toothache would give him Mr. Avery can arrange casually a system admitting the everlasting torture of millions. Mr. Avery's theology is parochial:

Now my friend the parson is the outgrowth of the New England theocracy, about the simplest, purest, and least objectionable state of society that the world ever saw. He has a good digestion, a healthy mind in a healthy body; he lives in a village where there is no pauperism, and hardly any crime,—where all the embarrassing, dreadful social problems and mysteries of life scarcely exist. But I, who have been tumbled up and down upon all the shores of earth, lived in India, China, and Polynesia, and seen the human race as they breed like vermin, in their filth and contented degradation,—how can I think of applying the measurements of any theological system to a reality like this?

In questioning the possibility of any theological measurement of the universe, Harriet made through her assumed personality a speculation far more heretical than anything we can discover in Emerson, whose central impulse was to vindicate the

All-Powerful, the All-Lovely, to reconcile God, Man, and
Nature. Jonathan is almost a modern Existentialist. At moments he has envisioned the human race as "bred like fish-
spawn on a thousand shores, by a Being who has never interested himself to care for their welfare, to prevent their degradation, to interfere with their cruelties to each other, as they have
writhed and wrangled into life, through life, and out of life
again." He writes that he is "not one of the shallow sort, who
think that everything for everybody must or ought to end with
perfect bliss at death. On the contrary, I do not see how anything but misery in eternal ages is to come from the outpouring
into their abyss, of wrangling, undisciplined souls, who were a
torment to themselves and others here, and who would make this
world unbearable, were they not all swept off in their turn by
the cobweb brush of Death."

Remembering Uncle Tom and Little Eva, we may rub our
eyes at finding such observations in a book by Harriet Beecher
Stowe; but in *Oldtown Folks* Harriet was surpassing herself
in almost every respect and writing one of the unquestionable,
but still generally unacknowledged, masterpieces of New England, indeed of American, literature. And her mastery was not
simply a matter of brilliant parts. To a degree usually unnoticed *Oldtown Folks* is an artistic unity. In savoring the
qualities in Jonathan's letter from Yankee humor to a surprisingly modern pessimism, we should not forget that this is Horace
Holyoke quoting, for it is Horace's free-ranging, skeptical intelligence which permits the inclusion of such an item. At first
glance, and somewhat at later glances, *Oldtown Folks* may seem
to confirm Henry James's generalization in the preface to *The
Ambassadors* that "the first person, in the long piece, is a
form foredoomed to looseness. . . ." But from a considerable
distance, Harriet in *Oldtown Folks* seems to have sensed with
James the possibility of telling a story through a "central intelligence" and it even seems probable that like James she discovered that possibility in Hawthorne's *The Blithedale Romance*
(1852), all of which is told through the mind and imagination
of Miles Coverdale.

The direct evidence on this point is not impressive. In *House and Home Papers,* she represented Christopher as reading *Twice-Told Tales* or *Mosses from an Old Manse* for the "two hundredth time" but she made through him only one reference, in passing, to *The Blithedale Romance.* Much, however, as Miles stands in imperfect sympathy with the communist experiment at Blithedale, Horace stands in imperfect sympathy with the religious urgency of his friends and relations. His grandmother lives and breathes Calvinism; his best friend, Harry Percival, is destined to be an Episcopal clergyman; Horace is well-acquainted with the Kitterys and Mr. Avery, but he plans to be a lawyer rather than a minister because of his religious difficulties. The plots of the books are surprisingly similar. In both, the hero-narrator is defeated, that is until the very close of *Oldtown Folks,* by a dynamic, spiritually corrupt rival, who likes to call himself his friend. In both, the rival deserts a beautiful, morally confused woman. There would seem to be more than accident in the fact that much as Miles loves Priscilla, who marries Hollingsworth, Horace loves Tina Percival, who marries Ellery Davenport, and that just as Hollingsworth deserts Zenobia, Ellery deserts Emily Rossiter, his mistress and the mother of his child.

These similarities indicate, I believe, that *The Blithedale Romance* was at the back of Harriet's mind as she wrote *Oldtown Folks* and that Hawthorne deserves partial credit not only for "the central intelligence" who narrates the action but for the essentially unsentimental story Horace manages to tell in the midst of reconstructing late eighteenth-century New England. The fact that Harriet was thus under the influence of a master craftsman helps to explain the nice returns of her novel. The Dench house, where Tina hides at the beginning of the story, becomes her home with Ellery at the close, and the beautiful woman, whose portrait startled her there as a child, materializes as Emily waiting for Ellery at the close of the wedding journey. Finally, there is the return, after Ellery's death, of Tina and Horace, now man and wife, to Oldtown and the warm affection they felt for each other as children.

With the spirit of art upon her, Harriet even managed in the midst of her many complications to give her book artistic unity through repetition of theme. Horace noted in his preface that "any one who may be curious" would find the Dench House in Elias Nason's *Sir Charles Frankland, Baronet; or Boston in the Colonial Times.* This volume, appearing in 1865, at the very time Harriet was planning *Oldtown Folks,* tells the story of a famous colonial scandal with a happy ending. In 1742 Sir Charles, Collector of Customs in Boston, saw sixteen-year-old Agnes Surriage scrubbing a tavern floor at Marblehead, Massachusetts. With intentions we shall probably want to question more than the Reverend Elias Nason, Sir Charles took Agnes to Boston, where she "was taught reading, writing, grammar, music, dancing, embroidery, and whatever graces and accomplishments were thought requisite to form a fashionable and perfect lady." Or, we should add, a perfect mistress, for that is what Agnes became. Colonial Boston was shocked and Sir Charles moved to the Dench House near Hopkinton, not very many miles from Calvin Stowe's birthplace and childhood home, Natick. Years later during the famous Lisbon earthquake of 1755 Sir Charles was pinned under a building and was saved only through the efforts of Agnes in securing help. As a reward for her good behavior, Sir Charles married her, thus rejoicing the hearts of both Boston and Hopkinton, and, I suppose, of Marblehead.

Early in *Oldtown Folks* Horace's Aunt Lois tells this story of Agnes and Sir Charles, which, as we learn at the end of the book, has been partially repeated in the very Dench House itself in the relations of Ellery Davenport and Emily Rossiter. A few pages after Aunt Lois' story of Agnes, we learn that Tina's father, an aristocratic British officer, kept secret his marriage to Tina's mother, a poor curate's daughter, and finally deserted her and his two children, denying the validity of his marriage and letting it be supposed (this echoes the story of Sir Charles and Agnes) that she was his mistress. Roughly a hundred pages later, Tina as a little girl sees Emily's picture in the Dench House; another hundred pages and we learn that

Miss Mehitable Rossiter keeps her large old home as a refuge to which her sister Emily may return; another hundred pages and Tina, who has been adopted by Miss Mehitable, discovers Emily's picture in the garret on a rainy day; we then have a letter from Miss Mehitable to Jonathan discussing Emily's revolt into radical behavior. It is unnecessary to multiply details. Though *Oldtown Folks* has much of the looseness James thought inevitable in telling a story in the first person, Harriet gave it considerable artistic unity through repetition of theme, as well as through the device of the "central intelligence," Horace Holyoke.

IV

The crucial factor unifying *Oldtown Folks* is, however, Horace Holyoke's thesis that Jonathan Edwards was a dangerous innovator in New England theology and ecclesiastical practice. Stated bluntly, this conviction may stand without serious criticism. Edwards' grandfather and predecessor in the Northampton pulpit, Solomon Stoddard, took an important step in humanizing the Puritan church when in 1700 he permitted the unconverted as well as the converted to participate in the Lord's Supper; and the record of new members supports his conviction that such a practice would strengthen rather than weaken piety on the New England frontier. In attempting in 1749 to reverse his grandfather's practice, which he himself had followed for twenty-three years, Jonathan Edwards may with considerable justice be called a dangerous innovator; the subsequent spiritual strivings of New England, those morbid inner states in the Mary Scudders as well as the Mrs. Marvyns, certainly leave Edwards open to humanitarian indictment. But Harriet made her case against him on other grounds, and on grounds far less secure.

It seems virtually certain that Harriet's charge against Edwards was suggested by Catharine Beecher. In *Religious Training of Children in the School, the Family, and the Church* (1864), Catharine argued that it was disastrous for the religious history of New England that Edwards returned the Puritan church to the stern Separatist pattern where membership was limited to "a *portion* of the Christian congregation, who unite by a profession and covenant as *regenerated* persons, believing a certain creed, and admitting by majority vote only such as, on examination, give evidence of such regeneration and belief." Catharine believed the root of the trouble was the doctrine of Original Sin as rigorously maintained by Puritan clergymen. She argued that a far more sensible view was to be found in the Episcopal Church, where clergy and laity had ceased contention as to the theory of transmitted infant damnation, and the remedy, and had trained all children "on the assumption that they are lambs of Christ's fold, and that the 'Grace' needful to their successful training for heaven will be bestowed in exact proportion to the faithfulness of parents and children in striving to understand and obey the teachings of Christ."

So wrote Catharine, whose latest spiritual revolution had carried her beyond her program of "common sense" to membership in the Episcopal Church. As words of an elder sister who had always exerted considerable influence, *Religious Training* could hardly fail to have impressed Harriet. But she did not rest on Catharine's arguments; she consulted the record for herself. Turning to Book V of the *Magnalia Christi Americana* (1702), Harriet found passages in which Cotton Mather muffled the original Puritan exclusiveness concerning membership and baptism. She stated in introducing one of these passages, "Old Cotton waxes warm in arguing this subject," but it seems unlikely that she knew he was masking and muffling the original rigidity in his enthusiastic defense of that expedient arrangement, the Half-Way Covenant of 1662, which secured baptism and "church-watching" for descendants of the regenerate. She copied out passage after passage from the *Magnalia* which apparently established the warm liberalism of the sevententh-century Puritan church, for example the following:

The way of the Ana-baptist, to admit none unto membership and baptism, but adult professors, is the straitest way; one would think it should be a way of great purity; but experience hath shew'd that it has been an inlet unto great corruption, and a troublesome, dangerous underminer of reformation. If we do not keep in the way of a converting, grace-giving covenant, and keep persons under those church-dispensations, wherein grace is given, the church will die of a lingring, though not violent, death. The Lord hath not set up churches only, that a few old Christians, may keep one another warm while they live, and then carry away the church into the cold grave with them, when they die; no, but that they might with all care, and with all the obligations and advantages to that care, that may be, nurse up still successively another generation of subjects to our Lord, that may stand up in his kingdom, when they are gone.

What was Harriet's conclusion? Simply this: "The colonists who founded Massachusetts were men whose doctrine of a Christian Church in regard to the position of its children was essentially the same as that of the Church of England. . . . The colony under Governor Winthrop and Thomas Dudley was, in fact, composed of men in all but political opinion warmly attached to the Church of England." She reduced the actual seventeenth-century Puritan majority to "a party in New England who maintained that only those who could relate a change so marked as to be characterized as supernatural should hope that they were the true elect of God, or be received in churches and acknowledged as true Christians."

Like other students of the New England mind before Perry Miller, Harriet had only a glimmering at best of the Non-Separatist position whereby the Puritan leaders of Boston Bay in their religious and political strategy with the mother country claimed that they were still of the Church of England. She did not understand that Mather not only quite intentionally obscured the background of the Half-Way Covenant but that he also stated truth with artful ambiguity in the first sentence of Book V when he wrote: "It was once an *unrighteous* and *injurious* aspersion cast upon the churches of *New-England,* that *the world knew not their principles:* whereas they took all the occasions imaginable to make all the world know, *that in the doctrinal part of religion, they have agreed entirely with the reformed churches of Europe:* and that they desired most particularly to maintain the *faith* professed by the churches of *Old England,* the country whereto was owing their original."

Having accepted Mather literally, Harriet went on to make a serious misreading of Jonathan Edwards' role in New England intellectual history. Critically, I believe, we can drive her into a corner where she could make no reasonable excuse for herself. Did she not know in her very bones that however original he might be, Edwards was actually clarifier and codifier of New England Puritanism? Had she not read, was she not in fact still using in writing *Oldtown Folks,* Sereno E. Dwight's *The Life of President Edwards* (1830), which made clear that in his proposals concerning church membership Edwards reverted essentially to the principles of that conventional Puritan, Eleazar Mather, the predecessor of Solomon Stoddard? Certainly Harriet knew better than she wrote. But she was doubtless charmed to discover that by the light of the *Magnalia* a convert of Anglicanism might really be an archetypal Puritan and in enthusiasm she found it easy to forget conflicting evidence and to shape this central thesis for *Oldtown Folks:*

Jonathan Edwards, a man who united in himself the natures of both a poet and a metaphysician, all whose experiences and feelings were as much more intense than those of common men as Dante's and Milton's, fell into the error of making his own constitutional religious experience the measure and standard of all others, and revolutionizing by it the institutions of the Pilgrim Fathers.

Regeneration, as he taught it in his "Treatise on the Affections," was the implantation by Divine Power of a new spiritual sense in the soul, as diverse from all the other senses as seeing is from hearing, or tasting from smelling. No one that had not received this new, divine, supernatural sense, could properly belong to the Church of Christ, and all men, until they did receive it, were naturally and constitutionally enemies of God to such a degree, that, as he says in a sermon to that effect, "If they had God in their power, they would kill him."

It was his power and his influence which succeeded in completely upsetting New England from the basis on which the Reformers and the Puritan Fathers had placed her, and casting out of the Church the children of the very saints and martyrs who had come to this country for no other reason than to found a church. . . .

Those very persons whom President Edwards addresses in such merciless terms of denunciation in his sermons, telling them that it is a wonder the sun does not refuse to shine upon them,—that the earth daily groans to open under them,—and that the wind and the sun and the waters are all weary of them and longing to break forth and execute the wrath of God upon them,—were children for uncounted generations back of fathers and mothers nursed in the bosom of the Church, trained in the habits of daily prayer, brought up to patience and self-sacrifice and self-denial as the very bread of their daily being, and lacking only this supernatural sixth sense, the want of which brought upon them guilt so tremendous. The consequence was, that immediately after the time of President Edwards, there grew up in the very bosom of the New England Church a set of young people who were not merely indifferent to religion, but who hated it with the whole energy of their being. . . .

The danger of all such violent recoils from the religion of one's childhood consists in this fact,—that the person is always secretly uncertain that he may not be opposing truth and virtue itself; he struggles confusedly with the faith of his mother, the prayers of his father, with whatever there may be holy and noble in the profession of that faith from which he has broken away; and few escape a very serious shock to conscience and their moral nature in doing it.

Recognizing the basic historical error in Harriet's statement that Edwards virtually broke with Anglicanism, we may be tempted to read *Oldtown Folks* out of court as a reliable witness on the New England mind, particularly on Edwardean Calvinism. But I believe that without stretching generosity too far, we may say that her error in history was by no means fatal to the historical truth of her novel. She was, of course, far less than just to Edwards' subtle and beautiful, and, as she could not know, very modern psychological insights in *A Treatise Concerning Religious Affections* (1746). Edwards' perception that man is a passionate creature whose essential nature determines both his thought and his action should have won comment from Harriet, who knew from her own religious experience the depth of the Edwardean reading of human nature. Also the novelist who had charted the operation of a divine and supernatural light in the heroine of *The Minister's Wooing* might have found at least some morsel of praise for Edwards's expression of the almost inexpressible through his skilful employment of metaphor in distinguishing the sensations of saintliness from all merely "natural" sensations. But even as Anglican, Harriet still recognized that Edwards was a genius belonging in the company of Dante and Milton; and she was quite right in stating that Edwards' extraordinary experience as poet-metaphysician was the root of his doctrine and that it was his error to make his experience the yardstick for measuring the experience of others. Harriet's collection of thoroughly ungenerous denunciations of the "ungodly" was unfortunately typical of one side of Edwards' preaching, in which, to be sure, he more generally sought to lead his listeners into his own realm of pure and blinding light.

Moreover, when we consider late seventeenth- and early eighteenth-century modifications of Puritanism and Edwards' interruption of the inclination toward an increasingly humane religion, she was accurate in terms of broad historical developments. Edwards' insistence that a merely humane religion was irrelevant and that salvation depended entirely on the divinely illuminated heart and mind did produce in instance after instance anxiety closely approximating hatred of religion. Certainly we may read anxiety approximating hatred in the case of Catharine Beecher in her theological struggles after the death of her fiancé; and Harriet herself in her inner history almost perfectly illustrates the person who, recoiling from her childhood faith, was secretly uncertain whether or not she had repudiated truth and virtue itself in her confused struggle with the faith of her mother, the prayers of her father. She spoke also for many in her generation when she represented Anglicanism as a possible solution for the perplexities of the Puritan. Consequently, the contrasts Harriet drew in the lives of her four chief characters possess historical validity. Ellery Davenport and Emily Rossiter, who agonize before the rungless ladder of Edwardean Calvinism and ultimately fall into spiritual and moral revolt, and Harry Percival and Esther Avery, who find security in the Anglican Church, illustrate a thesis, but they also illustrate truths discovered through a lifetime of intense experience and meditation.

On our first encounter with Ellery Davenport, supposedly the grandson of Jonathan Edwards, he makes this confession to staunchly Anglican Miss Debby:

". . . your catechism is much better for children than the one I was brought up on. . . . Now it's a true proverb, 'Call a man a thief, and he'll steal'; 'give a dog a bad name, and he'll bite you'; tell a child that he is 'a member of Christ, a child of God, and an inheritor of the kingdom of heaven,' and he feels, to say the least, civilly disposed towards religion; tell him 'he is under God's wrath and curse, and so made liable to all the miseries of this life, to death itself, and the pains of hell forever,' because somebody ate an apple five thousand years ago, and his religious associations are not so agreeable,—especially if he has the answers whipped into him, or has to go to bed without his supper for not learning them."

Later, Harriet made it even clearer that Ellery's mockery of all things religious (except when he talked Edwardean Calvinism, and even Edwards' aesthetic theories, for the intellectual exercise) and his utter selfishness, signalized in his exploitation of Emily Rossiter and his desertion of her, could all be traced to his ultra-Calvinistic training. He belonged to that generation after Edwards when the intellectual faculties were stimulated by hard and subtle doctrines but the heart was revolted by a God inconsistent with the teachings of Jesus. The implication of Ellery's history is unmistakable: if he had been brought up in the Episcopal Church, he would not have been distorted in this fashion; in all likelihood he would have developed into an admirable human being.

Far more interesting than Ellery, who is essentially another version of Aaron Burr in *The Minister's Wooing,* is Emily Rossiter, who, like her brother Jonathan, is an indigenous product of that Puritan family who came to New England with John Winthrop and who with the passage of years had developed these qualities:

There was in them a sort of intellectual vigor, a ceaseless activity of thought, a passion for reading and study, and a quiet brooding on the very deepest problems of mental and moral philosophy. The characteristic of such families is the greatly disproportioned force of the internal, intellectual and spiritual life to the external one. Hence come often morbid and diseased forms of manifestation. The threads which connect such persons with the real life of the outer world are so fine and so weak, that they are constantly breaking and giving way here and there, so that, in such races, oddities and eccentricities are come to be accepted only as badges of family character.

Emily's father, Parson Rossiter, was given to paroxysms of gloom; her brother Theodore had run a brilliant course in college, but he "was full of disgusts, and repulsions, and dislikes; everything in life wounded and made him sore; he could or would do nothing reasonably or rationally with human beings, and to deaden the sense of pain in existence, took to the use of opiates. . . ." Her sister, Miss Mehitable, has quite appropriately named her home Doubting Castle, the dwelling, it will be recalled, of Giant Despair in *Pilgrim's Progress.* For years her every cry of misery, her every breath of anguish has been choked by the logical proof of theology that she is God's enemy or he is hers.

Writing to Jonathan, early in *Oldtown Folks,* Miss Mehitable argues that there was great excuse for Emily's going astray, as it seems likely, "in the worst sense that a woman can." With her great beauty, her highly nervous and excitable Rossiter temperament, she was a perilously organized human being, and what had they done with her? After her mother's death, they had sent her to Uncle and Aunt Farnsworth where she experienced "glacial, gloomy, religious training," and the violent and terrible remedies of the family minister, Dr. Moses Stern. His theory was "that a secret enemy to God was lying latent in every soul, which, like some virulent poisons in the body, could only be expelled by being brought to the surface; and he had sermon after sermon, whose only object appeared to be to bring into vivid consciousness what he calls the natural opposition of the human heart." Emily's was a nature that would break before it would bow; only love could have subdued her. Unable to distinguish between "the word of God and the cruel deductions of human logic, she trod both under foot in defiant despair" when Dr. Stern preached a funeral sermon assigning her brother Theodore, the opium addict, to hell.

Sent to spend the winter in Boston with a worldly aunt, who was proud of her niece's beauty and talents and who introduced her into sophisticated society, Emily became acquainted with a French family and soon expended her passion for ideas on French literature. She found Voltaire too cold and cynical but Rousseau exactly suited her, particularly in his *Julie, ou La Nouvelle Héloïse.* After her return to the Farnsworths, she interspersed in her notebook quotations from this novel with quotations from Dr. Stern's sermons, and after a period of deceitful quiet, and under the pretense of a visit to her aunt in Boston, she finally escaped to Europe with the Marquis de Conté and his lady. In France, Emily became acquainted with Ellery Davenport, at the time suffering the misfortune of an insane wife, and having been taught by Dr. Stern "to think and reason boldly, even when differing from received opinions," she constructed her own system of morals and became Ellery's mistress. Reading Emily's letters at the close of *Oldtown Folks,* Tina sees "she was grand and unselfish in her love, that she was perfectly self-sacrificing." Tina believes that "because Jesus understood these things in the hearts of women" he uttered his memorable saying about casting the first stone at the woman taken in adultery. But the point of Emily's story, like the point of Ellery's, is poisoning from an overdose of Calvinism in childhood. Emily too might have been a happy as well as a noble woman, had she been reared in the Episcopal Church.

As a variation on this theme we have the story of Tina's brother, Harry, and Esther Avery, with whom he falls in love at Jonathan Rossiter's school at Cloudland. Trained by his mother in the prayers and catechism of the Church of England, Harry has been insulated against the Calvinism of Oldtown, and when he meets Esther, he is able through his gentle confidence in God to save her from the kind of Puritan tragedy that has overtaken Ellery and Emily. Harriet was thinking, at least in part, of herself. One of Esther's most notable compositions for Mr. Rossiter attempts to answer the question, "Can the

Benevolence of the Deity be proved by the Light of Nature?"
If we turn to Charles Edward Stowe's *Life,* we find that at
twelve Harriet wrote for John Pierce Brace of Litchfield Academy an astonishingly mature composition in answer to the question, "Can the immortality of the soul be proved by the light
of nature?"   She was virtually describing her own essay when
she wrote of Esther's: "It was condensed and logical, fearfully
vigorous in conception and expression, and altogether a very
melancholy piece of literature to have been conceived and written
by a girl of her age."

For the most part, however, Harriet in creating Esther was
moving well beyond the boundaries of self-portraiture. As I
have noted in an earlier chapter, Esther stands for all those
"intense, silent, repressed women that have been a frequent
outgrowth of New England society," a woman whose face
recalled John Donne's line, "One might almost say her body
thought," and whose character unfortunately illustrated Plato's
ideal of the Man-Woman. From a long line of scholar-preach-
ers, Esther has inherited inclinations for viewing the world in
purely intellectual terms; from an equally long line of saintly
and tender women, exquisite moral perceptions, and "all that
flattering host of tremulous, half-spiritual, half-sensuous intuitions that lie in the borderland between the pure intellect and
the animal nature." In Esther, heart is always rebelling against
the conclusions of head; she is Mary Scudder and Mrs. Marvyn
locked in one body. Her case, indeed the case of all sensitive
and thinking women under Puritanism, is inevitably tragic
because woman's nature was never consulted in those theologies
originating in Augustine and other men, who looked on woman
only in her animal nature and regarded her primarily as a
snare and a temptation. Quite rightly, Harry says that Esther
"both thinks and feels too much on all subjects." Through
his central conviction that God loves man (this was Henry
Ward Beecher's basic message), Harry is instrumental in turning Esther from a pale image of abstract thought to a woman
of warm flesh and blood. In marrying Harry, who becomes a
priest in the Church of England, Esther, of course, is united

with Anglicanism and thus further insulated against Puritanism.

Abstracted in this fashion, Harriet's central thesis verges on oversimplification, but in the context of *Oldtown Folks* it is constantly modified by the experience and comments of Horace, who saves the book from overneatness and endows it with the complexity of actuality.   In the first chapter, Lady Lothrop, the Episcopal wife of Congregational Parson Lothrop, gives Horace "The Mourner's Companion," consisting mainly of selections from the Book of Common Prayer, to comfort his mother during his father's dying hours. But Mrs. Holyoke never reads Horace any of the prayers, and shortly after his father's death, he goes to live with his grandparents, where he is exposed almost daily to "the battle of the infinities" between Arminian Deacon Badger and ultra-Calvinistic Grandmother Badger, who uses every weapon in her theological armory to save her husband. Grandmother's favorite reading is that grim masterpiece of New England theology, *True Religion Delineated,* by Jonathan Edwards' disciple, Joseph Bellamy, and she is given to reading aloud from Cotton Mather's *Magnalia.*   Here, as in the Rossiter and Davenport households, there would seem to be a breeding ground for revolt from the ancestral faith, but his grandparents do not force their views on Horace, and when he goes to church, he does not listen to a fiery Dr. Moses Stern, but to Parson Lothrop, who preaches moral platitudes in the cooling down of Puritanism.   At the end of the book, with a truly artistic impulse, Harriet resisted the temptation to make Horace another convert to Anglicanism; the most she would permit was Horace's acknowledgment that he now felt more devotion toward Mme Kittery than toward Grandmother Badger.

His habit, as he describes it, of "looking at everything from so many sides, that it was difficult to get a settled assent to anything" makes Horace an extraordinarily perceptive student of the New England mind.   Consider, for example, the following passage:

The ministers of the early colonial days of New England, though well-read, scholarly men, were more statesmen than theologians.   Their minds ran upon the actual arrangements of so-

ciety, which were in a great degree left in their hands, rather than
on doctrinal and metaphysical subtleties. They took their confession of faith just as the great body of Protestant reformers left
it, and acted upon it as a practical foundation, without much further
discussion, until the time of President Edwards. He was the first
man who began the disintegrating process of applying rationalistic
methods to the accepted doctrines of religion, and he rationalized
far more boldly and widely than any publishers of his biography
have ever dared to let the world know. He sawed the great dam
and let out the whole waters of discussion over all New England,
and that free discussion led to all the shades of opinion of our
modern days. Little as he thought it, yet Waldo Emerson and
Theodore Parker were the last results of the current set in motion
by Jonathan Edwards.

Rather obviously this is an unconventional analysis of New
England intellectual history. In the nineteenth-century it was
virtually the universal assumption that Emerson and Theodore
Parker represented a complete break with the past of American
religion, and Edwards, as almost everyone supposed, was the
essence of the past. But now that Perry Miller has edited Edwards' *Images or Shadows of Divine Things* (1948), we are able
to perceive that Edwards' "rationalistic methods" made him an
anticipator of Emerson in reading nature symbolically as the
Word of God. We should be willing to acknowledge at least
some propriety in Miller's quoting Horace's analysis in the
notes to *Images*. But was not Horace still wrong in stating
that Edwards actually set in motion the current producing the
"newness"?

His error would seem to be the fallacy, *after this, because
of this*. The obvious explanation for Emerson and Parker
would seem to be not Edwards but the heady excitement produced by the conjunction of democracy and the romanticism
coming to New England via Coleridge and Carlyle. With
romantic and platonic idealism in the air, it was all but inevitable
that bold spirits like Emerson and Parker would rise up against
early nineteenth-century Unitarianism with its unexciting insistence that man could know God and the realm of the spirit
only through the testimony of the Gospels. If Emerson in "The
Over-Soul" with his doctrine of the indwelling God was sur-

prisingly like Edwards in his sermon "A Divine and Super-natural Light Immediately Imparted to the Soul by the Spirit of God . . . ," if Emerson in *Nature* sometimes wrote apparently in the tradition of Edwards in *Images,*—why these were simply accidents of history, not cause and effect.

But were they simply accidents of history? In his masterly biographical sketch of his aunt, Mary Moody Emerson, delivered in Boston the year *Oldtown Folks* appeared, Emerson began with the statement that her life was "a fruit of Calvinism and New England" and at the close he acknowledged the debt of certain boys (his hearers would have understood him and his brothers) to her high counsels. Between these points, he selected passages from Aunt Mary's journals which parallel again and again not only his own writings but the more exuberant passages in Edwards' sermons and in his "Personal Narrative" where he responded poetically to the natural world. We seem justified in concluding that Emerson was at least partially prepared for the break with Unitarianism by the current of thought and feeling reaching him in his impressionable years from that Edwardean Calvinist, Aunt Mary. A different case would have to be made for Parker. He would seem to belong to the Edwardean tradition primarily because of his intense, rationalistic concern with the relations between God and man; as a master in New England theology he was, of course, well acquainted with the works of Jonathan Edwards.

Or we might substantiate Horace's generalization concerning Edwards as father of Transcendentalism in yet another way. William Ellery Channing, the "apostle" of Unitarianism and a kind of John the Baptist to Parker and Emerson, clearly opposed significant aspects of the New England past in such sermons as "The Moral Argument against Calvinism" (1820). But it can be demonstrated, I believe, that Channing's moral and religious idealism owed something at least to the theology of that famous disciple of Jonathan Edwards, Dr. Samuel Hopkins, of whom Harriet wrote in *The Minister's Wooing*. As a young man Channing sat under the preaching of Hopkins in Newport and in maturity sometimes spoke of Hopkins with admiration. It is not particularly difficult to trace a line of influence from Edwards to Hopkins to Channing to Emerson. In any case, Horace's point of view is confirmed not only by Perry Miller but also by another fine student of the New England past, Thomas H. Johnson, who has written: "The voice, through these many American years, is the voice of Hawthorne, and Melville, and Emerson, and Whitman, and Adams. But the hand is the hand of Jonathan Edwards."

For Horace, however, Edwards was a paradoxical figure, facing both toward the past and the future. Reflecting on Edwards and his disciple, Joseph Bellamy, Horace concluded: "These theologies were not formed by the Puritans; they were their legacy from past monarchical and mediaeval ages." Edwards' *The Nature of True Virtue* was primarily devoted to inculcating supreme devotion to the good of all, but it might also be read as an argument for the supreme right of the King and upper classes, once its theology was translated into politics. Yet Edwardean Calvinism, whatever its monarchical bias, had actually helped Americans win their independence from the British Crown. As Horace wittily observed: "They who had faced eternal ruin with an unflinching gaze were not likely to shrink before the comparatively trivial losses and gains of any mere earthly conflict. Being accustomed to combats with the Devil, it was rather a recreation to fight only British officers." And it was not only during the Revolution that Puritanism made men champions of democracy. Dr. Moses Stern, whose grim preaching tortured Emily Rossiter and sent her into revolt, was an antislavery man and once graced an Abolitionist meeting with his presence, though advised against it by his conventional well-wishers. The more one looked, the deeper the paradox grew. Calvinism without churches or cathedrals or rites to quicken the poetic side of human nature had still managed to redeem men by "the poetry of ideas." Was it not perhaps too early to dispense with Puritanism altogether? Spain, which like New England had recently experienced revolution, would have been better prepared for national independence by a set of schoolmasters and ministers

like Mr. Rossiter and Mr. Avery working together than by all
the pictures, statues, incense, architecture, and "all the sentimental paraphernalia of ritualism." When one looked nearer
home, the worldly superiority of New England over Catholic
Canada could be explained by reference to Puritanism, which
had preached not asceticism but the faith of the Old Testament
"in which material prosperity is always spoken of as the lawful
reward of piety, in which marriage is an honor, and a numerous
posterity a thing to be desired."

In his (and, of course, Harriet's) struggle with the whole,
complex, unsimplifiable truth of Puritan New England civilization, Horace inevitably ran into contradiction. The lives of
Ellery Davenport and Emily Rossiter seemed to prove a case
against Jonathan Edwards and more broadly against Puritanism which reflection on other facts of New England experience
did not sustain. Through Horace's meditations on the lives
of friends, Puritan and Anglican, *Oldtown Folks* develops a
unifying central thesis but it is not a thesis-ridden book. In
far more than a pictorial sense Horace became New England's
looking-glass reflecting with remarkable clarity the full image
of his world. The nearest, perhaps, that he came to a general
conclusion was his belief that "while the Bible comes from
God, theology is the outgrowth of the human mind, and therefore must spring from the movement of society." The human
mind could not "bear to relinquish more than a certain portion
of its cherished past ideas in one century," but time and "the
principles of a true Christian democracy" on which Americans
had founded their new state had already modified Puritanism
almost beyond recognition. Whether time and democracy might
not also call Anglicanism in question Horace did not say.

V

One of Horace's most illuminating comments is that the New
England mind united the utmost extremes of the material and
spiritual. The extremes, he believed, were represented by those
two native New Englanders, Benjamin Franklin and Jonathan
Edwards: "Put these two together, and you have the average

New England character,—that land in which every *ism* of social and religious life has had its origin,—that land whose hills and valleys are one blaze and buzz of material and manufacturing production." Horace did little more than refer to the industrial aspects of New England civilization; but he did paint with remarkable relish the materialistic as well as the spiritual qualities of life in Oldtown and Cloudland. Through Horace, Harriet indulged to the full not only her Puritan concern with inwardness but her humorous-realistic Yankee concern with outwardness. She delighted in recording the realistic details of her New England village world, some of which will surprise the modern reader, such as the Yankee anticipation of the deep-freeze in the stowing away of pies at Thanksgiving in a cold northern chamber. She reported that "the pies baked at Thanksgiving often came out fresh and good with the violets of April."

But the most vivid testimony to Harriet's practice of New England doubleness is her ability to realize at one extreme the Rossiters, connected by only weak threads with the outer world, and at the other extreme characters rooted in the outer world almost as firmly as the elms of Oldtown. Such for example is the Yankee giant, Heber Atwood, who contributes his best oak to the annual woodspell, paying part of Mr. Avery's salary. As he sits with a great block of cake and a mug of flip (this was the refreshment served by Lyman Beecher at woodspells in Litchfield), Heber looks like a cross between a polar bear and a man. He is completely down to earth in his philosophy: "Man he regarded in a physical point of view as principally made to cut down trees, and trees as the natural enemies of man." Heber can remember "the time when I had fourteen good, straight boys,—all on 'em aturnin' over a log together"; as for daughters, "There's been a gal or two 'long, in between, here an' there,—don't jest remember where they come; but, anyway, there's plenty of women-folks 't our house."

Miss Nervy, actually Miss Minerva, Randall, Jonathan Rossiter's housekeeper, is equally at home in this world. On a voyage to the Mediterranean, when her brother the captain came down with a fever, she not only nursed him but navigated the ship home, an exploit quite in keeping with her character, which only remotely suggests femininity: "There was a sort of fishy quaintness about her that awakened grim ideas of some unknown ocean product,—a wild and withered appearance, like a wind-blown juniper on a sea promontory,—unsightly and stunted, yet not, after all, commonplace or vulgar." She is the happiest woman Horace has ever met, for she has just as much of exactly the two things she most loves, books and work. What gives piquancy to her discourse is the fact that though she is "a dead shot" in the difficulties of Latin and Greek, she still clings to the racy and ungrammatical dialect of her childhood. Confronted in her kitchen by a Cloudland Academy boy or girl puzzled by a hard Latin sentence, Miss Nervy says:

"Why, don't you know what that 'ere is? . . . That 'ere is part of the gerund in *dum*; you've got to decline it, and then you'll find it. Look here!" she would say; "run that 'ere through the moods an' tenses, and ye'll git it in the subjunctive"; or, "Massy, child! that 'ere is one o' the deponent verbs. 'T aint got any active form; them deponent verbs allus does trouble boys till they git used to 'em."

As they neared Oldtown, on their way home from Mr. Rossiter's school, Tina and Harry Percival might easily have reflected on the dark days at Needmore (Harriet's name for Needham, a short distance from Natick), where before their escape to Grandmother Badger they labored under the stern eyes of Crab Smith and his sister, Miss Asphyxia. These Yankees typify the "sour, cross, gnarly natures that now and then are to be met with in New England, which, like knotty cider-apples, present a compound of harshness, sourness, and bitterness." Crab is a petrified man, walled out from all neighborhood sympathies. When Mrs. Percival, seeking her husband, arrives in exhaustion with her small children at his farm and Mrs. Smith builds a fire to make her some tea, Crab sees the smoke from afar and mutters: "So, burning out wood,— always burning out wood. I told her that I wouldn't have tea got at night. These old women are crazy and bewitched after tea, and they don't care if they burn up your tables and chairs to help their messes." When he learns that Mrs. Percival is dying, he only thinks of the expense of burying her. The day after her funeral he puts Harry to work digging potatoes: "Poor folks like us can't afford to keep nobody jest to look at, and so he'll have to step spry and work smart to airn his keep." Generally speaking Crab is convincing but Harriet blurred her picture in imagining that he saw Harry's mother in vision and was thus prevented from whipping him. Here Crab relapses into Simon Legree, and Miss Asphyxia also carries us momentarily back to *Uncle Tom's Cabin*. She is like Miss Ophelia in her conviction that she stands "sword in hand against a universe where everything was running to disorder,— everything was tending to slackness, shiftlessness, unthrift, and she alone was left on the earth to keep things in their places. . . . she slept, as it were, in her armor, and spent her life as a sentinel on duty." But Miss Asphyxia is not so much "a bond-slave of the ought" as she is a harsh, insensitive woman, who values persons and things only for their usefulness. As her hired man Sol says of her, "that 'ere critter ain't got no more bowels than a file."

Harriet was at her realistic and humorous best, however, in creating her Oldtown characters, based on the personalities Calvin Stowe recalled from his childhood in Natick, Massachusetts. But we misunderstand badly, I believe, if we suppose that at Hartford and later at Mandarin, Florida, Calvin performed a daily stint of reminiscence which his wife immediately turned into copy. As an eager and expert teller of anecdotes, Calvin could hardly have kept Sam Lawton (Harriet would call him Sam Lawson) and other Natick personalities to himself that long. Harriet must have known them in imagination for thirty years or more when she sat down to write *Oldtown Folks*. Long acquaintance is probably the explanation for her ability to range them vividly in a kind of New England Chaucer's *Prologue* in the chapter "The Old Meeting-House."

Since Natick was established by John Eliot in the seventeenth century as a community for Indian converts, Harriet quite appropriately began with the Indians in the central portion of the house. Here sits Justice Waban (Harriet remembered that Chief Thomas Waban had co-operated with Eliot) and Deacon Ephraim, undoubtedly a descendant of the first Deacon of Eliot Church. Their grave and reverend aspect marks them as little different from the white New Englanders in the side pews, but Ephraim's wife, Old Keturah, though baptized, is still a savage. Horace (or Calvin) remembered that during "thunderstorms and other convulsions of nature she would sit in a chimney corner and chant her old Indian incantations to my mingled terror and delight," particularly the three syllables "Ah-mah-ga, ah-mah-ga." Also notable is Dick Obscue, who perambulates the countryside, making stations at various kitchen firesides where he tells stories, moralizes, and drinks cider till the cider or the patience of his hosts runs out, when with a nod he says, since he is a Yankee Indian, "Wal, naow, 'f you can spare me I'll go."

The Negroes in the side gallery are quite as interesting Yankee men and women of color. There is, for example, Boston Foodah, once an African prince, but now an old man proudly erect with woolly white hair. He was servant to General Hull during the Revolution and at spring training, fall muster, and on Thanksgiving Day, he arrays himself, sword in hand, with a three-cornered hat and a uniform with epaulets, given him by his master. Also back from adventures is Primus King, a retired whaleman, much in demand as a butcher. Of less repute but still important is Aunt Nancy Prine, famous for making election-cake and ginger-pop, who saved her money and bought herself a mulatto husband in Boston, but who has often said she would never buy another "nigger."

The choir also comprises some richly individualistic personalities. One of the principal bass singers is Joe Stedman, who asserts his democratic rights by appearing every Sunday in a clean leather apron of precisely the kind he wears in his weekly work. The upper classes objected at first, and the minister told him that his apron was a form of pride, but Joe settled the matter (here we have the key to Puritan village individualism) by declaring "that the apron was a matter of conscience with him, and of course after that there was no more to be said."

At the head of the upper classes, of course, stand Parson and Lady Lothrop. Next is Captain Browne, a retired merchant and shipowner, who wears a scarlet cloak, white vest and stock, and long silk stockings with sparkling knee and shoe buckles. Behind the Captain, in darned laces, and a satin gown that has been made over countless times, sits Miss Mehitable, a member of the aristocracy by right of descent from Parson Rossiter. In the same pew with her is Squire Jones, wealthy ex-Tory, who like the historical Tory, William Boden, once King's Justice in Natick, has been elected Sheriff of the County. Below these, but associating with them on terms of equality, are Major Broad, currently opposing ratification of the Constitution because it permits slavery. Horace's grandfather, justice of the peace, selectman, and deacon ; and Horace's granduncle, Eliakim Sheril, known popularly as Uncle Fly, the pudding-stick keeping all Natick in a perpetual stir. Parson Lothrop's "Let us pray" is followed Sunday after Sunday by the crash of Uncle Fly's wagon against the meetinghouse doorstep as he delivers the dry, forlorn, tremulous old ladies, whom he regards as his special charge.

It is Sam Lawson, however, who most vividly brings Oldtown alive in our imaginations. Of a Sunday he shows off his miscellaneous accomplishments by pitching the tunes on his pitch pipe, playing the bass viol accompaniment, and singing tenor, treble, and counter, successively, during the rendering of one hymn. It is not only in music that Sam's range is wide. He is an expert in at least five or six different handicrafts : he is blacksmith, barber, nurse, undertaker, and laborer at anything that calls out his artistic nature, such as old clocks, broken china, and decrepit fire irons. But as he explains to Horace's Aunt Lois when he has the parts of the Badger clock strewn all over the kitchen, "Ef I work tew long on one thing, my mind kind o' gives out" ; he would rather discuss the Millennium with Aunt Lois than fix the clock and get paid immediately.

There can be no doubt of the genuineness of his interest in theology, for he not only attends church in Oldtown but walks around to sample doctrine in the neighboring parishes. Here is his vivid report on Parson Simpson of North Parish:

"Parson Simpson's a smart man; but, I tell ye, it's kind o' discouragin'. Why, he said our state and condition by nature was just like this. We was clear down in a well fifty feet deep, and the sides all round nothin' but glare ice; but we was under immediate obligations to get out, 'cause we was free, voluntary agents. But nobody ever had got out, and nobody would, unless the Lord reached down and took 'em. And whether he would or not nobody could tell; it was all sovereignty. He said there wa'n't one in a hundred,—not one in a thousand,—not one in ten thousand,—that would be saved. Lordy massy, says I to myself, ef that's so they're any of 'em welcome to my chance. And so I kind o' ris up and come out, 'cause I'd got a pretty long walk home, and I wanted to go round by South Pond, and inquire about Aunt Sally Morse's toothache."

Sam has bottomless curiosity, not only caring for all details concerning the living but also for details concerning the dead: he haunts the Indian burying ground and can often be seen perching on a fence, like a vulture, waiting for some sick person to die so that he can be first to see the body, which he will "lay-out" in expert fashion. His interest does not even stop here: he is avid for knowledge of the "sperit world." Pumping his friend Jake Marshall, he has discovered that it was through old Indian Keturah's black magic that Dench got the money to buy the house of Sir Charles Frankland at Hopkinton. Sam is very tolerant of Keturah, who, he admits, would certainly have been taken up for a witch in the old days: "Ef there be sperits, and we all know there is, what's the harm o' Katury's seein' on 'em?" Besides Keturah is an Indian, and "them wild Indians, they ain't but jest half folks, they're so kind o' wild, and birchy and bushy as a body may say. Ef they take religion at all, it's got to be in their own way. Ef you get the wild beast all out o' one on 'em, there don't somehow seem to be enough left to make an ordinary smart man of, so much on 'em's wild."

Keturah told Dench exactly how to get the great carbuncle out of Sepaug River: "You was to fast all the day before, and go fastin', and say the Lord's prayer in Injun afore you went; and when you come to where 't was, you was to dive after it. But there wa'n't to be a word spoke; if there was, it went right off." Keturah had quite a time teaching Jake and Dench the Lord's prayer in Indian (her fee was ten dollars) to pacify the Indian spirits guarding the carbuncle but finally they learned their lesson and there came a beautiful moonlight night:

"Jake says it was the splendidest moonlight ye ever did see,— all jest as still,—only the frogs and the turtles kind o' peepin'; and they didn't say a word, and rowed out past the pint there, where the water's ten feet deep, and he looked down and see it a shinin' on the bottom like a great star, making the waters all light like a lantern. Dench, he dived for it, Jake said; and he saw him put out his hand right on it; and he was so tickled, you know, to see he'd got it, that he couldn't help hollerin' right out, 'There, you got it!' and it was gone. Dench was mad enough to 'a' killed him, 'cause, when it goes that 'ere way, you can't see it agin for a year and a day. But two or three years arter, all of a sudden, Dench, he seemed to kind o' spruce up and have a deal o' money to spend. He said an uncle had died and left it to him in England; but Jake Marshall says yo'll never take him in that 'ere way. He says he thinks it's no better'n witchcraft, getting money that 'ere way. Ye see Jake was to have had half, if they'd 'a' got it, and not gettin' nothin' kind o' sot him to thinkin' on it in a moral pint o' view, ye know."

In writing American folk speech with supreme artistry Harriet anticipated Mark Twain in *Huckleberry Finn*. Mark certainly might have been proud of Sam's marvelous résumé of Indians as "birchy and bushy, as a body may say," with not enough left to make "an ordinary smart man of" once you got the wild beast out of them; and Jake's moral indignation is that perfect twist of irony with which Mark again and again rounded out Huck's anecdotes. Mark, incidentally, was acquainted with Sam. In "The Man that Corrupted Hadleyburg," Jack Halliday is described as the "typical 'Sam Lawson' of the town."

Sam's cross is his wife, Hepsy. When he sees Horace's Aunt Keziah and Aunt Lois cutting cowslip greens across the river, he says to himself, "Lordy massy, I wish't I was an old maid." Sam is the decided do-nothing, which every Yankee village must have for lubrication or burn out its bearings; Hepsy is the more conventional Yankee do-something, "a gnarly, compact, efficient little pepper-box of a woman, with snapping black eyes, pale cheeks, and a mouth always at half-cock, ready to go off with some sharp crack of reproof at the shoreless, bottomless, and tideless inefficiency of her husband." By going out to do washing, scrubbing, and cleaning for her neighbors, by making vests and binding shoes for the shoemaker, and hoeing the garden between whiles, she manages to provide food and clothes for the six Lawson children, or perhaps we should say seven, and include Sam. Because of Hepsy's temper, Sam has to do a good deal of what he calls "Indianing round," that is, going off on one-man expeditions into the country to let her cool off. At the end of her life, as we learn toward the last of *Oldtown Folks*, Hepsy still found Sam a trial. As he tells Horace in a startling revelation:

"Wal, jest half on her was clear paralyzed, poor crittur; she couldn't speak a word; that 'ere was the gret trial to her. I don't think she was resigned under it. Hepsy had an awful sight o' grit. I used to talk to Hepsy, an' talk, an' try to set things afore her in the best way I could, so's to git 'er into a better state o' mind. D' you b'lieve, one day when I'd ben a-talkin' to her, she kind o' made a motion to me with her eye, an' when I went up to 'er, what d' you think? why, she jest tuk and BIT me! she did so!"

But even through such extensive quotation as I have practiced, a critic can do no more than suggest the meaning and flavor of *Oldtown Folks*. The charm of certain chapters, such as those dealing with school life in Cloudland, where Harriet re-created her Litchfield education under John Pierce Brace, now called Jonathan Rossiter, can be appreciated only in a full reading. *Oldtown Folks*, to be sure, is not a perfect book. Harriet could not completely escape her age and its over-valuation of sentiment. In an early chapter, "The Day in Fairy-Land," which describes the woodland adventures of little Tina and Harry Percival after they have escaped Miss Asphyxia and Old Crab Smith, Harriet was a typical sentimental Victorian novelist. But chapters like this are few and seem concessions to popular taste rather than Harriet's own vision of things.

That vision was primarily shrewd, witty, and—there would seem to be no other word—masculine. As we read *Oldtown Folks,* we are almost completely unconscious that the book is the work of a woman; we feel we are being addressed by a thoroughly mature and full-blooded Puritan-Yankee like Lyman Beecher. Undoubtedly the essential clue to the tone of *Oldtown Folks* is Harriet's invention of her masculine narrator, Horace Holyoke. But we should not forget that even in her earliest stories Harriet had sought to identify herself with her father and her husband; and the masculine mind and imagination, the masculine handling of character and anecdote and language, these rather than the typically feminine had always been Harriet's ideals even as she won an international reputation as feminine sentimentalist. Augustine St. Clare in *Uncle Tom's Cabin* and Edward Clayton in *Dred* are early studies for the wit and vigor typical of Horace Holyoke. The tone of *Oldtown Folks* represents, in short, the triumph of an ideal in seeing, feeling and saying toward which Harriet had been moving for almost a half century. In *Oldtown Folks* we reach at last in concentrated form the essential Harriet Beecher Stowe, the more masculine than feminine artist depicting Puritan inwardness and Yankee realism and humor.

But *Oldtown Folks* is a good deal more than Harriet's charming expression of an ideal self slowly forming through a lifetime. Her novel is large, comprehensive, various. In its perceptive reading of New England intellectual history, in its expression through symbolic action of a major change in American religious alliance, in its marvelous rendering of the bold phrasing and varying rhythms of Yankee talk, in its huge gallery of vividly realized personalities from all levels of the New England village world, *Oldtown Folks* is a central New England and American book.

HOLIDAY IN YANKEEDOM

In March, 1869, Harriet wrote James T. Fields that there was "an amount of curious old Natick tradition" which she could not work into *Oldtown Folks* without making the book too bulky but which she had been writing out to divert herself and make herself "laugh and dream." She was not sure how a book of Yankee tales might fare but she had found them fascinating to write. She enclosed one for sampling. Did he want the set for the *Atlantic?* Fields would have been justified in being annoyed. Not long before, he had offered her $6,000 for the magazine and book rights to *Oldtown Folks* for one year in America and England and she had refused, arguing that it better suited her purposes to have her book read at once and that the *Atlantic,* particularly in the person of Dr. Holmes (she must have been thinking of *Elsie Venner* and *The Guardian Angel*) had been irritating "*my* people (i.e. the orthodox)" and ridiculing them when "after all, they are not ridiculous." Apparently, she was saying her scraps would do for the *Atlantic.* But if he was annoyed, Fields wisely did not allow his annoyance to keep him from the enclosed story, "The Widow's Bandbox." Harriet here delightfully unfolded the history of Commodore (then Captain) Tucker's near capture, during the Revolution, by a British officer posing as a pathetic widow who must get her husband's body (actually a confederate hidden in a bandbox) to Boston. Tom Toothacre of Harpswell Point sensed that the "widow" was a man and Yankee cleverness saved the *Brilliant* for the American cause. But what must have led Fields immediately to accept the set of stories was Sam Lawson and the Yankee rhythms and phrases in which he told the tale. Always on the lookout for the authentic expression of America, Fields must have felt the indigenous note readers of 1869 were beginning to discover in Mark Twain as Sam unobtrusively and perfectly caught the look of Camden, particularly in his marvelously exact image for hens on a lazy afternoon:

"Wal, we wus a-lyin' at Camden there, one arternoon, goin' to sail for Boston that night. It was a sort o' soft, pleasant arternoon, kind o' still, and there wa'n't nothin' a-goin' on but jest the hens a-craw-crawin', and a-h'istin' up one foot, and holdin' it a spell 'cause they didn't know when to set it down, and the geese a-sissin' and a-pickin' at the grass. Ye see, Camden wasn't nothin' of a place,—'t was jest as if somebody had emptied out a pocketful o' houses and forgot 'em."

Oldtown Fireside Stories (1872), in which Harriet collected "The Widow's Bandbox" and nine other yarns, is a good deal more than postscript or appendix to *Oldtown Folks*. The rich humor of her previous books, in general, derived from the need to escape momentarily the self-consuming seriousness imposed by conscience and religious perplexities. But after joining the Episcopal Church and making her "résumé of the whole spirit and body of New England" in *Oldtown Folks*, she was no longer victim of those lifelong compulsions which had driven her through *Uncle Tom's Cabin* and *The Minister's Wooing*. She was now writing, as she told Fields, to divert herself and make herself "laugh and dream."

On the surface, this program is not so promising as the half-conscious scheme of "symbolic action" giving form and substance to her earlier work. But in diverting herself, Harriet was not simply scribbling. Much as Mark Twain in 1865 in "The Celebrated Jumping Frog" had committed to writing a Western oral tale, she was putting in black and white the oral tales Calvin Stowe had heard in his childhood in Natick. Like Mark Twain, she also had learned valuable lessons from her predecessors in fixing the indigenous in print. A reference to the Yankee peddler Sam Slick in her *Mayflower* sketch "The Canal Boat" indicates her early acquaintance with Thomas

Chandler Haliburton's *The Clockmaker* (1837), and it seems likely, as Walter Blair suggests, that she borrowed from Haliburton the happy device of the framework depicting the scene and the storyteller and making a vivid contrast with the story itself. Doubtless she had also learned lessons in creating Yankee monologue from Seba Smith's *The Life and Writings of Major Jack Downing* (1834), so seemingly authentic that Emerson's stepgrandfather, Ezra Ripley, thought Jack an actual man. In view of her obvious delight in racy American humor, she was probably, like Emily Dickinson, an eager reader of the Western oral tales finding their way into various newspapers. In any case, *Oldtown Fireside Stories* is not a collection of oral tales sprawled in print. Harriet's self-amusement took the form of developing, with the skills learned through a lifetime, the possibilities of native art and native materials.

This is not all. Her accusing Holmes, in the letter to Fields, of ridiculing "*my* people" when "after all they are not ridiculous" indicates that though she was working in the tradition of Down East humor, she brought to that tradition an essentially new attitude. Her affectionate respect for village characters and village ways makes her an anticipator of Robert Frost, who has also spoken of Yankees as "my people," and stated "They are much the same as we are," and not to be represented by having them "hop a little as if they were going over clods." Every now and then we catch in Smith and Haliburton the wink of superiority and that wink is virtually a habit in the pointless bad spelling in Lowell's *Biglow Papers* and Holmes's New England novels. As insider rather than outsider, Harriet in her holiday in Yankeedom was laughing *with,* not *at* her people. In knowledge, skill, and attitude, she was, in short, prepared to create a permanently interesting and significant revelation of New England.

Harriet did not, like her predecessors in Down East humor, imagine a Yankee spokesman: she became the Yankee spokesman, projecting herself, as Richard M. Dorson has written, "within the psyche of Sam Lawson." So complete was her imaginative identification that Sam never relapses into omnis-

cient author, or, for that matter, into Calvin Stowe.   The
stories are Sam's from the ground up.   In most instances, he
remembers just where he picked up his information.   Sometimes
his source was a single person, as, for example, the driver
Cap'n Eb Sawin who told him "The Ghost in the Mill," but
for "The Sullivan Looking-Glass," he had had to piece together reports from Aunt Polly Ginger, Mehitable Ginger,
Abner Ginger, Granny Badger, and Lady Lothrop.   In "The
Ghost in the Cap'n Brown House," Sam was faced with irrefu-
table, contradictory evidence.   Cinthy Pendleton, "a good, pious
gal," told him that a ghostly woman stood by her bed when
she spent a week tailoring at the Brown house; Aunt Sally
Dickerson, "a good woman and a church member," insisted that
one night when she sat up in a neighboring home with a corpse,
she saw an obviously mortal woman leave the Brown house in
a carriage.   Had there been a ghost or a mistress haunting Oldtown?   Several of Sam's stories grew from his own adventures.
He himself had been present but had no part (conscience for-
bade) in the digging for Captain Kidd's money.

In her identification, Harriet thought not *for*, but *with* Sam,
who is exactly the reverse of her last "central intelligence," that
skeptic, Horace Holyoke.   Sam follows his "gran'ther's" doctrine, "Boys, if ye want to lead a pleasant and prosperous life,
ye must contrive allers to keep jest the *happy medium* between
truth and falsehood."   Horace's Aunt Lois, the very impersonation of obstinate New England rationalism, is his mighty
opposite as he lingers on that "happy medium" before the
Badgers' kitchen fire.   She is "so large and commandin' in
her ways, and so kind o' up and down in all her doin's" that
Sam likes "once and a while to sort o' gravel her," as, for
example, by setting the boys after her for information concerning her friend Ruth Sullivan's gift of seeing through walls
and houses, into people's hearts, and "what's to come."   Later
by way of preface to "The Ghost in the Cap'n Brown House,"
Sam tells the boys they should mind Granny Badger, who believes Cotton Mather's *Magnalia*, rather than Aunt Lois: "You
look at the folks that's allus tellin' you what they don't believe,—

they don't believe this, and they don't believe that,—and what sort o' folks is they? Why, like yer Aunt Lois, sort o' stringy and dry. There ain't no 'sorption got out o' not believin' nothin'."

For Sam, keeping "the happy medium between truth and falsehood" means recognition that this is a world of hard facts and marvelous providences. The miller Cack Sparrock may help his father stow the corpse of the peddler Jehiel Lommedieu "up chimbley" at the mill, but God will use old Indian Keturah to call Jehiel down piece by piece in vision and draw a confession from Cack. In "The Sullivan Looking-Glass," General Sullivan's nephew, Jeff, may ship a will to England so he can inherit all the Sullivan fortune, but God has seen to it that Ruth Sullivan was born with a veil over her face, thereby earning the gift to see in her looking-glass the very room and cabinet where the will is hidden. Deliverance Scranton of Sherburne told Sam a story indicating that God's providence operated even in the brutalities of Indian warfare. The night the Indians attacked it was a remarkable providence first that the family reading in the Bible should have come just to the passage "The race is not to the swift, nor the battle to the strong," and second that the Colonel's Sunday shoes with shiny buckles should be standing where he could easily slip into them. When, after his capture, the Colonel was tied to a tree and most of the Indians were off gathering pine knots and slivers with which to torture him, the shoe-buckles caught the eyes of his Indian guard, who concluded that he might as well have them as anyone else. When he laid down his tomahawk and was working to get off the buckles, the Colonel, who had loosened his bonds, had his chance. With one blow, he split open the Indian's skull and remembering the text of the evening before, that the race is not to the swift, he ran praying to God until he fell safe and exhausted near his home. Sam quotes approvingly the Colonel's conclusion: "There's a providence in everything, even down to shoe-buckles."

Harriet also understood what Sam would think as henpecked husband. In view of Hepsy's sharp ways, even more "up and down" than those of Aunt Lois, Sam appropriately compares his reflections on his beautiful and pleasant cousin, Huldy, whom he might have had, to wintergreen: "it comes up jest so fresh and tender every year, the longest time you hev to live; and you can't help chawin' on 't though 't is sort o' stingin'. I don't never get over likin' young wintergreen." He can remember the days when he used to walk ten miles over to Sherburne of a Sunday just to play the bass viol in the same "singers' seat" with Huldy. She would have made the perfect wife for him: there was "no gal in Sherburne that could put sich a sight o' work through . . . and yet, Sunday mornin', she always come out in the singers' seat like one of these 'ere June roses, lookin' so fresh and smilin', and her voice was jest as clear and sweet as a meadow lark's." But she was destined to be Mrs. Parson Carryl. After the death of the first Mrs. Carryl, Huldy had moved in as housekeeper and with charming modesty had so skilfully managed "temporals" for the un-worldly minister that when the old ladies "fussed and fuzzled and wuzzled till they'd drinked up all the tea in the teapot" doubting her merits and ultimately questioning the propriety of her living at the minister's, Parson Carryl drove her over to Oldtown, where they were married by Parson Lothrop.

Huldy is not the only "might-have-been" Sam remembers in his stories. There was also Black Hoss John's daughter Miry, "one o' your briery, scratchy gals, that seems to catch fellers in thorns. She allers fit and flouted her beaux, and the more she fit and flouted 'em the more they'd be arter her." She was amazingly strong. When Tom Beacon came up from Cambridge to rusticate in Oldtown (this means that he was suspended for a period from Harvard), he put his arm around Miry as they walked home from a quilting past an orchard, whereupon she grabbed him by the shoulders and threw him over the fence. But Sam thought her beautiful when she came into church with her red cheeks and her bonnet tipped with "laylock." He was, however, cut out by Bill Elderkin, who took the academy. Bill didn't play fair: "He would have it that he sung tenor. He no more sung tenor than a skunk-blackbird, but he made b'lieve he did, jest to git next to Miry in the singers' seat." Their performance shocked Sam. They tore out all the leaves in the hymnbooks, and the singing books besides, writing notes, and Sam used to see Bill "a-lookin' at her all through the long prayer, in a way that wa'n't right, considerin' they was both professors of religion." But it was all Black Hoss John's fault. He wanted Miry to marry Tom Beacon from Cambridge and was "snarlier than a saw" whenever Bill called. When Bill went up to Bowdoin College, Black Hoss tried to intercept his letters, but Sam, who by this time had seen he could get Hepsy and couldn't get Miry, obligingly beat him to the postoffice and brought Miry her mail. Black Hoss John's final mean turn was to leave Miry only an old pitcher apparently full of sand. She was so mad she threw it across the room and out rolled gold pieces thick as dandelions all over the parlor. Mis' Elderkin's pitcher was not the least of Miry's attractions as Sam reflected that he might have had her.

But Huldy, or Miry, or Hepsy—it would have been much the same. Take Cap'n Brown's "old black Guinea nigger-woman," Quassia:

"She wa'n't no gret beauty, I can tell you; and she used to wear a gret red turban and a yaller short gown and red petticoat, and a gret string o' gold beads round her neck, and gret big gold hoops in her ears, made right in the middle o' Africa among the heathen there. For all she was black, she thought a heap o' herself, and was consid'able sort o' predominative over the cap'n. Lordy massy! boys, it's allus so. Get a man and a woman together,—any sort o' woman you're a mind to, don't care who 't is,—and one way or another she gets the rule over him, and he jest has to train to her fife. Some does it one way, and some does it another; some does it by jawin', and some does it by kissin', and some does it by faculty and contrivance; but one way or another they allers does it. Old Cap'n Brown was a good stout, stocky kind o' John Bull sort o' feller, and good judge o' sperits, and allers kep the best in them 'ere cupboards o' his'n; but, fust and last, things in his house went pretty much as old Quassia said."

As a poor man, Sam may think momentarily with longing of Mis' Elderkin's pitcher and Cap'n Brown's liquor, but it is

more characteristic of him to defend his poverty and poverty
in general on spiritual grounds. After describing the splendors
of General Sullivan's mansion in loving detail, Sam tells Horace
and Harry:

"Ye see, the Gineral was a drefful worldly old critter, and was
all for the pomps and the vanities. Lordy massy! I wonder what
the poor old critter thinks about it all now, when his body's all gone
to dust and ashes in the graveyard, and his soul's gone to 'tarnity!
Wal, that 'ere ain't none o' my business; only it shows the vanity
o' riches in a kind o' strikin' light, and makes me content that I
never had none."

Ruth Sullivan is a heroine after Sam's own heart because,
though the General "dressed her up in silks and satins, and she
had a maid to wait on her, and she hed sets o' pearl and dia-
mond," she was lonesome: "ye see, Ruth wan'n't calculated for
grande'r. Some folks ain't."

Like Thoreau, who mocked his worldly neighbors, Sam
cannot resist making fun of miserly Black Hoss John:

"You ought to 'a' seen him. Why, his face was all a perfect
crisscross o' wrinkles. There wa'n't a spot where you could put a
pin down that there wa'n't a wrinkle; and they used to say he held
on to every cent that went through his fingers till he'd pinched it
into two. You couldn't say that his god was his belly, for he hed
n't none, no more'n an old file: folks said that he'd starved himself
till the moon'd shine through him."

Black Hoss John's miserliness is the subject of Sam's last story,
"How to Fight the Devil." Being "ugly jest for the sake o'
ugliness," Black Hoss, Sam feels, could have set right "these
'ere modern ministers that come down from Cambridge college,
and are larnt about everything in creation . . . [and] say there
ain't no devil, and the reason on 't is, 'cause there can't be
none." Old Sarah Bunganuck, one of the converted Indians,
who made baskets and brooms, picked young wintergreen to
sell in bunches, and dug sassafras and ginseng to make beer,
had gotten a piece of land beside Black Hoss's white-birch
woodlot. Black Hoss said she was an old witch and thief,
that she stole things off his grounds. He used to jaw at her

by the hour over the fence, and getting no response, he tried to scare her away by wrapping himself in a bull's skin with the horns on his head, telling her he was the devil. But Sarah, who was cutting white-birch brush for brooms, merely said, "Ye be? Poor old critter, how I pity ye!"

What offended Sam most was Black Hoss's violation of the New England principle favoring the poor:

"As to her stealin', she did n't do nothin' but pick huckleberries and grapes, and git chestnuts and wannuts and butternuts, and them 'ere wild things that's the Lord's, grow on whose land they will, and is free to all. I've hearn 'em tell that, over in the old country, the poor was kept under so that they couldn't shoot a bird, nor ketch a fish, nor gather no nuts, nor do nothin' to keep from starvin', 'cause the quality folks they thought they owned everything, 'way down to the middle of the earth and clear up to the stars. We never hed no sech doin's this side of the water, thank the Lord! We've allers been free to have the chestnuts and the wannuts and the grapes and the huckleberries and the strawberries ef we could git 'em, and ketch fish when and where we was a mind to."

This unwritten law would persist in the habits of the people. In his poem "Blueberries" in *North of Boston* (1914), Robert Frost wrote of a Yankee named Loren who was able to feed his brood "like birds" on wild berries because New Englanders like Patterson continued the tradition:

> He won't make the fact that they're rightfully his
> An excuse for keeping us other folk out.

Sam, of course, is an amusing character, but he is no clown. Through imaginative identification, Harriet made him a figure, like Huck Finn, whom we can take seriously as an embodiment of his culture. In his acceptance of providences, for example, Sam walks a well-worn New England path. His assumptions may be found in Winthrop's *Journal* and Mather's *Magnalia;* and in Urian Oakes' sermon "The Sovereign Efficacy of Divine Providence" (1677), the classic New England Puritan exposition of the matter, we can see that these assumptions were not ignorant superstition. They rested on the belief that God is the first supreme cause and that events, even the most

trivial and the most terrible, must be either ordered or permitted by him.   Like Sam in his story of "Colonel Eph's Shoe-
Buckles," the Reverend Mr. Oakes, insisting that all is in God's
hand, returned again and again to the text, "The race is not
to the swift, nor the battle to the strong."   How traditionally and
thoroughly Puritan Sam was in his interpretation of Colonel
Eph's adventure can be seen from one of Mr. Oakes's most
memorable illustrations:

> No Contingency, or Emergency, or Accident so casual, but it is
> ordered & governed by the Lord. The Arrow that was shot at a
> venture, and smote *Ahab* throw the joints of his Harness, was
> directed at him by the Hand of God. So in that case of Man-
> slaughter, and killing a man casually, as if a man be hewing Wood,
> and his hand fetcheth a stroke with the Axe, to cut down a Tree,
> and the head slippeth from the helve, and lighteth upon his Neigh-
> bour that he die, *Deut.* 19.5 God is said in that case, to *deliver*
> that man that is slain, *into his hand,* Exod. 21.13.   God ordereth
> that sad event.

Being a "do-nothing," and, generally speaking, a nonpro-
vider for his wife and children, Sam, of course, does not live
up to the Puritan standard stated by John Cotton: "Faith
drawes the heart of a Christian to live in some warrantable
calling; as soone as ever a man begins to looke towards God,
and the wayes of his grace, he will not rest, till he find out
some warrantable Calling and imployment."   But Sam is more
New England than we may at first recognize in his attitude
toward wealth and worldly success.   We can easily make more
than we should of the intimate historical relations of piety and
the rise of capitalism.   Cotton not only bade men to look for
"a warrantable Calling"; he also insisted in orthodox Puritan
fashion that the Christian *"uses the world as if he used it not,
1. Cor. 7.31.*   This is not the thing his heart is set upon, hee
lookes for greater matters then these things can reach him, he
doth not so much look at the world as at heaven."   We may
read in the sermon of Oakes, to which I have referred above,
that "It is ordinarily seen in the World, that the thriving men
in Estates, are none of the most understanding & judicious.

Many a man hath this world-craft, that yet is a man of no deep or solid Understanding." In noting the pomps and vanities of General Sullivan and the miserliness of Black Hoss John, and in remaining content with his own poverty, Sam, however much in self-defense, was speaking underlying convictions of his society just as he was in voicing his belief in the providence of shoe-buckles.

Sam is such a delightful revelation of what it means to see, to feel, to think, to talk as Yankee that it does not seem unjust to say of *Oldtown Fireside Stories* what Mark Twain wrote Joel Chandler Harris concerning his *Uncle Remus: His Songs and Sayings* (1880) : "You can argue *yourself* into the delusion that the principal life is in the stories themselves and not in the setting ; but you will save labor by stopping with that solitary convert, for he is the only intelligent one you will bag. In reality the stories are only alligator pears—one merely eats them for the sake of the salad-dressing." The point of every one of Sam's stories is less in the happenings than in the self-portraiture and Sam's method of telling a story, which, Harriet wrote in "The Widow's Bandbox," was "like the course of a dreamy, slow-moving river through a tangled meadow-flat,— not a rush nor a bush but was reflected in it. . . ."

This suggests literary slow motion, but that, as the stories obviously demonstrate, was not what Harriet had in mind. Something is always happening and happening quickly and dramatically in Sam's stories. In "The Ghost in the Mill," old Keturah calls, "Come down, come down," and the various parts of Jehiel Lommedieu obligingly and frighteningly seem to assemble on the hearth. In "Colonel Eph's Shoe-Buckles," we have not only his escape from the Indians but a series of extras, by way of preface, describing other violent encounters with savages. In "Mis' Elderkin's Pitcher," as I have noted, Miry hurls a beau over a fence and throws her pitcher across the room. Even in "The Minister's Housekeeper," essentially a celebration of Huldy, the lovely, the lost, the "facultized," there is something happening on practically every page. Parson Carryl tries to make his tom turkey hatch eggs and Tom fights the parson, strides around with a basket on his head when the parson tries to keep him in place, and smashes the eggs when the parson weighs him down with a stone. Later the parson throws a pig in a well, thinking it is the new pigpen. In "The Bull-Fight," Sam tells of a bull who chases Bill Moss into the kitchen, smashes the looking glass, overturns furniture, and is finally brought down by a well-directed shot, after which the "old critter" lies kicking and bleeding on the carpet.

What Harriet had in mind in writing that Sam's method was "like the course of a dreamy, slow-moving river through a tangled meadow-flat,—not a rush nor a bush but was reflected in it" is the device of circumstantiality. In *Uncle Tom's Cabin* her enlivening her page with details was an important factor in throwing a nation into turmoil and encouraging it to Civil War. This circumstantiality is the device above all others making us feel that we were there, we lived the life, in her New England novels, and it is the essence of Sam's art in *Oldtown Fireside Stories*. Instinctively, Sam practices all the necessary arts of the narrator, delay, suspense, climax, anti-climax, but we stay with him primarily because his details, item by item, build up a world of such convincingness that momentarily we do not question the questionable. The happy success of *Oldtown Fireside Stories,* and its authenticity, as a development of native art and native materials, derived from the fact that a great artist in detail was working in a tradition where, as witness Walter Blair's anthology *Native American Humor (1800-1900)*, circumstantiality is the major literary device.

The story most stretching belief, "The Ghost in the Mill," amply illustrates Sam's art of taking us in. Quite appropriately, since it is an evening when the winds shriek around the house and roar and tumble down the chimney, the boys ask for "Come down, Come down," as they call "The Ghost in the Mill." Sam begins, after artful delay, by establishing the authority of his source: Cap'n Eb Sawin was a respectable man, a deacon in the church, and a patriot who arrived at Lexington when the first shot was fired against the British. Futhermore,

he married Lois Peabody, a "A rael sensible woman," and Sam
has heard her tell the story just as the Captain told it to him.

Sam now turns to making the peddler Jehiel Lommedieu
live in our imaginations. No one knew where Jehiel had
come from, but the women all liked him: "Women will like
some fellows, when men can't see no sort o' reason why they
should; and they liked this 'ere Lommedieu, though he was
kind o' mournful and thin and shad-bellied, and hadn't nothin'
to say for himself." It got to be the custom for women to
calculate Jehiel's arrival weeks ahead of time, and make up
gingersnaps and preserves and pies and "make him stay to tea
at the houses, and feed him up on the best there was." One
year he wrote Phebe Ann Parker, whom he was supposed to be
courting, that he would be along about Thanksgiving time, but
he didn't come then, nor even the next spring, and finally, he
was gone out of folks' minds "much as a last year's apple
blossom." Sam thinks it quite affecting "how little these 'ere
folks is missed that's so much sot by."

We now come to Cap'n Eb's discovery of what became of
Jehiel. Sam does not say "a long time after"; no, it was the
nineteenth of March, memorable for the greatest snowstorm
in those parts, and not just for snow but "this 'ere fine, siftin'
snow, that drives in your face like needles, with a wind to cut
your nose off: it made teamin' pretty tedious work." Cap'n
Eb was the toughest man in those parts but by sundown he
was so bewildered that he got off the road to Boston and came
out at a pair of bars at old Cack Sparrok's mill near Sherburne.

Sam continues to particularize almost as if he were giving
testimony in court under oath. Ahead of Cap'n Eb is a dark
piece of woods where he knows the light "will give out clean,"
so he "driv his oxen up agin the fence, and took out the hoss,
and got on him, and pushed along through the woods, not
rightly knowin' where he was going." When he reaches the
mill, where Cack sits before a blazing fire with a rum jug at
his elbow, Cap'n Eb, like a good and convincing teamster, remembers his "critters." Cack gets out his "tin lantern" and
back they go through the drifts to get Eb's team: "He told

him he could put 'em under the mill-shed. So they got the
critters up to the shed, and got the cart under; and by that
time the storm was awful."

Through the device of circumstantiality, Sam has built up
a world in which we can believe so easily that with further
specific details he can make us momentarily accept the impossible. When Keturah knocks at the door, Cack and Cap'n
Eb wait a moment and hear only the wind screeching in the
chimney, and since no one, of course, can be paying a visit
such a night, Cack is about to go on with his story, when
another rap comes harder than ever. Cack's response is what
we might expect from "a drefful drinkin' old crittur, that
lived there all alone in the woods by himself a-tendin' saw
and grist mill." He says: "Wal, if 'tis the Devil, we'd jest
as good's open, and have it out with him to onct." Sam makes
us understand, through other choice details, why the smile
should fade from Cack's face and the laugh die in his throat,
when he finds Keturah at the door. When everyone else rises
in church as Parson and Lady Lothrop come down the broad
aisle, Keturah remains seated, and when, after meeting, Lady
Lothrop bows and smiles graciously to her as she comes back
down the broad aisle, Keturah looks "jest as if she was a-workin'
up to spring at her." Rumor holds that Keturah's father was a
great powwow out on Martha's Vineyard and that she had been
set apart as a child to the service of the devil. This may possibly
explain why it makes people dizzy to look into her snaky eyes
and why she is always winking and blinking "as if she saw more
folks round than you did, so that she wa'n't no way pleasant
company."

Cack pours her out a mug of hot toddy but quite understandably her presence in the chimney corner "sort o' stopped
the conversation," particularly since she keeps muttering to herself and looking "up chimbley," from which come the worst
yells and screeches Cap'n Eb has ever heard. But the Cap'n
is a brave man. He is not going to have conversation stopped
by any woman, witch or no witch. He says: "Well, Ketury,
what do you see? . . . Come, out with it; don't keep it to your-

self." An evil smile creeps over Keturah's face. She rattles her necklace of bones and snakes' tails; her eyes snap, and she looks up the chimney, calling out, "Come down, come down! let's see who ye be." When Jehiel's feet come down the chimney, they are not shadowy ectoplasm: "a pair of feet come down the chimbley, and stood right in the middle of the haarth, the toes p'intin' out'rds, with shoes and silver buckles a-shinin' in the firelight." Keturah can't frighten Cap'n Eb. When she has called down legs which co-operatively join the feet,' he says, "Wal, we're in for it now. Go it, Ketury, and let's have the rest on him," and when all is finished save the head, he tells her, with New England practicality, "Wal, Ketury, this 'ere's getting serious. I 'spec' you must finish him up, and let's see what he wants of us." Cap'n Eb knows Jehiel Lommedieu immediately when he sees his face and asks him, "What do you want, now you hev come?" But Jehiel can only point "up chimbley" and moan. As Sam explains, as if he had considerable experience in such matters, it "isn't often that his sort o' folks is permitted to speak." There is suddenly a screeching blast of wind that blows the smoke and fire out into the room and blows the door open, a whirlwind and darkness and moans and screeches, and Cap'n Eb finds himself alone with Cack, who rolls on the floor moaning and groaning.

After Cap'n Eb has picked him up and built up the fire, Cack tells how his father murdered Jehiel for his money, how he helped his father hide the body in the chimney, and how he has had no peace of mind since. Sam does not even leave circumstantiality here. Cap's Eb gets Parson Carryl and one of the selectmen in Sherburne to take Cack's deposition, and Cack, conveniently dying of shock, gives signs that he may be saved; at least he is distressed that he can't live to be hanged: "He sort o' seemed to think, that if he was fairly tried, and hung, it would make it all square." The final detail taking us in is that Cap'n Eb was one "of a party o' eight" who pulled down the chimney and found Jehiel's skeleton.

Not until Robert Frost in "The Witch of Coös" would have "Mother" search her button box for one of the finger pieces of a skeleton that mounted the stairs from cellar to attic one interesting night, would any New England writer so skilfully manage detail to make us believe, even while we smile, in the delightful horrors of a Yankee ghost story. Here again, as in her respect and affection for village ways and village characters, Harriet recalls her most distinguished twentieth-century successor in the art of seeing New Englandly, and looking back through *Oldtown Fireside Stories,* we can see that on her Yankee holiday she was very close to fulfilling Frost's definition of poetry:

> It begins in delight and ends in wisdom. . . . It begins in delight, it inclines to the impulse, it assumes direction with the first line laid down, it runs a course of lucky events, and ends in a clarification of life—not necessarily a great clarification, such as sects and cults are founded on, but in a momentary stay against confusion.

In Sam's stories Harriet did not make the profound clarification and stay against confusion which Frost would make again and again in his speculative monologues and in his lyrics. But her achievement, if prose may be compared with poetry, is comparable to Frost's dramatic poems. She made a clarification, a stay against confusion, a portion of wisdom, in realizing beautifully and realistically, with delightful humor, the village world already crumbling into farce and stereotype in the work of her contemporaries; and we repeatedly smile the smile of recognition as Sam in lively Yankee phrases clarifies human nature and human experience. Harriet would never write a more nearly perfect book than *Oldtown Fireside Stories;* as art it stands above *Oldtown Folks* and it is only less her masterpiece because it is less searching, less various, less comprehensive in its vision.

VINDICATION OF A FRIEND

SOMETHING of Harriet's enduring appreciation of New England Puritanism should be traced to her early acquaintance with her father's maiden sister, Aunt Esther Beecher, whose darkest moods, we learn in *House and Home Papers,* "were so lighted up and adorned with an outside show of wit and humor, that those who had known her intimately were astonished to hear that she had ever been subject to depression." Aunt Esther was a noble and charming woman. With her proud and sensitive nature, she had never found the hero who could meet her requirements of ideality, but she had not therefore withdrawn from the domestic trials befalling the women of her generation. She served as housekeeper for Lyman Beecher after the death of his first wife, later helped Catharine and Harriet keep house for their students at the Hartford Seminary, and finally accompanied the Beechers to Cincinnati, where, as Harriet wrote, "She was the one who thought for and cared for and toiled for all, yet made never a claim that any one should care for her." Her neat parlor, a half-minute's walk from the Litchfield parsonage, was Harriet's early refuge from the noise and dominance of her brothers, and there Aunt Esther used to serve tea in delicate India china cups and delight Harriet with New England legends and with choice bits from her wide reading. Aunt Esther had the head of a student and confessed that she would like to live in a Protestant convent where she could devote herself to reading and meditation without interruption. Believing that what interested her would interest her little niece, she gave Harriet at six or seven on one of her visits Byron's

recently published poem *The Corsair* to appease her appetite
for reading. Harriet was astonished and electrified, calling to
Aunt Esther's attention the wonderful things she found and asking her what Byron could have meant by some of his lines, for
example, "One I never loved enough to hate."

Harriet went home absorbed with Byron, and paid careful
attention to all her stepmother and her father now said at the
table concerning him, particularly discussion of the poet's
separation from his wife in 1816 and in 1824 Lyman Beecher's
announcing to Mrs. Beecher, "My dear, Byron is dead—*gone*,"
and after a moment of silence, his lament, "Oh, I'm sorry that
Byron is dead. I did hope he would live to do something for
Christ. What a harp he might have swept!" Lyman's statements made a solemn and painful impression on little Harriet.
That afternoon she went off by herself to pick strawberries on
Chestnut Hill, but she was too dispirited. She lay down among
the daisies and "looked up into the blue sky, and thought of that
great eternity into which Byron had entered, and wondered
how it might be with his soul." Her father furnished some
answer the next Sunday when he preached a funeral sermon
on Byron, taking as his text "The name of the just is as brightness, but the memory of the wicked shall rot." Lyman instructed his congregation that some of Byron's verses were
as "imperishable as brass," but that the impurities in other
poems, notwithstanding the beauty of language, would sink
them in a few years into oblivion. This funeral sermon was one
more example of Lyman's interest in great lost souls. Harriet
remembered his reading *Paradise Lost* aloud and bursting into
tears over Satan and also his search of the memoirs emanating
from St. Helena in the desire to shape out some hope for
Napoleon's eternal future. In view of his successes with stubborn, hardheaded Yankee farmers and Litchfield aristocrats,
Lyman was confident that if Byron "could only have talked with
Taylor [Nathaniel W. Taylor, Dwight Professor of Didactic
Theology in Yale Divinity School] and me, it might have got
him out of his troubles." It might also have gotten him into
other troubles: Lyman was capable of embracing inconsistences;

Taylor's favorite motto was "Follow truth if it carries you over Niagara."

At fourteen, during her first year at Hartford Seminary, Harriet in imagination did what her father and Professor Taylor could not do in reality: she converted Byron. Her means was a verse drama, *Cleon*. Like Byron, who swam the Hellespont, Cleon is a fine athlete, in fact, an Olympic champion, and also like Byron he is, as his teacher Diagoras tells him, the common talk for waste, outstripping even these "degenerate days," that is, the days of Nero, in "riot and loose luxury." But behind the façade of worldliness, Cleon is a Christian. When Nero pardons his apostasy, telling him

> My lord, we cannot think that you will hold it.
> We are persuaded of your better reason
> To be a follower of a crazy Jew,

Cleon will not promise to keep his faith to himself:

> It is my settled purposes while I live
> To leave no word or argument untried
> To win all men to reverence Him.

At this point, Catharine Beecher pulled down the curtain on *Cleon,* telling Harriet that she should not waste her time writing poetry but should discipline her mind by the study of Butler's *Analogy*. But it is easy to see that Cleon is destined for those tortures made famous years later in *Quo Vadis* and recently refurbished in the popular imagination through technicolor.

In *Poganuc People,* Harriet reported that among the students in the law offices and the young ladies of the first families in the Litchfield of her childhood "There were promising youths who tied their open shirt-collars with a black ribbon, and professed disgust at the hollow state of human happiness in general, and there were compassionate young ladies who considered the said young men all the more interesting for this state of mysterious desolation, and often succeeded in the work of consoling them." In writing *Cleon,* Harriet, of course, participated in an essentially traditional fashion in this Byron craze, for the common assumption was that Byron epitomized all noble youths who had been led into erratic behavior through the tears of things and the lack of understanding and love. But in making Cleon a Christian, willing to die for his faith, Harriet went well beyond contemporary girlish enthusiasm: she did not console some imitation Byron; in imagination, she saved Byron himself.

When we notice that on the last evening of his life the aristocratic worldling Augustine St. Clare reads the Bible aloud, sings the "Dies Irae," resolves to do his duty to the poor and lowly, and dies exclaiming that his mind "is coming HOME, at last! at last! at last!" we can see that her spokesman in *Uncle Tom's Cabin* is another version of Byron saved, and that possibly Eva (there is even a verbal echo) is Byron's daughter Ada, and that Marie St. Clare, the neurotic, the selfish wife, may be Lady Byron as she was popularly interpreted by her husband's worshipers. After *Uncle Tom's Cabin,* however, Harriet fictionalized Byron very differently. In *The Minister's Wooing* Aaron Burr toys with the seduction of Mme de Frontignac because he feels artistic pleasure "in the beautiful light and heat." In *Oldtown Folks,* Ellery Davenport goes even further, actually seducing Emily Rossiter and becoming the father of her child.

This change in pattern came from Harriet's friendship with Lady Byron, beginning in 1853, and from Lady Byron's disclosure in 1856 of the true cause of her separation from her husband, her discovery that he had committed incest with his half sister, Augusta, and that he was apparently continuing this doubly criminal relation (Augusta was Mrs. Leigh) after marriage. Lady Byron sought Harriet's counsel as to the advisability of making the facts known in view of a new edition of Byron's poems, which, rumor reported, was to be promoted by the old story of his domestic misfortunes. After discussing the matter with her sister Mary, who had accompanied her to Europe, Harriet advised silence; and for thirteen years the only sign she herself gave of her knowledge was the alteration in the Byronic hero, which, of course, the world at large would scarcely notice and if it did notice, would not understand.

But the afternoon when Lady Byron told her secret was undoubtedly one of the most dramatic moments in Harriet's long life. She already knew the story of incest from other English friends, but to have Lady Byron bare her soul, ask her advice, and discuss Byron's spiritual state (he was, she told Harriet, made desperate by his inability to reason his way out of Calvinistic Christianity)—here, indeed, was an almost fairy-story sequence of events for a woman who had been fascinated with Byron since six or seven, who at thirteen had been too dispirited to pick strawberries when her father had announced "Byron is dead—*gone*," and who in Cleon and Augustine St. Clare had twice saved Byron in imagination. As Harriet wrote Lady Byron in 1857: "I often think how strange it is that I should *know* you—you who were a sort of legend of my early days; that I should love you is only a natural result."

It was equally a natural result, given Harriet's Puritan New England background, her personal history, her character, and the state of nineteenth-century literary criticism, that someday she would tell the world what she knew. In *Crusader in Crinoline*, Forrest Wilson assumes that "Whether she recognized it or not, a small, selfish voice was whispering to her that in telling this unsavoury story she was proclaiming to the world the glamorous, stupendous fact that she, Harriet Beecher Stowe, had been the bosom friend of Byron's wife and widow, the sharer of her most intimate secrets." This, like his later statement that her book was based on a deliberate misrepresentation because she wrote that she answered the *Blackwood's* review of the Guiccioli book rather than the book itself, is not perceptive criticism. It is undoubted fact that Harriet had placed her essay "The True Story of Lady Byron's Life" in Osgood's hands in June and that the *Blackwood's* review did not appear until July, but she must have seen that review before her article was published or she could not have referred to it, and it seems possible that she revised her essay after reading the review. In any case, Mr. Wilson has gone too far in referring to his discovery as an "astonishing fact" and in declaring dramatically that "Not one critic or enemy ever found it, and Harriet died with her guilty secret intact."

Mr. Wilson's charge that "she had rushed out with her scandal in order to flatter her own vainglory" cannot, of course, be proved or disproved. Quite obviously, she delighted in her closeness to Lady Byron, and considered her friendship with her "a stupendous fact," but Puritanism rather than egotism would seem the obvious explanation for Harriet's disclosure. For nine years after Lady Byron's death, she waited in vain for the English critic with enough courage to risk his reputation in a statement of the facts that would vindicate her friend. But no one dared speak what so many knew or surmised. The accepted program of Victorian England was to let sleeping dogs lie, and if they seemed to be waking to put them to sleep again. This, of course, was not the program of New England Puritanism, which typically found itself in opposition to the world, and which, as we can see in Thoreau's "Civil Disobedience" and *Uncle Tom's Cabin,* imprudently spoke the truth when duty and justice demanded it. For two generations Lady Byron had been vilified by romantic critics around the globe and now, as it seemed to Harriet in 1869, she was again being held up to scorn in *My Recollections of Lord Byron,* by his mistress, Countess Guiccioli. If no one else would defend Lady Byron's memory, Harriet must, come what would. God expected no less of the writer he had made powerful and influential.

Harriet's essay, "The True Story of Lady Byron's Life," appearing in the *Atlantic* for September, 1869, and her book *Lady Byron Vindicated,* appearing the next year, made Victorian England and Victorian America reel with shock and disgust, and in.the ferocious counterattack her critics ferreted out all discoverable errors in an attempt to discredit her and attributed to her the lowest motives they could imagine for writing her book. But Harriet was not in error on major points. Weighing the evidence dispassionately as a lawyer fifty-five years after Harriet shocked the world, Sir John C. Fox in

The Byron Mystery (1924) concluded that Byron committed incest with Augusta before his marriage and that, though it cannot be proved that he continued the offense after marriage, he did attempt it, and thus gave Lady Byron just cause for separating from him. In *The Romantic Rebels* (1935), Frances Winwar has vindicated Lady Byron with the facts Harriet first ventured to bring forward, and with other details far more incriminating than anything Harriet wrote.

Lady Byron Vindicated deserves our respect not only as a courageous statement of fact but as an interpretation of Byron. Harriet postulated not a moral monster but a sick man. She believed that Byron was originally a fine and sensitive, but perilously organized, individual, and that his degeneration could be explained by what she called the "Physiological Argument." Alternately the pet and victim of his mother's tumultuous nature, essentially undisciplined at school and college, where he combined drinking and licentiousness, Byron managed at first to save himself through physical exercise. But even as a young man there were danger signs which the perceptive might have read. With his abiding belief in Christianity Calvinistically interpreted, Byron would pass from violent excesses in eating and drinking to unnatural abstinence, which made the succeeding debauch all the worse: "He was like a fine musical instrument, whose strings were every day alternating between extreme tension and perfect laxity." At twenty-one he was prematurely exhausted, but he now imposed further burdens on himself with his literary labors. Harriet suspected that he drew on his active imagination in his account of some of his amorous activities, but his violent pursuit of pleasure, his constant driving of himself through poem after poem, and his inner conflict finally reduced him, she believed, to that state of exhausted vitality, characteristic of Greece and Rome in decline, where, dead to normal pleasures, "the mind delights to dwell on horrible ideas, which give a shuddering sense of guilt and crime." In this half-insane state, Byron committed incest with Augusta, but

A most peculiar and affecting feature of that form of brain-disease which hurries its victim, as by an overpowering mania, into crime, is, that often the moral faculties and the affections remain to a degree unimpaired, and protest with all their strength against the outrage.   Hence come conflicts and agonies of remorse proportioned to the strength of the moral nature.   Byron, more than any other one writer, may be called the poet of remorse.   His passionate pictures of this feeling seem to give new power to the English language. . . .

Harriet, of course, had been reading Byron's poems critically since that day in her childhood when she asked what he could possibly have meant by "One I never loved enough to hate." With the master clue confirmed by Lady Byron, she now demonstrated what no critic had dared to demonstrate before, the significance of the incest theme in "Manfred," "Cain," and other poems, and she indicated for the first time that those moments when Byron cast himself on the world's sympathy as the nobly misunderstood were parts of an intentional program of deception, calculated to put the blame for the failure of his marriage on the already overburdened shoulders of his wife. Of the later and greater Byron of *Don Juan,* Harriet was unappreciative, but though the world shouted her down, she had inaugurated the modern study of one of the major romantic poets. *Lady Byron Vindicated* quite obviously damaged Harriet's reputation: James T. Fields published no more of Sam Lawson's stories for eight years; the polite and cautious, misunderstanding her motives, wrote her down as a scandalmonger. But in the more candid atmosphere of the mid-twentieth century, *Lady Byron Vindicated* seems another reason for attributing courage and intelligence to Harriet Beecher Stowe.

THE LAST NOVELS

I

BETWEEN 1870 and 1881, when her writing career drew to a close, Harriet wrote, in addition to *Lady Byron Vindicated* and *Oldtown Fireside Stories,* which she expanded in a later edition, an account of her life in Florida, two popular religious studies, a brief volume of stories and sketches, two books for children, and four novels. This is an impressive record of virtuosity. Quite obviously, she was now more the professional writer, more the journalist shrewdly estimating what her readers wanted and doing her best to supply them with it. As we should expect, most of these books hurried into print make no new revelation of Harriet Beecher Stowe. But the novels, contributed to the *Christian Union,* of which she became an owner in 1870, still merit consideration. The last, *Poganuc People* (1878), the fictionalizing of her childhood in Litchfield, is one of her most charming books, and the novels of contemporary life, *Pink and White Tyranny* (1871), *My Wife and I* (1871), and *We and Our Neighbors* (1875), while far below her best work, are at least significant for what they tell us of her reaction to the Gilded Age.

We may often wish to smile at *Pink and White Tyranny* for its crude diatribe, but it has the large virtue of attacking those aspects of the Gilded Age deserving satire. Harriet's primary target was the newly rich like Dick Follingsbee, "one of those shoddy upstarts, not at all our sort of folks . . . a vulgar sharper, who has made his money out of our country by dishonest contracts during the war." Follingsbee glows with the bright colors of decay. His wife, an unscrupulous social climber, lives for show and, taking her cue from cheap French novels, carries on a tepid amour with her interior decorator, Charlie Ferrola. Harriet's description of Charlie shows her awareness of the essential decadence of that world given as the prize of virtue by Horatio Alger to his Ragged Dicks and Tattered Toms: "He was one of those blossoms of male humanity that seem as expressly designed by nature for the ornamentation of ladies' boudoirs, as an Italian greyhound: he had precisely the same graceful, shivery adaptation to live by petting and caresses. His tastes were all so exquisite that it was the most difficult thing in the world to keep him out of misery a moment. His profession was nominally that of architecture and landscape gardening; but, in point of fact, consisted in telling certain, rich, *blasé,* stupid, fashionable people how they could quickest get rid of their money. He ruled despotically in the Follingsbee halls. . . ."

The Follingsbees' great admirer, Lillie Ellis, twenty-seven and "shopworn," who tricks the hero John Seymour into marriage, but whom, Harriet argued, Seymour should not divorce, is rather obviously overdone, but through her Harriet let the world know that the newly rich, unlike the families of inherited wealth, represented by the New England Seymours, felt no commitment to the laboring classes and were without moral responsibility in business matters. When Seymour invites, as is his custom, his mill workers to his birthday party, Lillie, hoping to discourage further visits, lies about their behavior, saying they left grease spots on the sofa and ground cake and raisins into the carpet, whereas they actually conducted themselves with quiet dignity. At the end of the book, Lillie advises her husband to cheat his way out of his responsibilities to Clapham & Company, which has failed: ". . . Dick Follingsbee said that there were ways in which people could put their property out of their hands when they got caught in such scrapes as this. . . . He told me of plenty of people that had done that, who were living splendidly, and who were received everywhere; and people thought just as much of them."

My Wife and I and its sequel, *We and Our Neighbors,* are more sophisticated novels. The narrator of *My Wife and I,* Harry Henderson, an aspiring writer, leaves New England to make his way in the New York world of smart literary adventurers. His talents win him a place on the "Great Democracy," which its owner, Mr. Goldstick, describes as "not primarily a money-making enterprise—it is a great moral engine; it is for the great American people, and it contemplates results which look to the complete regeneration of society." Harry soon discovers, however, that Mr. Goldstick wants only general moral fervor; he will not publish specific criticisms of political corruption. This is typical of New York, the Vanity Fair of the world, where everything has its market value and where "Hand out your wares! advertise them, and see what they will bring seemed the only law of production." In "the first blast and blare of its busy, noisy publicity and activity," Harry feels his "inner spirits shrink and tremble with dismay."

In *My Wife and I* Harriet again drew the contrast between the old and new aristocracy. The Van Arsdels, like the Seymours, come of respectable New England stock, and though they play the game of fashion, they do not have the hard glitter of Wat Sydney, "a man, heart, soul, and strength, interested in that mighty game of chance and skill by which, in America, money is made. He is a railroad king—a prince of stocks—a man going with a forty-thousand steam power through New York waters." Sydney courts Eva Van Arsdel but she resists the temptation of a life of ease without love and marries Harry Henderson, the man of principles. Her sister, Ida, who aspires to a career in medicine, is even more clearly a reversion to the New England type. As Eva informs Harry: "Blood will tell; there's the old Puritan broken loose in Ida. She don't believe any of their doctrines, but she goes on their track. . . . Ida is as bent on testifying and going against the world as any old Covenanter." Ida says she likes "hardness and simplicity. I am sick to death of softness and perfumed cushions and ease." She spends her evenings in her father's study, to which the old New England furniture has been relegated, where she carries on the traditional Puritan concern with ideas. Currently, she is reading Charles Darwin's *Origin of Species,* which deeply interests her, and which she feels is not necessarily in conflict with Christianity.

Harry's New England cousin, Caroline Simmons, who finally accompanies Ida to Europe, is another illustration of the non-doctrinal Puritan. It was early her fate (could Harriet possibly have heard rumors of Emily Dickinson?) to have her father drive off her lover, who taught at the local academy, and since that time she has confined herself to a lonely and intensely intellectual existence at home. Caroline believes that her father really loves her and that far within the frozen circle of his repression he is a lonely prisoner, longing to express himself and unable: "The hard skies of our New England, its rocky soil, its severe necessities, make characters like his; and they intrench themselves in a similar religious faith which makes them still harder. They live to aspire and to suffer, but never to express themselves; and every soft and warm heart that is connected with them pines and suffers and dies like flowers that are thrown upon icebergs." We may well wish that Harriet had gone into more detail concerning Caroline, particularly in regard to those poems of "subdued fire" that she sends Harry's friend, Bolton, the young man her father long ago drove off. But Harriet was interested in Caroline, as in Ida, primarily as an illustration of the fact that some women because of fate or temperament are not meant for the conventional responsibilities of wives and mothers.

Harriet here dealt, of course, with the "woman question" currently agitating America. As the American woman who had made the most conspicuous public success in her generation, Harriet, we might suppose, would have encouraged any reform giving new freedom and a greater measure of equality to women, but she insisted that the woman question must be answered in a Christian spirit with the proper reverence for marriage as a sacrament. In Audacia Dangyereyes, she expressed her disapproval of Victoria Woodhull, Tennie Claflin, Elizabeth Cady Stanton, Susan Anthony, and other female reformers, who seemed to her to be running true reform into the ground. Harriet undoubtedly thought of herself when she had Bolton tell Harry in his disgust with Audacia, ". . . you're not the first reformer that has had to cry out, 'Deliver me from my friends.' Always, when the waters of any noble, generous enthusiasm rise and overflow their banks, there must come down the driftwood—the wood, hay, and stubble. . . . If I could have been made a pro-slavery man, it would have been by reading anti-slavery papers, and *vice-versa*. I had to keep myself on a good diet of pro-slavery papers, to keep my zeal up."

As I have indicated in discussing *Uncle Tom's Cabin,* Harriet was a radical democrat, like Orestes Brownson approaching Karl Marx in her sympathy with a world-wide revolt of the masses, but in the early 1870's she perceived, as some American liberals would not perceive until the 1940's and 1950's, that there is a significant difference between Christian-democratic revolution and the atheistic revolution encouraged by Communism. It was the tie-in between French Communism and the demand for equal rights for women which primarily distressed her as we can see from her long but extremely illuminating comment on Audacia Dangyereyes' paper, "Emancipated Woman":

The bold intrusion of Miss Audacia Dangyereyes into my apartment had left a most disagreeable impression on my mind. This was not lessened by the reception of her paper, which came to hand in due course of next mail, and which I found to be an exposition of all the wildest principles of modern French communism. It consisted of attacks directed about equally against Christianity, marriage, the family state, and all human laws and standing order, whatsoever. It was much the same kind of writing with which the populace of France was indoctrinated and leavened in the era preceding the first Revolution, and which in time bore fruit in blood. In those days, as now, such doctrines were toyed with in literary salons and aristocratic circles, where their novelty formed an agreeable stimulus in the vapid commonplace of fashionable life. They were then, as now, embraced with enthusiasm by fair illuminati, who fancied that they saw in them a dawn of some millennial glory; and were awakened from their dream, like Madame Roland, at the foot of the guillotine, bowing their heads to death and crying, "O Liberty, what things are done in thy name!"

The principal difference between the writers on the "Emancipated Woman" and those of the French illuminati was that the
French prototypes were men and women of elegance, culture, and
education; whereas their American imitators, though not wanting
in a certain vigor and cleverness, were both coarse in expression,
narrow in education, and wholly devoid of common decency in
their manner of putting things. . . . Society assumed the aspect
of a pack of breeding animals, and all its laws and institutions were
to return to the mere animal basis.

We and Our Neighbors is a disappointing sequel to *My
Wife and I,* giving the impression again and again that Harriet
wrote a long book because she did not have time for a short
one. The neighbors are potentially interesting but Harriet
dealt with them, apparently, only when she remembered her
title. Her primary concern was that profound attraction for
the Catholic Church, which she had indicated thirteen years
before in *Agnes of Sorrento.* She now examined the problem
as Episcopalian, and we are probably justified in reading autobiographical significance into Eva Van Arsdel's deserting the
conventional Episcopal Church of her parents for the chapel
of Mr. St. John, a New England Puritan, who became an Anglican through reaction and now inclines toward Rome in his
reading of Francis de Sales, Thomas à Kempis, and other
Catholic writers. Editorializing, Harriet stated that "the most
stringent Protestant" should not fail "to honor that rich and
grand treasury of the experience of devout spirits of which the
Romish Church has been the custodian." Reading Mr. St.
John's "ritualistic books," Eva and Harry are charmed, and
though Eva agrees with Harry, who is still a Congregationalist,
that "they lead right back into the Romish Church," she thinks
the way they offer is "enticingly beautiful." But nothing comes
of all this. Mr. St. John marries Eva's sister, Angelique, thus
removing the possibility that he will become a Catholic priest,
and Eva finds an outlet for religious devotion in the practice
of radical Christianity, symbolized by her sensitive and generous treatment of her cook's daughter, Maggie, who has been
a prostitute and almost reverts into that profession when her

mother and her Uncle Mike, unlike Eva, keep her sin before her eyes.

With *We and Our Neighbors,* Harriet came to a weak conclusion in her fictionalizing of the Gilded Age, but in her three novels she had still managed, not only to make perceptive comments, but to record a significant change in American life, the migration of New Englanders to New York and their increasing involvement in a world hostile to the traditional assumptions and practices of the Puritan village world. She here opened a new literary frontier, blazing the way hurriedly and sometimes crudely for later writers such as Howells, Henry James, and John P. Marquand.

II

In *Poganuc People,* Harriet concluded her career, as she had begun it in "A New England Sketch," with a fictionalizing of Lyman Beecher; and, though she now described her father in his Litchfield ministry rather than in his youthful Yankee cleverness, there is an interesting similarity between these portraits forty-five years apart. In both, she was primarily interested, not in the Puritan clergyman, but in the warm and generous human being. Parson Cushing, as she now called her father, is completely charming. Though he is a docile and tracable husband, he retains "here and there certain wild male instincts," and has been known to upset all Mrs. Cushing's yarn baskets, stocking baskets, and patch baskets, pouring the contents on the floor, in eager preparation for those nutting expeditions with his children when he scales the tallest chestnut trees in the neighborhood. At dinner, while he pursues the deeper mazes of theology, he sometimes becomes so abstracted (so at least Mrs. Cushing likes to suppose) that his soul does not notice that his body is feeding the family dog, Spring, under the table, as he has forbidden his children to do. When Colonel and Mrs. Davenport come to tea and the Colonel confides that George Washington cursed and swore to rally his troops during the Long Island retreat, Parson Cushing, who believes he himself would have sworn under such circumstances, explains: "My

children, to use the name of the great God solemnly and earnest-
ly for a great and noble purpose is not to 'swear.' Swearing is
taking God's holy name in vain, in a trifling way, for a trivial
purpose—a thing which our great and good general never did.
But this story I would rather you would never repeat. It
might not be understood."

In making the central event in *Poganuc People* the crisis
of 1817-1818 when the Democrats defeated the Federalists and
introduced a new constitution separating Church and State, thus
bringing an end to the Connecticut theocracy, Harriet fictionalized the occasion above all others which demonstrated her
father's sincerity and his good sense. As Puritan clergyman,
Lyman quite naturally aligned himself with the standing order
but he was completely free of those worldly concerns for power
and prestige which closed the ranks of Federalist gentlemen.
He opposed religious toleration and the widening of the suffrage
for lofty reasons, believing that once orthodoxy was denied
official support, the plain people, not always wise in their own
interests, would be led astray by irresponsible demagogues.
After the Democratic victory, however, Lyman was quick to
see that his fears had magnified the danger and that in being
thrown more on God and on themselves, the Puritan clergy
were actually strengthened for their tasks:

> When the theocracy had passed away, they spent no time lament-
> ing it. They let the cocked hat, gold-headed cane, gown and bands
> go down-stream; they let all laws protecting their order go by; and
> addressed themselves simply to the work of leading their people,
> as men with men, only by seeking to be stronger, wiser, and better
> men. To know more, to have more faith in the Invisible and
> Eternal, to be able to argue more logically to convince and to per-
> suade—these were now their ambition. Dr. Cushing was foremost
> in this new crusade of earnestness.

Perhaps Harriet was led into this generous tribute by the
feeling that she had not been quite fair to Lyman Beecher in
fictionalizing him as Mr. Avery in Jonathan Rossiter's letter
in *Oldtown Folks*. But I think we are justified in suspecting
deeper reasons and in supposing that here once again, as in all

her best books, we have an attempt to encompass a spiritual and intellectual situation through "symbolic action." In *Oldtown Folks* she had justified her "signing off" to the Episcopal Church by reference to the distortions of ultra-Calvinism, but there still lurked in her mind and heart, I believe, some feeling of uncomfortableness for having broken with the ancestral faith. What she wished was her father's blessing on her new alliance, and being a novelist, she could bestow that blessing by returning in imagination to the 1817-1818 crisis when her father, as a man of good sense and warm humanity, had accepted the principle of religious toleration. Surely, he would not have objected very much if as a child she had run off to a Christmas illumination at the Episcopal Church and later had expressed her enthusiasm for its beautiful ritual. He had always been generous and affectionate; she remembered her "easy conversion" of 1825 and made it a major event of Dolly's childhood.

If poetry is truer than history, there is probably considerable truth in Harriet's reshaping of the facts to fit her heart's desire. Her father's *Autobiography* confirms her picture of a lovable and charming man, who urged his children to think for themselves and to state their own ideas. We catch Lyman's spirit when we read in the *Autobiography* Charles Beecher's statement that at Lane Theological Seminary

. . . the atmosphere of the class-room was the atmosphere of the family. He was father; the students were all sons. He was at home with them, and they with him. Never was a student put down for asking hard questions on ticklish points of theology. The trouble was, he could not get them quite unceremonious enough. He wanted them to come in and grapple with him as his own flesh and blood were wont to do. It cost him no small pains to divest them of their too scrupulous reverence.

But there is still a large element of wishful thinking in *Poganuc People*. Doubtless Lyman encouraged his children to attend Episcopal family prayers on their visits to Grandmother Foote at Nutplains, and he may even have advised their attending the Episcopal Church, but not, it seems certain, without strong reminders that Episcopacy was a danger. It is difficult to believe that he ever went quite so far as Parson Cushing, who tells Dolly about to visit the Kitterys, her cousins whom we have already met in *Oldtown Folks:*

Of course, while with them you will attend the services of the Episcopal Church; for that you have my cordial consent and willingness. The liturgy of the Church is full of devout feelings, and the Thirty-Nine Articles (with some few slight exceptions) are a very excellent statement of truth. In adopting the spirit and language of the prayers in the service you cannot go amiss; very excellent Christians have been nourished and brought up upon them. So have no hesitation about uniting in all Christian exercises with your relatives in Boston.

The subsequent history Harriet imagined for herself is even more obvious wishful thinking. Dolly does not immediately become an Episcopalian but at sixteen or seventeen, following her father's recommendation, she attends the Episcopal Church and reports home: "When the communion service came I went with grandmamma and knelt at the altar. It seemed as if Christ himself was there giving me the bread and the wine. I never felt so near to him. . . . I was so full that I could not speak. No one else seemed to feel as I did—they were all used to it—but it was all new and wonderful to me, and made heavenly things so real that I felt almost averse to coming back to every-day life." In Boston, Dolly falls in love with her Anglican cousin, Alfred Dunbar, who has recently come from England. He is not so intolerant as the Kitterys of Parson Cushing and New England Puritanism nor so enthusiastic about the Episcopal Church as Dolly, but quite clearly, after their marriage, Dolly and Alfred will attend the Episcopal Church and Dolly will be spared that lifetime of strugle with Calvinism, which produced *Uncle Tom's Cabin, The Minister's Wooing, Agnes of Sorrento,* and *Oldtown Folks,* and which Harriet now brought to a beautiful and gentle conclusion in *Poganuc People.*

Her final novel, however, is much more than a consoling dream. As in her previous books, Harriet registered not simply inner concern but her realistic and humorous awareness of New England life and history. By supposing the Episcopal Church was of recent origin at Poganuc Center in 1811 (it had been actually established at Litchfield in 1745), she was able to concentrate history and demonstrate in brief compass the various causes which had made Yankees "sign off" to Anglicanism and thereby strengthen the Democratic hand in its destruction of the theocracy. One of those causes, as she indicated in Dolly's stealing off to the first Christmas illumination, was the excitement created in a nonritualistic community by such simple matters as a star cut out of gilt paper. Inevitably children, young people, and "all that floating populace who might be desirous of seeing or hearing some new things" were interested and some persons were thus drawn into the new church. But they were a minor matter, as were those merchants like the storekeeper Lucius Jenks, who joins the Episcopal Church to get the trade of certain wealthy Episcopalians.

The cause above all others for "signing off" was discontent with the established order. The Episcopal Church was associated with the persecution which had driven the Puritans out of England; it was the Church of that party whose intolerance and tyranny had brought on the Revolution; there was "no religious organization in the world in its genius and history less likely to assimilate with a democratic movement than the Episcopal Church," and Connecticut was by inclination democratic. But Congregationalism—or, as the common people called it, Presbyterianism—was the state church, levying its tax on every householder and demanding by stringent law and custom attendance at two Sunday services. No allowance was made for difference of religious opinion; Sabbath-keeping was enforced with more than Mosaic strictness; for years eligibility for some public offices was restricted to church members; generally speaking, New England justified the sarcasm which said that Puritans had left the Lords Bishops to be under the Lords Brethren. Harriet believed that in the very nature of things such a state of society could not endure, and she recalled that even before the Revolution Ethan Allen in Litchfield had advertised his farm and stock for sale, indicating his determination at any cost to get out of "this old holy state of Connecticut."

Desiring, however, to create a charming and lovable Parson Cushing, Harriet specified only amusing instances of "signing off" at Poganuc Center. For example, there is the case of Uncle Sol Peters, thus described by Hiel Jones, the stage-driver:

"You know he's kind o' crazy to sing, and he hain't got no ear, and no more voice 'n a sawmill, and they wouldn't hev 'im in our singer seats, and so he went off to the 'Piscopals. And he bought an orgin right out and out, and paid for it, and put it in this church so that they'd let him be in the singin'. You know they can make noise enough with an orgin to drown his voice."

The case of Zeph Higgins has even less to do with religion. He is, says Hiel Jones, "nothin' but a mad Presbyterian, like a good many o' the rest on 'em." Zeph's apostasy comes from his disagreement over five and sixpence with Deacon Dickenson, to whom he once traded some potatoes. Zeph had insisted that the Deacon cheated him; the Deacon had insisted that he was in the right. Finally, the matter came up before the church. Mindful of his official position, the Deacon there agreed that he would pay the money if Zeph would take back the statement that he was a cheat, but Zeph would take nothing back, the church suspended him, and over he went to the "Episcopals." Being, as Hiel describes him, "one o' them ropy, stringy fellers, jest like touchwood—once get 'em a-burnin' and they keep on a-burnin' night and day," Zeph has not become one whit more Christian by entering the Episcopal Church. The Deacon and he have an unsettled case before the court (Zeph's lawyer is the Episcopal Squire Lewis) to determine whether Zeph was within his rights in taking up wooden pipes carrying water across his land to the Deacon's house.

The political contest of Democrats and Federalists gives Zeph a chance, of course, to make one more attack in the battle of the five and sixpence by voting against the party of Deacon Dickenson. But Harriet indicated that much more was involved than a trivial quarrel. Like so many New Englanders shaped in the Calvinistic mold, Zeph is a creature born to oppose. Taking a thirteen-acre lot so rocky that a sheep could hardly find a blade of grass, he had dug and blasted, ploughed and planted, and finally raised crop after crop of good rye: "He did it with heat, with zeal, with dogged determination; he did it all the more because neighbors said he was a fool for trying, and that he could never raise anything on that lot. There was a stern joy in this hand-to-hand fight with nature. He got his bread as Samson did his honeycomb out of the carcass of the slain lion." Knowing his natural combativeness, Israel Dennie, Federalist high sheriff of the county, has some illuminating fun when Zeph arrives at the polls:

"Hulloa, Higgins; step this way; here's Mr. Adams to give you your vote. You're going to vote the Democratic ticket, you know."

"No, I ain't, nuther," said Zeph, from the sheer mechanical instinct of contradiction.

"Not going to vote with the Democrats, Higgins? All right, then you're going to vote the Federal ticket; here 't is."

"No, I ain't, nuther. You let me alone. I ain't a-goin' to be dictated to. I'm a-goin' to vote jest as I'm a mind ter. I won't vote for nuther, ef I ain't a mind ter, and I'll vote for jest which one I want ter, and no other."

"So you shall, Higgins,—so you shall," said Squire Dennie sympathetically, laying his hand on Zeph's shoulder.

"I sha'n't, nuther; you let me alone," said Zeph, shaking off the sheriff's hand; and clutching at the Democratic ticket, he pushed up towards the polls.

"There's a fellow, now," said Sheriff Dennie, looking after him with a laugh. "That fellow's so contrary that he hates to do the very thing he wants to, if anybody else wants him to do it. If there was any way of voting that would spite both parties and please nobody, he'd take that. The only way to get that fellow to heaven would be to set out to drive him to hell; then he'd turn and run up the narrow way, full chisel."

Squire Dennie has perfectly caught Zeph's essential character, but Zeph, nevertheless, is of usefulness to Poganuc, where, as in the typical democratic Yankee village, everything is debated and redebated with agonizing slowness in town meeting, as, for example, the moving of the shanty schoolhouse at public expense. Almost everyone favors moving it, but the complicating factor is that Zeph, in talking for the cause, has been so combative that his neighbors, as freeborn Yankees who will not be pushed around, have quite naturally been forced to take the other side. Finally convinced somewhat paradoxically that "It's a sin to keep up these 'ere quarrels among neighbors," Zeph braces himself with an evening reading of Samson's carrying off the gates of Gaza and the next morning, with the help of his sons, moves the schoolhouse to a sensible location. For months everyone discusses the propriety of Zeph's *coup d'état,* but no one proposes moving the schoolhouse back.

Clearly Zeph illustrates the natural combativeness and independence developed in the New England character by Calvinism and the hard conditions of New England life. Men and women of his stamp would sooner or later "sign off" from an oppressive established church. There is no reason to question Harriet's sociological insight at this point. But we are likely to be somewhat confused by the conclusion of Zeph's story. He does not remain an Anglican. After experiencing lonely agony on his wife's death, he finally returns to the Puritan church when Dolly convinces him of Jesus's love.

Once we recognize, however, the primary point in *Poganuc People,* Harriet's attempt to win in imagination her father's approval for her "signing off" to Anglicanism, Zeph's return to Parson Cushing's church assumes its natural place in the book. It was only just that she give her father, symbolized in Parson Cushing, something in return for his freeing her from latent guilt for having left his church. What was more natural than that she should give him back that rebel of rebels, Zeph Higgins, and what touch could be more appropriate than her making herself in Dolly the vehicle for Zeph's return to the fold?

Harriet's symbolic action, her strategy for encompassing the last difficulty in her struggle with the ancestral faith, apparently convinced her if it does not convince us. *Poganuc People* is the gayest as well as the briefest of her New England novels. There are shadows in the picture such as the tragic death of Mrs. Higgins, but primarily Harriet treats us to spots of light: the apple bees, the Fourth of July celebrations, the amusing

Yankee courtship of Hiel Jones and Zeph's daughter, Nabby, the crisp, fresh beauties of nature in Connecticut, the lovable eccentricities of Yankee character, Dolly's affectionate relations with her charming and ultimately tolerant father.

With her last novel, Harriet's career came full circle. She had now again reached that happy reconciliation with her region and its culture which she had known momentarily as a girl a half-century before in her "easy conversion" of 1825. But if *Poganuc People* thus brings the pattern of her career to a neat and charming conclusion, we must also recognize that it sounds the nostalgic note (Harriet's last paragraphs are an elegy of her village world) and that this nostalgic note is prophetic of a similar mood in a whole generation of minor writers who already had begun to express New England in the *Atlantic Monthly* and other magazines. In its final impetus, Harriet's career inclined toward the nostalgic, the minor, the evasive expression of her culture rather than toward the impressive realism of Mary E. Wilkins Freeman's "A New England Nun."

But we read Harriet all wrong, of course, if we take the mood of *Poganuc People* as representative. It is simply the final scene in the symbolic action of her career and that career was clearly not characterized by evasion or nostalgia. Writing in the *New Yorker* of March 14, 1953, Edmund Wilson suggests the true significance of her work. Seeking some parallel for Lincoln's apocalyptic interpretation of the Civil War, Wilson writes that like "most of the important products of the American mind at that time, it grew out of the religious tradition of the New England theology of Puritanism" and he continues: "Of this mental and moral atmosphere you will find a brilliant expression in the novels of Mrs. Stowe."

We may wish to argue with Mr. Wilson as to the degree in which American culture a century ago was an outgrowth of New England Puritanism but the more we know, not only of Lincoln in his apocalyptic phase, but of Emerson, Thoreau, Emily Dickinson, Hawthorne, and Melville, the more we are likely to find justification for his hyperbole and for his assertion concerning the importance of Harriet Beecher Stowe. Obvious-

ly the major writers of our American Renaissance were power-
fully influenced by English, French, and German romanticism,
either directly or indirectly, and profoundly shaped by democratic doctrine.   But when we read the novels of Harriet
Beecher Stowe, particularly her New England novels, we discover again and again in her people habits of thought and feeling and action which remind us of Emerson and Thoreau, Emily
Dickinson, Hawthorne, and Melville.   In some instances, ad-
mittedly, Harriet like her more artful contemporaries was expressing an almost universally diffused romanticism.   But as I
have shown, her books, generally speaking, were products of her
own experience and observation buttressed by family reminiscence and a wide and deep knowledge of New England intellectual history. We are completely safe in accepting Mr. Wilson's
belief that her books are "a brilliant expression" of the mental
and moral atmosphere of her culture.   As such, they serve the
important function of indicating the basically Puritan pattern of
American culture a century ago and of suggesting the interesting
probability that on many occasions our major artists found in
Wordsworth, Coleridge, and Carlyle not so much new insight as
confirmation of assumptions inherited, often unconsciously, from
Jonathan Edwards and even further back from seventeenth-
century Puritanism.

But the final claim for Harriet Beecher Stowe must rest
on her ability to give us a balanced and immediate sense of the
vital and complex Puritan past.   It was here that she made
a permanently significant contribution to American culture, for
it is only as Puritan New England comes to life in our imaginations and our emotions as well as in our understandings that
we can discover how "usable" a past we actually possess. A
study such as I have written is no substitute for *The Minister's
Wooing, The Pearl of Orr's Island, Oldtown Folks, Oldtown
Fireside Stories,* and *Poganuc People.* Harriet Beecher Stowe
gives us something far better than an interpretation; she gives
us at a single remove in the world of imagination a deep and
moving and often beautiful experience.   Reading her novels
we are likely to discover that we have surprising sympathies

with the intellectuality, the moral boldness, the intense soul-searching, the warm and vital humor and humanity of New England Puritanism. We are likely to discover a new source of refreshment in a return to our intellectual and spiritual roots in the New England village.

NOTES

Since the reader will be able to locate quotations from the novels and stories easily from my discussion, I have not identified them by volume and page in the standard edition, *The Writings of Harriet Beecher Stowe,* 16 volumes (Cambridge, Mass., 1896). I have, however, identified all passages from HBS not collected in this edition. I have used the following shortened titles for primary sources:

The Autobiography—The Autobiography, Correspondence, Etc., of Lyman Beecher, D.D., 2 volumes (New York, 1864).

Stowe, *Life—Life of Harriet Beecher Stowe, Compiled from Her Letters and Journals,* by her son, Charles Edward Stowe (Boston and New York, 1890).

Fields, *Life—Life and Letters of Harriet Beecher Stowe,* ed. Annie Fields (Boston and New York, 1897).

Wilson—Crusader in Crinoline: The Life of Harriet Beecher Stowe, by Forrest Wilson (Philadelphia, London, and New York, 1941).

Preface

P. viii.　　James Baldwin, "Everybody's Protest Novel," *Partisan Review,* XVI, 578-585 (June, 1949).
Increasing recognition of HBS's depiction of Puritan New England: Among the studies calling attention to her as fictionalizer of her native region are the following:
Edmund Wilson, *New Yorker,* March 14, 1954, p. 110, particularly. I quote from Mr. Wilson's review on p. 241.
Van Wyck Brooks, *The Flowering of New England 1815-1865* (New York, 1936), p. 420. "Her mind had the swing and rhythm of the great story-tellers, like

Dickens, Cooper, Scott and Victor Hugo, and she showed in her later novels, *The Pearl of Orr's Island* and *The Minister's Wooing,* how little she needed a moral thesis to bring all her gifts into play."

Van Wyck Brooks, *New England Indian Summer 1865-1915* (New York, 1940), pp. 82-83. "At this very moment, in *Old Town Folks* [*sic*] and *The Minister's Wooing,* she was recalling the poetry of a bygone era, the fears and sorrows of heart of the Puritans whom she had known as a child for the perfect church and state they had hoped to establish. In these books, as nowhere else, one found the roots of the Yankee mind, in the Hebraistic air of an earlier epoch, when all were of one blood and race and the sentiments of justice and moral indignation, in view of cruelty and crime, were uncomplicated as yet by mundane interest. In *Old Town Folks,* especially, the spirit of her grand progenitors rose in Mrs. Stowe's mind at moments, and she was often inspired and often happy. . . ."

George F. Whicher, in *Literary History of the United States,* by Robert Spiller, Willard Thorp, Thomas H. Johnson, Henry Seidel Canby, and others (New York, 1948), I, 584-585: *"The Minister's Wooing* with its plot based on a succession of fine-spun renunciations is not a great novel, but it is a masterly revelation of the springs of Puritan character. The light it throws on the inner life of an intensely native New England poet like Emily Dickinson can never be too insistently brought to the attention of readers who have not cultivated a historical imagination. . . . The . . . leisurely exposition of New England ways in *Oldtown Folks* (1869) crowned her work as the interpreter of a peculiar people whose institutions and habits of thought had for nearly two centuries suffered little by its abrasion from the rest of the world. The descriptive chapters in this novel and its varied gallery of village characters place Mrs. Stowe at the head of the school of New England realists."

Perry Miller, editor of *Images or Shadows of Divine Things,* by Jonathan Edwards (New Haven, 1948), p. 144, in reference to the passage from *Oldtown Folks* quoted on pp. 189-190 of this study: "Harriet Beecher Stowe, brought up in the Edwardsean tradition, understood many of its implications better than the theologians who endeavored to follow him, and could evaluate his achievement in terms that are fundamental for understanding American culture."

V. L. Parrington, *The Romantic Revolution in America*, Vol. II of *Main Currents in American Thought* (New York, 1927 and 1930), pp. 371-378. One of the best statements.

F. O. Matthiessen, *American Writers on American Literature*, ed. by John Macy (New York, 1931). Matthiessen observes, p. 410, in discussing New England stories that *Uncle Tom's Cabin* has made us forget that HBS was "one of the first to make articulate her reasons for writing about New England."

A. H. Quinn, *American Fiction: An Historical and Critical Survey* (New York and London, 1936), pp. 159-163. "Mrs. Stowe's place in our fiction will probably be determined by a book, *Uncle Tom's Cabin,* which is far from her best work." Mr. Quinn finds her best work in *The Minister's Wooing* and *Oldtown Folks.* He also suggests, p. 160, that a passage in *The Minister's Wooing,* the third paragraph of chap. xxi, may be the original of Emily Dickinson's poem "The bustle in a house."

Walter Blair, *Native American Humor (1800-1900)* (New York, Cincinnati, and Chicago, etc., 1937). Mr. Blair notes HBS's early place in the local color movement with "A New England Sketch." On p. 126 he writes: "But her art reached its greatest heights, when, after years of occasional writing about New England, she produced *Oldtown Folks* and *Sam Lawson's Fireside Stories.*" On pp. 482-502 he anthologizes her "Captain Kidd's Money," from *Oldtown Fireside Stories.* Later in *The Literature of the United States,* ed. Walter Blair, Theodore Hornberger, and Randall Stewart (Chicago, Atlanta, Dallas, 1947), II, 381, Mr. Blair in introducing this same story writes of *Oldtown Fireside Stories* that "in addition to being authentic, the yarns are charming and comic—the mature creations of a great author."

Catherine Gilbertson, *Harriet Beecher Stowe* (New York and London, 1937).

Margaret Farrand Thorp, in *American Issues, Volume Two—The Literary Record,* ed. Willard Thorp, Merle

Curti, and Carlos Baker (Chicago, Philadelphia, and New York, 1941), pp. 547-548. "The heavy weight of the fame of *Uncle Tom's Cabin* has almost obliterated Harriet Beecher Stowe's real importance as a novelist of New England. Even her literary contemporaries spoke of the book as the high-water mark to which her genius—George Sand said that she had genius but not talent—never rose again. To the modern reader the best character in *Uncle Tom's Cabin* is a minor one, the New England spinster, Miss Ophelia, aunt to St. Clare. . . . *Oldtown Folks* (1869), [is] the best of her books. . . ."

Kenneth R. Andrews, *Nook Farm: Mark Twain's Hartford Circle* (Cambridge, 1950), p. 200: "Just as *The Minister's Wooing* is chiefly the history of a phase of Calvinism, *The Pearl of Orr's Island* is a study of character. Late in the sixties, Harriet brought her experience in both subjects to the composition of *Oldtown Folks,* the masterpiece of her long career."

Perry D. Westbrook, *Acres of Flint: Writers of Rural New England* (Washington, 1951). I quote Mr. Westbrook on p. 150 of this study.

Ruth Suckow, "An Almost Lost American Classic," *College English,* March, 1953. This extremely fine study of *Oldtown Folks* appeared after I had written my own chapter on the novel. I regard Miss Suckow's essay as an important supplement to my discussion.

P. x.   *F. O. Matthiessen: American Renaissance: Art and Expression in the Age of Emerson and Whitman* (London, Toronto and New York, 1941), p. 229.

P. xi.   *Mark Twain on the native novelist:* "What Paul Bourget Thinks of Us," *The Writings of Mark Twain,* Hillcrest Edition (Hartford, 1903), XXII, 145-146.

EPIGRAPH

Benjamin Colman: Quoted in *The Puritans,* ed. Perry Miller and Thomas H. Johnson (New York, Cincinnati, etc., 1938), p. 392.

Jonathan Edwards: Images or Shadows of Divine Things, ed. Perry Miller, p. 109.

CHAPTER I
NEW ENGLAND DOUBLENESS

P. 3.   *Harriet's Litchfield Academy Composition:* This remarkable essay is printed in Stowe, *Life,* pp. 15-21.

In one of the chapters of reminiscence she contributed to her father's autobiography (I, 536), HBS made it clear that this essay was not self-assigned, neither an original question nor an original answer: "The subject assigned me was one that had been very fully discussed in the school in a manner to show to the utmost Mr. Brace's peculiar power of awakening the minds of his pupils to the higher regions of thought. The question was, 'Can the immortality of the soul be proved by the light of nature?'

"Several of the young ladies had written strongly in the affirmative. Mr. Brace himself had written in the negative. To all these compositions and the consequent discussions I had listened, and, in view of them, chose the negative."

HBS's abiding admiration for John Pierce Brace is evident from *Oldtown Folks* (1869), where she re-created him as Mr. Jonathan Rossiter.

HBS's first story: "A New England Sketch" was reprinted as "Uncle Tim" in *The Mayflower,* as "Uncle Lot" in the second issue of *The Mayflower* in 1855, and finally as "Uncle Tim" again in *The Writings of Harriet Beecher Stowe.* Lyman Beecher was apparently undisturbed by HBS's fictionalizing. In *The Autobiography,* I, 24, he wrote: "Uncle Lot Benton was a substantial farmer, an upright, tall, bright, dark-eyed man of pleasant countenance. Uncle Lot Griswold, in the 'Mayflower,' is a pretty good picture of him. He had strong feelings, hid under a don't-care look, yet spilling over at the corner of his eye." Why HBS should have made her many changes of name is a mystery.

P. 4.   To give the complete flavor of the original (there are slight differences between the first edition and *The Writings*) I have drawn my quotations from the early stories, except in writing "Uncle Lot" as in the *Western Monthly* version, from *The Mayflower; Or, Sketches of Scenes and Characters Among the Descendants of the Pilgrims* (New York, 1844).

P. 7.   *HBS to Georgianna May in 1832:* Stowe, *Life,* p. 50.

Pp. 7-8.   *HBS to Georgianna May in 1833:* Stowe, *Life,* p. 67.

P. 8.   *LB's "running-down": The Autobiography,* II, 117-118.

P. 9.   *Calvin Stowe's childhood adventures:* Stowe, *Life,* pp. 422-438.

              Passage suggesting "Love versus Law": Stowe, *Life,* p. 440.

P. 10.   *Hawthorne's journal: The American Notebooks,* by Nathaniel Hawthorne, ed. Randall Stewart (New Haven, 1932), pp. 30-71.

              Robert Frost's formula: Introduction to *King Jasper,* by Edwin Arlington Robinson (New York, 1935), p. xiii.

P. 11.   *"Mirth is the mail of anguish":* Last stanza of "A wounded deer leaps highest," *The Poems of Emily Dickinson,* ed. Martha Dickinson Bianchi and Alfred Leete Hampson (Boston, 1931), p. 6 (cited hereinafter as *The Poems of Emily Dickinson*). In quoting this particular poem, I have, however, accepted the reading "cautious" rather than "caution" and the punctuation found in *Poems by Emily Dickinson,* ed. Mabel Loomis Todd and T. W. Higginson (Boston, 1906), p. 20. It seems probable to me that Mrs. Todd's transcription is more accurate than that of Mme Bianchi.

CHAPTER II
"THAT TRIUMPHANT WORK"

P. 12.   *Henry James on Uncle Tom's Cabin: A Small Boy and Others* (New York, 1913), pp. 158-160.

P. 13.   *Lucy Poate Stebbins and Richard Poate Stebbins: The Trollopes: The Chronicle of a Writing Family* (New York, 1945), p. 79.

              Herbert Brown on similarities of Uncle Tom's Cabin to popular sentimental novels: The Sentimental Novel in American 1789-1860 (Durham, N. C., 1940), pp. 268, 276, 301, 304-307.

P. 14.   *Jonathan Edwards on Richardson:* see Brown, *The Sentimental Novel,* p. 29, and also Perry Miller, *Jonathan Edwards* (New York, 1949), p. 137: "The story of Abigail carries us forward to Edgar Poe's Annie, but Phoebe anticipates the stereotype of little Eva, except that Phoebe did not die and Edwards did not write her up as a stereotype."

P. 15.   *HBS on Defoe: Sunny Memories of Foreign Lands* (Boston, 1854), II, 30.

   HBS's discovery of Don Quixote: The Autobiography, I, 526.

Pp. 15-16.   *HBS's reading of Scott: The Autobiography,* I, 525-526, tells of the contest and her reading of *Ivanhoe*. For her reading of Scott in 1850, see Fields, *Life,* p. 128.

Pp. 16-17.   *Daniel Drake on the West:* Harriet Martineau, *Retrospect of Western Travel* (London and New York, 1838), II, 42, 43.

P. 17.   *Miss Martineau on the diversity of East and West at Cincinnati parties in the 1830's: Retrospect of Western Travel,* II, 49.

P. 18.   *Harriet's use of Weld, Lewis, and Douglass* is clear from chap. iv in *A Key to Uncle Tom's Cabin* (Boston, 1853), pp. 13-21.

P. 19.   *Harriet's forgetfulness:* Fields, *Life,* p. 256. See also *Wilson* for her great carelessness in money matters. The works show again and again her surprising retentiveness. I am responsible for this inner dialogue. As will be noted, it is based substantially on sources.

Pp. 19-20.   *HBS's visions:* Fields, *Life,* p. 163: ". . . it all came before me in visions, one after another, and I put them down in words."

P. 20.   *The meeting with Henson in Boston: Wilson,* p. 249.
   The writing at Andover of the chapter dealing with Uncle Tom's death: Fields, *Life,* pp. 163-164.
   HBS to Mrs. Howard: Fields, *Life,* p. 163.

P. 21.   "The Author's Introduction" is reprinted in the *Writings,* Vol. 1.

   Mrs. Howard's reminding Harriet of her discrepancy: Fields, *Life,* p. 165.

   Annie Fields's clarification: Fields, *Life,* p. 165.

P. 22.   *Cincinnati in the 1830's and 1840's: Wilson,* pp. 210-234.

   End of the Semi-Colon Club: Wilson, p. 197.

P. 23.   *HBS's easy conversion of 1825:* Stowe, *Life,* pp. 33-34.
   The examination by the Hartford pastor: Stowe, *Life,* p. 36.
   HBS's wishing she could die young: Stowe, *Life,* p. 37.

HBS at the center of the Calvinistic web: Stowe, *Life,* p. 47.

Pp. 23-24. *Charles's fatalism from reading Edwards: The Auto-biography,* II, 461.

P. 24. *HBS's reaction to the death of George: The Auto-biography,* II, 494.

The letter to Thomas, the basic document in under-standing HBS, is printed in *The Autobiography,* II, 487-498.

Pp. 24-25. *HBS's failing health but abiding faith:* Stowe, *Life,* pp. 111-112.

P. 25. *Brattleboro:* Stowe, *Life,* pp. 113-114.

HBS's strange state: Fields, *Life,* p. 115. HBS wrote the information in a letter to Georgianna May.

Fires of soft coal: Wilson, p. 227.

One hundred and twenty burials: HBS to Calvin Stowe, Stowe, *Life,* p. 121.

P. 26. *HBS during the cholera epidemic:* HBS's diary writ-ten for her husband, Stowe, *Life,* pp. 120-124.

Pp. 26-27. *Mrs. Edwards' response to her husband's death:* Letter to Mrs. Burr in Sereno Edwards Dwight, *The Life of President Edwards* (New York, 1830), p. 580. Harriet was undoubtedly familiar with this book; it was here that she found the youthful Edwards' description of his future wife which she incorporated in *The Minister's Wooing.*

P. 27. *HBS to Mrs. Follen:* Stowe, *Life,* pp. 198-199.

P. 28. *Edward Beecher's discussion of the Fugitive Slave Law:* Stowe, *Life,* p. 144.

Mrs. Beecher's suggestion: Stowe, *Life,* p. 145.

P. 31. *Henson's relation with his master:* "Truth is Stranger than Fiction," *An Autobiography of the Rev. Josiah Henson (Mrs. Harriet Beecher Stowe's "Uncle Tom"), from 1789 to 1879,* with a preface by Mrs. Harriet Beecher Stowe (Boston, 1879), p. 41. This is an ex-pansion of the volume of 1858.

P. 33. *Douglass as George Harris:* The account Douglass wrote of life under slavery in *Narrative of the Life of Frederick Douglass: An American Slave* (1845) he expanded in *My Bondage and My Freedom* (New York and Auburn, 1855). Unlike Henson, Douglass did not try to capitalize on *Uncle Tom's Cabin*. He made in his volume of 1855 only one brief reference, p. 183, to *UTC*.

P. 39.   *HBS's description of her mother:* The *Autobiography*, I, 307.

P. 41.   *Hepzibah Pyncheon: The Complete Works of Nathaniel Hawthorne,* Old Manse Edition (Boston and New York, 1900), VII, 351-352. Hereinafter, Hawthorne, *Writings.*

P. 45.   *Marie: A Key to Uncle Tom's Cabin,* p. 33.

P. 48.   *Charles Kingsley:* Letter reprinted in "The Author's Introduction," HBS, *Writings,* I, lxxi.

P. 49.   *Edmund Wilson:* Wilson's review of the Modern Library *UTC* in the *New Yorker,* Nov. 27, 1948, pp. 126-133.

P. 50.   *Brownson's essay "The Laboring Classes":* Reprinted in Perry Miller's *The Transcendentalists* (Cambridge, Mass., 1950), pp. 437-446. Hereinafter, Miller, *The Transcendentalists.*

P. 53.   *The Western Messenger:* Information drawn from Frank Luther Mott, *A History of American Magazines* (New York and London, 1930), pp. 658-663.

Pp. 54-55. *True Socialism: A Key to Uncle Tom's Cabin,* p. 33.

P. 55.   *HBS's persisting belief in a proletarian revolution: Men of Our Times* (Hartford, 1868), pp. 12-13.

Pp. 57-58. *Fredrika Bremer: The Homes of the New World: Impressions of America,* trans. Mary Howitt (New York, 1853), II, 108-109. My colleague Professor Grace Hunter called this passage to my attention; I am responsible, however, for matching it with HBS's letter and for making deductions. HBS reprinted the letter from Fredrika Bremer in "The Author's Introduction" of 1878, HBS, *Writings,* I, lxxiv-lxxv.

P. 59.   *Abraham Lincoln's description of HBS: Wilson,* p. 484. HBS spent a "brief hour" with Lincoln in Nov., 1862.

P. 62.   *Edmund Wilson on "UTC" and "Dead Souls":* In his *New Yorker* review.

CHAPTER III

TRANSITION

Pp. 64-65. *Letters from Maine:* Reprinted in *Uncle Sam's Eman-*
           cipation; Earthly Care, A Heavenly Discipline; and
           Other Sketches (Philadelphia, 1853). I quote from
           pp. 95, 97, 103, 99, 98-99 in that order.

P. 65.   *Need of another trip to Orr's Island and planning of a*
           letter on Hawthorne: Stowe, *Life,* p. 187.

           HBS's joy: Stowe, *Life,* p. 186.

           HBS's conviction she is God's betrothed; the read-
           ing of Chaucer: Fields, *Life,* p. 169.

P. 66.   *The "New York Journal of Commerce" and the black*
           and bloody ear: Wilson, pp. 297, 298.

           Invitation to visit the British Isles: Wilson, p. 328.

           Letter from British Women: Wilson, p. 341.

P. 67.   *Comment on the altar of Aberdeen Cathedral: Sunny*
           Memories of Foreign Lands, I, 103.

           Ruins left by Cromwell: Sunny Memories, I, 243-244.

           Allan Ramsay: Sunny Memories, I, 189-190.

P. 68.   *Calvinism and civil liberty: Sunny Memories,* II, 409.

           The Puritan Sabbath: Sunny Memories, II, 411-413.

           The Calvinistic facts of nature: Sunny Memories, II,
           277.

P. 69.   *Emerson in The Conduct of Life:* Emerson, *Writings,*
           VI, 35.

           Crushing out of the beautiful in New England: Sunny
           Memories, II, 392.

P. 70.   *HBS's part in "The Autobiography":* The Autobiogra-
           phy, II, 544.

P. 79.   *D. H. Lawrence: Studies in Classic American Litera-*
           ture (1924) in Wilson, *The Shock of Recognition*
           (Garden City, 1943), pp. 908 and 909.

P. 81.   *Roger Williams: Experiments of Spiritual Life &*
           Health, ed. Winthrop S. Hudson (Philadelphia, 1951),
           p. 41.

CHAPTER IV

"THE BRUISED FLAX-FLOWER"

Pp. 86-87. *The letter to James Fields:* Fields, *Life,* p. 315. HBS
           referred to *Oldtown Folks.*

Pp. 87-88. *Elizabeth West:* In William B. Sprague's *Annals of The American Pulpit* (New York, 1856), which HBS reviewed for the *Atlantic Monthly,* Feb., 1858, the biographer of Samuel Hopkins made this comment on Elizabeth West: "She was a lady of remarkable endowments, was a thoroughly read theologian, and not only understood well her husband's system, but was scarcely less capable than himself of defending it." In the 1866 edition of the *Annals,* this comment may be found in I, 432.

P. 88. *Hopkins' youthful love affair described by Patten:* William Patten, *Reminiscences of the Late Rev. Samuel Hopkins, D.D. of Newport, R. I. Illustrative of His Character and Doctrines, with Incidental Subjects. From an intimacy with him of Twenty-one years, while Pastor of a Sister Church in Said Town* (Boston and New York, 1843), pp. 31-32.

Pp. 88-89. *Park's quotation from Patten:* Edwards A. Park, *Memoir of the Life and Character of Samuel Hopkins, D.D.* (Boston, 1854), p. 55.

Stiles' signing of antislavery documents: Memoir . . . of Samuel Hopkins, pp. 132 and 136.

P. 89. *Park's knowledge of Catharine Beecher and Fisher:* Edwards A. Park, *Memoir of Nathanael Emmons; With Sketches of His Friends and Pupils* (Boston, 1861), "Professor Alexander Metcalf Fisher," pp. 234-236. The epitaph is identified as the work of Catharine in Lyman Beecher Stowe, *Saints, Sinners and Beechers,* p. 95.

The letter from Professor Pond: Park, *Memoir of Emmons,* p. 234.

P. 90. *Emily Dickinson on Park:* Mabel Loomis Todd, ed., *Letters of Emily Dickinson* (New York and London, 1931), p. 99.

Park's summary of HBS's letter concerning "The Minister's Wooing": Florine Thayer McCray, *The Life-Work of the Author of Uncle Tom's Cabin* (New York and London, 1889), pp. 281-282. HBS's letter to Park is not to be found in any of the important collections of her correspondence.

Pp. 90-91. *Kenneth Burke:* Robert Wooster Stallman, ed., *Critiques and Essays in Criticism 1920-1948* (New York, 1949), p. 249.

P. 91. *Henry's reburial and Harriet's vigil:* Stowe, *Life,* p. 324.

P. 92. *Park as last outstanding example of New England theology: Dictionary of American Biography,* ed. Allan Johnson and Dumas Malone (New York, 1928-1936), XVI, 205.

Park's insistence that the Council describe the Congregational Church as Calvinist: Debates and Proceedings of the National Council of Congregational Churches, Held at Boston, Mass., June 14-24, 1865. From the "phonographic" report by J. M. W. Yerrington and Henry M. Parkhurst (Boston, 1866), p. 357.

HBS as gardener: Letter to her daughters, Fields, *Life,* p. 324.

P. 93. *Henry to his mother on not being a Christian:* quoted by HBS in a letter to the Duchess of Sutherland, Stowe, *Life,* p. 317.

P. 93. *HBS and the slave woman:* Stowe, *Life,* p. 318.

Pp. 93-94. *John Calvin on infant damnation:* John Calvin, *Institutes of the Christian Religion* (Philadelphia, 1928), trans. John Allen, II, 516. Lyman Beecher was apparently thinking of this passage in the *Institutes* in his reference to Calvin in the *Autobiography,* II, 143. Lyman also believed that Jonathan Edwards stood in substantial agreement with Calvin on the doctrine of infant damnation, as may be seen from the *Autobiography,* II, 25-26. Some support for Lyman's conviction would seem to be furnished by Edwards' statement in *An Humble Inquiry . . . Concerning the Qualifications Requisite to a Complete Standing and Full Communion in the Visible Christian Church.* There, in *The Works of President Edwards* (Worcester, 1808-1809), ed. Samuel Austin, I, 155, we may read: "The revelation of God's word is much plainer and more express concerning adult persons, that act for themselves in religious matters, than concerning infants. The scriptures were written for the sake of adult persons, or those that are capable of knowing what is written: It is to such the apostles speak in their epistles, and to such only does God speak throughout his word: And the scriptures especially speak for the sake of those, and about those to whom they speak. And therefore if the word of God affords us light enough concerning those spoken of in the question, as I have stated it, clearly to determine the matter with respect to them, we need not wait until we see all doubts and controversies about baptized infants cleared and settled, before we pass a judgment with respect to the point in hand. The denominations, characters, and descriptions, which we find given in Scripture to visible Christians, and to the visible church, are principally with an eye to the church of Christ in its adult state and proper standing."

Pp. 94-95. *Catharine's history after Fisher's death: The Auto-biography,* I, 478-519. By the time he dictated his *Autobiography,* Lyman was inclined to be critical of Emmons. He described him, p. 503, thus: "He came out high, dry, and stiff that God was the author of sin."

P. 95. *Catharine's reluctance to credit HBS's conversion:* Stowe, *Life,* p. 35.

Pp. 95-96. *Catharine's orthodoxy in* 1836: Catharine E. Beecher, *Letters on the Difficulties of Religion* (Hartford, 1836), pp. 170, 324. Lyman Beecher Stowe misunderstood his famous grandaunt in *Saints, Sinners and Beechers,* pp. 96-97.

P. 96. *Catharine's radicalism in 1857:* Catharine E. Beecher, *Common Sense Applied to Religion, or, The Bible and the People* (New York, 1857), pp. xxv, 307.

Edward Beecher's use of Origen in saving some vestige of the Augustinian position: EB's attempt in *The Conflict of Ages* was to find some ground on which he could maintain the Augustinian doctrine of total depravity, modified by Jonathan Edwards, while defending God from the charge of injustice and cruelty in bestowing a fallen nature on new-created beings. This he believed he accomplished through the doctrine of pre-existence of souls. EB's doctrine was a complete reversal of Wordsworth's famous lines in the *Intimations Ode,* ". . . trailing clouds of glory do we come/ From God, who is our home." To EB's way of thinking we come trailing clouds of evil from a prior state of existence where we fell through voluntary choice.

This doctrine he apparently borrowed (though he did not acknowledge it in *The Conflict of Ages*) from Origen, whose view in the matter has been summarized by W. R. Inge, *Encyclopedia of Religion and Ethics*, ed. John Hastings (New York, 1913), p. 317: "The original creation, Origen teaches, was of innocent spirits, who shared 'accidentally' or precariously the perfection which God possesses 'essentially.' Their fall from perfection was voluntary. Some (the angels and stars, to which Origen attributed souls) remained in their first estate; others (sinful men and evil spirits) fell in various degrees, and can be restored only though the discipline of suffering. This world is constructed as the appropriate scene of their training, affording scope for the treatment proper to every degree of guilt. The fall of souls was thus antenatal, but Origen teaches no metempsychosis."

Lyman Beecher Stowe in *Saints, Sinners and Beechers*, p. 149, writes of *The Conflict of Ages*: "In this book by the demolition of the doctrines of 'original sin' and 'total depravity,' he did more than any one had previously done to abolish the belief in a literal Hell and to defend God's reputation." This obviously is a gross misinterpretation. EB's book was an ingenious attempt to defend the doctrine of "original sin," which he believed anyone must acknowledge from his own consciousness and his experience of the world, and to defend God's ways to man.

P. 97. *HBS's letter to Catharine on the attack of the Devil:* Stowe, *Life*, pp. 321-323.

P. 99. *Mrs. Sarah Osborne:* Samuel Hopkins, *Memoirs of the Life of Mrs. Sarah Osborne, Who Died at Newport, (Rhode Island), on the Second Day of August, 1796. In the Eighty-Third Year of Her Age* (2d ed.; Catskill, 1814), pp. 68-69.

HBS's golden hours of calm: Stowe, *Life*, p. 326.

P. 102. *HBS's letter to Lady Byron:* Stowe, *Life*, pp. 339-340.

Pp. 102-103. *HBS's letter to Georgianna May:* Stowe, *Life*, pp. 340-341.

P. 103. I owe the insight concerning Freud to Lionel Trilling's chapter, "Freud and Literature," in *The Liberal Imagination* (New York, 1950).

P. 104.   *Constance Rourke:* Constance Rourke, *Trumpets of Jubilee* (New York, 1927), p. 120.

            Lyman Beecher Stowe: Lyman Beecher Stowe, *Saints, Sinners and Beechers,* p. 202.

P. 105.   *Lionel Trilling's criticism of Parrington:* Trilling, *The Liberal Imagination,* p. 9.

P. 108.   *Edwards:* Clarence H. Faust and Thomas H. Johnson, *Jonathan Edwards: Representative Selections, with Introduction, Bibliography, and Notes* (New York, etc., 1935), p. 223. Hereinafter *Representative Selections.*

P. 109.   *The arguments of Dr. Mayhew:* The New England preacher and theologian Dr. Jonathan Mayhew (1720-1766) attempted to iron out the difficulties of Calvinism, but in some instances at least, he created new wrinkles. On the one hand, he argued that the Gospel promises salvation to all sinners who strive; on the other hand, he argued that the mere striving of the sinner is no guarantee that he will be saved. See Joseph Haroutunian, *Piety versus Moralism: The Passing of the New England Theology* (New York, 1932), pp. 46-50.

P. 115.   *HBS's use of her mother's letter:* My discovery of this fact started me on the revaluation of *The Minister's Wooing* in my article, "The Genesis of Harriet Beecher Stowe's *The Minister's Wooing,*" *New England Quarterly,* XXI (Dec., 1948), 493-517.

P. 118.   *Ward concerning Emily Dickinson: Letters of Emily Dickinson,* p. xxii.

P. 118.   *Emily Dickinson on "Ourself, behind ourself concealed":* Stanza four of "One need not be a chamber to be haunted." *The Poems of Emily Dickinson,* p. 188.

Pp. 118-119.   *Emerson:* Emerson, *Works,* IX, 92, and *Works,* II, 126-127.

P. 121.   The incident from Park's *"Memoir": Memoir of the Life and Character of Samuel Hopkins, D.D.,* by Edwards A. Park, p. 118.

Pp. 123 ff.   *New England Platonic love:* George F. Whicher in *This Was a Poet: A Critical Biography of Emily Dickinson,* (New York and London, 1938) made the important point that Emily sought "tutors" in her male friends.

I am indebted also to the very perceptive comment by Theodora Van Wagenen Ward in *Emily Dickinson's Letters to Dr. and Mrs. Josiah Gilbert Holland* (Cambridge, Mass., 1951), pp. 161-162.

CHAPTER V
"FICTITIOUS SHORES"

P. 129. *Emily Dickinson's poem: The Poems of Emily Dickinson,* p. 35.

Pp. 129-130. *HBS to Calvin:* Stowe, *Life,* p. 351.

P. 130. *The Florentine guitar:* Stowe, *Life,* p. 352.

Oliver Wendell Holmes on spiritualism and Calvinism: Fields, *Life,* p. 370.

HBS's outreachings after Henry: Stowe, *Life,* p. 350.

P. 131. *The continuing anguish:* Fields, *Life,* p. 281.

Holmes on the prenatal poisoning of Elsie Venner: The Works of Oliver Wendell Holmes, Standard Library Edition (Boston and New York, 1892), V, ix-x. Hereinafter, Holmes, *Works.*

P. 132. *Moral insanity:* Holmes, *Works,* V, 227.

HBS on "Elsie Venner": Stowe, *Life,* p. 362.

Abiel Holmes and Lyman Beecher: For details of this relation and its tragic consequence in causing Holmes to lose his pulpit, see Eleanor M. Tilton, *Amiable Autocrat: A Biography of Dr. Oliver Wendell Holmes* (New York, 1947), pp. 44-49.

Pp. 132-133. *Jonathan Edwards on Original Sin: Representative Selections,* pp. 324, 326.

Pp. 133. *All was the fault of "inherited congenital tendencies":* Holmes's essay on Jonathan Edwards, 1880, the final statement of his argument against Calvinism. This essay is reprinted in *Major American Writers,* ed. Howard Mumford Jones, Ernest E. Leisy, and Richard M. Ludwig (New York, 1951), Vol. I; I quote from p. 865.

Edwards confronted by a similar doctrine: Representative Selections, p. lxi.

P. 134. *HBS's approval of "Elsie Venner" in 1878:* Stowe, *Life,* p. 415.

P. 135. *The origin of Agnes as "a spontaneous tribute":* Fields, *Life,* p. 283.

Hilda's visit to St. Peter's: Hawthorne, *Writings,* X, 198.

Pp. 135-136. *Hilda's confession:* Hawthorne, *Writings,* X, 207-208.
"Eager Propagandists": Hawthorne, *Writings,* X, 289.

P. 136. *The letter from Father James O'Donnell:* Printed in the *Andover Advertizer,* Sept. 9, 1870.

Pp. 136-137. *Orestes Brownson on Unitarianism:* Miller, *The Transcendentalists,* p. 46.

P. 137. *George Eliot's plan for writing a historical romance: Letters and Journals of George Eliot,* ed. J. W. Cross (New York, 1885), II, 197.

P. 138. *Robert Frost on the revolt "sideways into Catholicism": Memoirs of the Notorious Stephen Burroughs of New Hampshire,* with a preface by Robert Frost (New York, 1924), pp. vi-vii. "In his [Burroughs'] lifetime, he made the only two revolts from Puritanism anyone has yet thought of, one backwards into Paganism and the other, let us say, sideways into the Catholic Church." Stephen Burroughs flourished in late eighteenth-century Massachusetts. One of his most interesting complaints was that they call this a free country and put a man in jail for making, that is counterfeiting, his own money. A completely charming account of Burroughs is George F. Whicher's "A Pelham Rogue" in *Mornings at 8:50* (Northampton, 1950), pp. 131-136. *Mornings at 8:50* is a series of witty and delightfully perceptive portraits of Connecticut Valley personalities, presented as chapel talks at Amherst College.

HBS to Fields that "Agnes" "must be written": Wilson, p. 464.

Pp. 143-144. *Edwards on the rotten covering of hell: Representative Selections,* p. 159.

CHAPTER VI

A NEW ENGLAND IDYL

P. 145. *Whittier's description of "The Pearl":* Stowe, *Life,* p. 327.

Pp. 145-146. *Sarah Orne Jewett's description of "The Pearl": Letters of Sarah Orne Jewett,* ed. Annie Fields (Boston and New York, 1911), pp. 46-47.

P. 149.   *Miss Roxy's story about Mrs. Titcomb:* HBS may
have remembered an incident in Cotton Mather's
Magnalia Christi Americana (1702), which she had
known since childhood. In II, 407, of the edition of
the *Magnalia* published at Hartford in 1820, we may
read of the wife of Mr. J. C., deacon at Charlestown,
who on her death, Aug. 31, 1684, asked who would
go with her, and at length said, "My son Robert will
go." At the time her son was in Barbadoes, but as
Mather noted, ". . . his friends here have since learn'd
that he also dy'd there, and this at the very *hour* when
his mother here gave up the ghost; and (which is
further odd) not *without* the like expressions concerning his mother, that his mother had concerning him."
President Appleton rather than President Averill:
Roxy was doubtless thinking of the Reverend Jesse
Appleton, who became President of Bowdoin College
in 1807. No Averill was ever president of this college.

P. 150.   *Perry D. Westbrook: Acres of Flint,* p. 23.

P. 154.   *Jonathan Edwards on all visions and dreams as natural
occurrences: Religious Affections,* pp. 242-249, in Edwards, *Representative Selections.*

P. 156.   *Alcott's comment on Thoreau's "A Week on the Concord and Merrimack Rivers": The Journals of Amos
Bronson Alcott,* ed. Odell Shepard (Boston, 1938),
pp. 213-214.

HBS on writing "The Pearl" with a shiver: Fields,
Life, p. 285.

P. 157.   *Tilton's announcement of "The Pearl" as* "MRS.
STOWE'S GREAT STORY": *Wilson,* p. 476.

P. 158.   *HBS's notice concerning "The Pearl" in the "Independent":* Fields, *Life,* p. 287.

*Sarah Orne Jewett's comment on the second part of
"The Pearl": Letters of Sarah Orne Jewett,* p. 47.

CHAPTER VII
NEW ENGLAND'S LOOKING-GLASS

P. 161.   *The Fall of the House of Beecher: The Autobiography,* I, 18.

*Characteristics of Henry Ward Beecher: Dictionary of
American Biography,* VII, 132.

P. 162. *HBS to Mrs. Follen:* Stowe, *Life,* pp. 197-198.

Mark Twain's recollection of HBS in her old age at Hartford: Mark Twain's Autobiography, The Complete Works of Mark Twain (New York, 1924), II, 243.

Emerson's observation: in "Inspiration," *The Complete Writings of Ralph Waldo Emerson,* Concord Edition, ed. Edward Waldo Emerson (Boston and New York, 1904), p. 289. Hereinafter, Emerson, *Writings.*

Pp. 162-163. *Hawthorne on HBS's A Reply to "The Affectionate and Christian Address of the Women of Great Britain and Ireland to the Women of the United States of America":* Wilson, p. 486.

Pp. 163-164. *HBS to Dr. Bacon:* Wilson, p. 495.

P. 164. *HBS's attempt to persuade her brother Charles to become an Episcopal clergyman:* Stowe, *Life,* p. 402. *Charles Edward Stowe's report on HBS and the Episcopal Church:* Stowe, *Life,* p. 402.

HBS on Charles Edward Stowe's "Life": Letter in facsimile prefacing the *Life.*

P. 168. *HBS's visit to her grandparents: The Autobiography,* I, 310-319.

P. 169. *Dr. Samuel Johnson and the Yale Commencement of 1722:* George Hodges, "The Episcopalians," *The Religious History of New England, King's Chapel Lectures,* by John Winthrop Platner and others (Cambridge, Mass., 1917), p. 220.

President Woolsey's comment: The Religious History of New England, p. 220.

Pp. 169-170. *Ezra Stiles on his invitations to enter the Episcopal Church:* quoted by Abiel Holmes in his *The Life of Ezra Stiles, D.D., LL.D.* (Boston, 1798), p. 40.

P. 171. *HBS to Annie Fields concerning her hard work on Oldtown Folks:* Fields, *Life,* p. 317.

P. 172. *An Adams worshipping the Virgin:* I refer to Henry Adams in *Mont-Saint-Michel and Chartres* (1904). T. S. Eliot, of course, is an Anglican. The poet Robert Lowell has been a Catholic; his present position is not clear. HBS would certainly be interested in Mr. Lowell and his religious problems. As he once told me in conversation, he is a descendant of Jonathan Edwards.

P. 176.   *Henry James in the preface to "The Ambasadors":*
              The Art of the Novel: Critical Prefaces by Henry
              James, with an introduction by Richard P. Blackmur
              (New York, 1934), p. 320.

P. 178.   *The training of Agnes Surriage:* Elias Nason, *Sir*
              Charles Frankland, Baronet: or Boston in the Colonial
              Times (Albany, 1865), p. 25.

Pp. 179-180. *Catharine Beecher on the Separatists: Religious Train-*
              ing of Children in the School, the Family, and the
              Church (New York, 1864), p. 61.

P. 180.   *CB on the Episcopal Church: Religious Training,* p.
              162.

Pp. 180-181. *HBS's quotation from the Magnalia: Magnalia Christi*
              Americana, edition of 1820, II, 264.

P. 181.   *Perry Miller: Orthodoxy in Massachusetts 1630-1650:*
              A Genetic Study (Cambridge, Mass., 1933), particular-
              ly pp. 73-101.

              Mather's first sentence: Magnalia, II, 155.

P. 182.   *HBS's use of Dwight in writing "Oldtown Folks":*
              It seems likely that her later observation concerning
              Edwards as bold rationalizer and anticipator of Emer-
              son and Theodore Parker was based in part on fresh
              awareness of Edwards' notes on "The Mind," col-
              lected by Dwight in the appendix to his *Life,* pp. 664-
              702. If she was thus reviewing Dwight, of whom she
              had made use in writing *The Minister's Wooing,* she
              could hardly miss, even in leafing through the book,
              the long discussion, pp. 300-448, of Edwards' attempt
              to reverse the practice of his grandfather and the con-
              sequent dismissal of Edwards from Northampton. On
              page 300 in Dwight, HBS might have found the fol-
              lowing statement concerning the practice of the North-
              ampton Church as established by Eleazar Mather:
              "The church of Northampton, like the other early
              churches of New-England, was formed on the plan
              of *Strict Communion:* in other words, none were ad-
              mitted to the sacrament of the Lord's Supper, but those
              who, after due examination, were regarded as re-
              generate persons. Such was the uniform practice of the
              church, from its formation, during the ministry of Mr.
              Mather, and for a considerable period after the settle-
              ment of Mr. Stoddard, the predecessor of Mr. Ed-

wards. How early Mr. Stoddard changed his sentiments, on this subject, it is perhaps, impossible to
decide. . . . Mr. Stoddard publicly avowed this change
of his opinions in 1704, when he had been in the ministry at Northampton *thirty-two years.* . . ."

I have accepted Ola E. Winslow's dating of 1700
for Stoddard's change of policy. In her *Jonathan
Edwards 1703-1758: A Biography* (New York, 1941),
pp. 241-261, she has written an authoritative and dramatic account of the dispute between Edwards and
his church.

P. 188.   *HBS's childhood composition:* Stowe, *Life,* pp. 15-22.

P. 190.   *Perry Miller's quotation of Horace's analysis: Images
or Shadows of Divine Things,* p. 144. I have quoted
Mr. Miller's comment on this passage on pp. 246-247.

Pp. 191-192. *Hopkins' influence on Channing:* In his "Christian
Worship," spoken in 1836 at the dedication of the
Unitarian Church in Newport, Rhode Island, Channing
said of the theology of Hopkins: "I need not be
ashamed to confess the deep impression which this
system made on my youthful mind. I am grateful
to this stern teacher for turning my thoughts and
heart to the claims and majesty of impartial, universal
benevolence." Also of significance in view of Horace's
comment on Edwards and the "Newness" is Channing's
observation on Hopkins: "The churches of New England received a decided impression from his views; and
though his name, once given to his followers, is no
longer borne, his influence is still felt. The conflict
now going on in our country, for the purpose of
mitigating the harsh features of Calvinism, is a stage
of the revolutionary movement to which he more than
any man gave impulse" (*The Works of William E.
Channing, D.D.,* Glasgow, Edinburgh, London, 1840,
IV, 345-346). Channing wrote a brilliant thumbnail
sketch of Hopkins in a long note, pp. 349-355. Harriet
undoubtedly read the passage concerning Hopkins and
the "Newness": Dr. Park quoted it in his *Memoir of
Samuel Hopkins,* p. 179.

P. 192.   *Thomas H. Johnson on the influence of Edwards:*
"Jonathan Edwards," in *Literary History of the
United States,* I, 81.

P. 194.   *The refreshment at Lyman Beecher's woodspells: The Autobiography*, I, 326.

P. 196.   *Sam Lawton as the original of Sam Lawson: The Story of Natick* (Natick, 1948), p. 17. This informative pamphlet was published by the Natick Federal Savings and Loan Association, John S. M. Gilden, President.

P. 197.   *Thomas Waban and Deacon Ephraim: The Story of Natick*, pp. 5, 7.

P. 198.   *William Boden: The Story of Natick*, p. 15.

CHAPTER VIII

HOLIDAY IN YANKEEDOM

P. 203.   *HBS to James T. Fields: Wilson*, pp. 531-532.

P. 205.   *Walter Blair on HBS's use of Haliburton: Native American Humor (1800-1900)* (New York, Cincinnati, etc., 1937), p. 136.

Ezra Ripley's belief in Jack Downing: "Ezra Ripley, D.D." in Emerson, *Writings*, X, 389-390.

Robert Frost on Yankees as "my people": "Poverty and Poetry" in *Biblia*, IX, No. I (Feb., 1938), Princeton. No page numbers; my quotations are from the first page of Frost's lecture.

Richard M. Dorson: Jonathan Draws the Long Bow (Cambridge, Mass., 1946), p. 218.

P. 211.   *Robert Frost in "Blueberries": Complete Poems of Robert Frost* (New York, 1949), p. 79.

P. 212.   *Urian Oakes's use of the text, "The Race is not to the swift . . .": The Puritans*, ed. Perry Miller and Thomas H. Johnson, pp. 352, 353, 355.

Oakes's memorable illustration in "The Sovereign Efficacy of Divine Providence": The Puritans, p. 358.

John Cotton on the Calling: The Puritans, pp. 319, 322.

Pp. 212-213. *Oakes on the "the thriving men in Estates": The Puritans*, p. 356.

P. 213.   *Mark Twain to Joel Chandler Harris:* Blair, *Native American Humor*, p. 157.

P. 218.   *Robert Frost's definition of poetry:* "The Figure A Poem Makes," *Complete Poems of Robert Frost*, p. vi.

CHAPTER IX
VINDICATION OF A FRIEND

P. 220-21.   *Aunt Esther's giving HBS "The Corsair" to read and HBS's question as to Byron's meaning: The Autobiography,* I, 528. Byron's line, "From one I never loved enough to hate," will be found in *The Corsair,* Canto II, Stanza XIV.

P. 220.   *Discussion of and response to Byron in Litchfield: The Autobiography,* I, 529.

Lyman Beecher's interest in great lost souls and his belief that he and Taylor could have gotten Byron out of his troubles: The Autobiography, I, pp. 530-531.

P. 221.   *Taylor's favorite motto: Dictionary of American Biography,* XVIII, 339.

Cleon: Fields, *Life,* pp. 46-49.

P. 223.   *Forrest Wilson's assumption: Wilson,* p. 536.

Pp. 223-224.   *Forrest Wilson's dating of "The True Story of Lady Byron" and his inferences: Wilson,* pp. 536-537; 549-551.

P. 225.   *HBS's comparison of Byron to a musical instrument: Lady Byron Vindicated, A History of the Byron Controversy, from Its Beginning in 1816 to the Present Time* (Boston, 1870), p. 377.

The state of exhausted vitality: Lady Byron Vindicated, p. 384.

P. 226.   *The affecting feature of Byron's "brain-disease": Lady Byron Vindicated,* p. 391.

CHAPTER X
THE LAST NOVELS

P. 230.   *The possibility that HBS heard rumors of Emily Dickinson:* By rumors I mean the guesses about her story which (according to George F. Whicher in *This Was a Poet,* pp. 81-82) were current in Amherst between 1850 and 1880. HBS might have heard such rumors from her brother, Henry Ward Beecher, who could have picked them up on one of his returns to Amherst College, from which he was graduated in 1834; but an even more likely source was her daughter Georgianna Stowe Allen, whose husband was Episcopal rector of Amherst in the 1870's.

With her intense interest in details of life in the New England village, and on the lookout for raw materials for novels and stories, HBS would have listened avidly to the gossip (I quote Mr. Whicher) which specified "a lover's meeting in the garden interrupted by lantern light, a stern father ordering the young man off the premises, a defiant Emily promising never to leave her home until her lover could claim her and to wear nothing but white for his sake, and a broken-hearted lover dying after a few years of agonized separation." The gossip might have interested HBS, in addition, because she may have once known Emily's grandfather. In 1833 Samuel Fowler Dickinson went to Cincinnati as fiscal agent for Lane Seminary, of which Lyman Beecher was President. Possibly, HBS may also have known Emily's tutor and "dearest earthly friend," Charles Wadsworth, not only as a distinguished Protestant clergyman, but as a childhood acquaintance from Litchfield, Connecticut, where he was born three years after HBS. All of this, however, is in the realm of conjecture.

P. 235.   *Charles Beecher's statement about his father in his classes at Lane Theological Seminary: The Autobiography, II, 568.*

P. 237.   *The Episcopal Church in Litchfield:* Payne Kenyon Kilbourne, *Sketches and Chronicles of the Town of Litchfield, Connecticut, Historical, Biographical, and Statistical, Together with a Complete Official Register of the Town* (Hartford, 1859), p. 177. Kilbourne notes the fact that the first service was performed by that apostate at the Yale Commencement of 1722, Dr. Samuel Johnson, whom I have discussed in writing of *Oldtown Folks.* How firmly the Episcopal Church was established in Litchfield in HBS's childhood can be seen from the following facts noted by Kilbourne: the first church building was erected in 1749; in 1797, the "Second Episcopal Society of Litchfield" was organized and amicably united with the original society in 1803; but in HBS's childhood and up at least to 1859 the two societies had different rectors; thus there were essentially *two* Episcopal churches in Litchfield in HBS's childhood.

P. 241.   *Edmund Wilson on Puritanism and the novels of HBS: New Yorker,* March 14, 1953, p. 110.

INDEX

Adams, Henry, 192, 263
Aiken, George L., vii, 34
A Kempis, Thomas, 232
Alcott, Amos Bronson, 156
Alger, Horatio, 228
Allen, Ethan, 237
Allen, Henry (HBS's son-in-law), 163, 267
Alton, Ill., 28
Andover, Mass., 20, 21, 65, 69-70, 72, 83, 86, 91, 92, 93, 130, 136
Andover Theological Seminary, 20, 65, 87, 91-92, 132, 163
Andrews, Kenneth R., 248
Anthony, Susan, 230
Appleton, Jesse, 149, 262
Arkansas, 78
Atlantic Monthly, 86, 87, 99, 100, 131, 138, 173, 203, 241
Arvin, Newton, 30
Augustine, Saint, 96, 144, 188, 257

Bacon, Leonard, 163
Baldwin, James, viii-ix
Beecher, Catharine (HBS's sister), 23, 25, 89, 91, 94-96, 97, 111, 113, 115-116, 179-180, 221
Beecher, Charles (HBS's brother), 6, 23, 70, 163-164, 235
Beecher, David (HBS's grandfather), 161
Beecher, Edward (HBS's brother), 20, 28, 94, 96, 163, 168-169, 171, 257-258
Beecher, Mrs. Edward (HBS's sister-in-law), 18, 28

Beecher, Esther (HBS's aunt), 219-220
Beecher, George (HBS's brother), 24
Beecher, Harriet Porter (HBS's stepmother), 6
Beecher, Henry Ward (HBS's brother), 5, 6, 18, 22, 79-80, 115, 157, 161, 188, 267
Beecher, Isabella (HBS's half-sister), 6
Beecher, James (HBS's half-brother), 6
Beecher, Joseph (HBS's great-great grandfather), 161
Beecher, Lyman (HBS's father), 8-9, 15, 23, 51, 54, 70, 72, 93, 94, 104, 115, 161, 162, 171, 174-175, 194, 219, 220, 233-236, 249, 256, 268
Beecher, Nathaniel (HBS's great grandfather), 161
Beecher, Roxana Foote (HBS's mother), 6, 39-40, 114-115, 118, 125, 171
Beecher, Thomas K. (HBS's half-brother), 6, 24
Bellamy, Edward, x
Bellamy, Joseph, 121, 131, 189, 192
Benton, Lot (HBS's granduncle), 7, 249
Birney, James, 22
Blair, Walter, 205, 214, 247
Boston, Mass., 8-9, 20, 23, 28, 33, 163, 165-168, 170, 178, 236
Boston Quarterly Review, 50, 53

Bowdoin College, 20, 65, 149, 209
Brace, John Pierce, 3, 188, 201, 249
Brattleboro, Vermont, 25
Bremer, Fredrika, 57-58, 253
Brook Farm, 136
Brooklyn, N. Y., 80, 161
Brooks, Congressman Preston S., 80
Brooks, Van Wyck, ix, 245-246
Brown, Daniel, 169
Brown, Herbert, 13
Brownson, Orestes A., 50, 53, 54, 55, 58-59, 136, 137, 231
Brunswick, Maine, 21, 29, 57, 64, 146, 149
Buchanan, President James, 80
Bunyan, John, 186
Burke, Kenneth, 90-91, 128
Burr, Aaron, 110
Burroughs, Stephen, 261
Butler, Senator Andrew P., 80
Butler, Bishop Joseph, 221
Byron, Lady, 102, 222-226
Byron, Lord, 82, 219-226

Caldwell, Erskine, 61
Calvin, John, 68, 93, 256
Calvinism; see Puritanism
Camden, Maine, 204
Canada, 33, 193
Carlyle, Thomas, 190, 242
Casco Bay, Maine, 64-65, 86, 151
Catherine de Médicis, 68
Catholicism, 68, 134-144, 232
Cervantes Saavedra, Miguel de, 15
Channing, Edward Tyrrell, 3
Channing, William Ellery, 53, 191-192, 265
Channing, William Henry, 54
Chaucer, Geoffrey, 65, 196
Christian Union, 227
Cincinnati, Ohio, 7, 13, 15, 16-17, 22, 23-25, 25-27, 32, 53-54, 57-58, 84, 95, 268
Claflin, Tennie, 230
Clark, Lewis, 18
Clarke, James Freeman, 53, 54
Clemens, Samuel L.; see Mark Twain

Colman, Benjamin, 8
Coleridge, Samuel Taylor, 30, 190, 242
Columbia University, 169
Committee of New Ladies' Anti-Slavery Society in Glasgow, 66
Committee of the Glasgow New Association for the Abolition of Slavery, 66
Communism, 51-57, 231-232
Cooper, James Fenimore, 60, 79
Cotton, John, 212
Council of Congregational Churches, 92
Courier, Natchez, 78
Covenanters, 67-68
Cranch, Christopher Pearse, 54
Cromwell, Oliver, 67, 168
Cutler, Timothy, 169

Dante Alighieri, 140, 143, 144, 182, 184
Darwin, Charles, 230
Dartmouth College, 92, 93
Davenport, John, 172
Deane, Samuel, 100-101
Defoe, Daniel, 15, 17, 30
DeForest, John W., x
Dickens, Charles, 10
Dickinson, Emily, ix, 11, 90, 106, 118, 124, 129, 143, 205, 230, 241, 242, 246, 267-268
Dickinson, Samuel Fowler, 268
Donne, John, 119-120, 188
Dorson, Richard M., 205
Douglas, Senator Stephen A., 79, 80
Douglas, Frederick, 18, 33, 74, 252-253
Drake, Daniel, 16, 17
Dred Scott Decision, 80
Dudley, Thomas, 181
Dwight, Sereno E., 182, 264-265

Eaton, Samuel, 101, 157
Edinburgh, Scotland, 67
Edwards, Jonathan, ix, x, 8, 14, 23, 26, 54, 57, 96, 101, 106, 108, 109, 110, 111, 121, 122, 131, 132-

133, 143-144, 154, 166, 168-169, 170, 174, 179-184, 185, 189-193, 242, 246-247, 250, 252, 256-257, 260, 263, 264, 265

Edwards, Sarah Pierrepont (Mrs. Jonathan Edwards), 26

Eliot, John, 196

Eliot, George, 137

Eliot, T. S., 53, 120, 263

Eliot, William G., 53

Emerson, Mary Moody, 191

Emerson, R. W., 10, 11, 53, 54, 69, 87, 118-119, 124, 162, 163, 175-176, 190-192, 205, 241, 242, 264

Emmons, Nathanael, 89, 91, 95, 101, 102, 111, 131

Engels, Friedrich, 51

Episcopal Church (also Anglican Church, Anglicanism, Episcopalianism), 169-171, 180-183, 184, 185, 236-238, 268

Evans, Mrs. Sarah, 14

Existentialism, 93, 176

Faulkner, William, viii, 61, 75

Fénelon, François de Salignac de la Mothe, 139

Fields, Annie, 21, 156, 171

Fields, James T., 86, 87, 138, 203-204, 205, 226

Fisher, Alexander Metcalf, 89, 90, 91, 94, 95

Flaubert, Gustave, 12

Flint, Timothy, 42

Florence, Italy, 123, 129-130, 137

Follen, Eliza Lee Cabot, 27, 63, 162

Foote, Mrs. Eli (HBS's grandmother), 168-169, 171, 172, 235

Foote, Harriet (HBS's aunt), 168, 171

Foote, Samuel (HBS's uncle), 22

France, 68, 69

Frankland, Sir Charles, 178

Franklin, Benjamin, 167, 193

Franklin, Mass., 89, 95

Freeman, James, 170

Freeman, Mary E. Wilkins, x, 241

French character, 109-110

French communism, 231-232

French Revolution, 68

French, Daniel Chester, 10

Freud, Sigmund, 103, 116

Frost, Robert, 11, 138, 148, 205, 211, 217-218, 261

Fugitive Slave Law, 28, 34

Fuller, Margaret, 53, 124

Fox, Sir John C., 224-225

Fox, John D., daughters of, 129

Gallagher, W. D., 53

Geneva, Switzerland, 68

Georgetown, Mass., 164

Gettysburg, Pa., 162

Gilbertson, Catherine, 247

Gilded Age, viii, 227-229, 233

Giotto, 123

Gogol, Nikolai, 62

Grayson, William J., 49

Great Barrington, Mass., 88

Grierson, Herbert J. C., 120

Guiccioli, Countess Teresa, 224

Guilford, Conn., 168

Gysin, Brion, 30

Hafiz, 162, 163

Hall, James, 16, 17

Halliburton, Thomas Chandler, 204-205

Hanover, N. H., 93, 96

Haroutunian, Joseph, 259

Harpswell, Maine, 152, 153, 157

Harris, Joel Chandler, 213

Hartford, Conn., 20, 23, 163, 196

Hartford Seminary, 219, 221

Harvard College, 170, 208, 210

Harvard Medical School, 134

Hawthorne, Nathaniel, x, xi, 9, 10, 12, 41, 59, 74, 79, 110, 126, 134-136, 139, 143, 164, 176-177, 192, 241, 242

Hawthorne, Rose (Sister Alphonsa), 136

Hemingway, Ernest, 75

Hemmenway, Moses, 100-101

Henson, Josiah, 18, 20, 30-33, 74

Higginson, T. W., 124

Holmes, Abiel, 132-134

Holmes, Oliver Wendell, 130, 131-135, 203, 205

Hopkins, Samuel (historical figure), 87-90, 91, 99, 101, 121, 122, 131, 138, 174, 191-192, 267
Hopkinton, Mass., 178, 199
Howard, Mrs. John T., 20, 21, 130
Howells, William Dean, 233
Hubbard, Mary (HBS's aunt), 112
Huntington, Frederick D., 170

Independent, N. Y., 157, 158
Indians, 199-200, 207, 210-211, 216-217
Inge, W. R., 258
Ingersoll, Joanna, 88

James, Henry, 9, 12, 59, 176, 179, 233
Jefferson, Thomas, 101, 166
Jewett, Sarah Orne, x, 145-146, 150, 158, 159
Johnson, Samuel (1696-1772), 169, 172, 268
Johnson, Samuel (1709-1784), 169
Johnson, Thomas H., 192
Journal of Commerce, New York, 66
Judd, Sylvester, x

Kansas, 80
Kansas-Nebraska Bill, 79, 80
Kentucky, 16, 36, 64
Kilbourne, Payne Kenyon, 268
Kingsley, Charles, 48

Lane Theological Seminary, 13, 235, 268
Lawrence, Amos, 54
Lawrence, D. H., 79
Lawrence, Kansas, 79
Lawrence, Mass., 136
Leigh, Augusta, 222
Leonardo da Vinci, 112, 123
Lexington, Mass., 214
Liberia, 34
Lincoln, Abraham, 56, 162, 163, 241
Litchfield, Conn., 3, 6, 23, 155, 194, 201, 219-220, 233-234, 237, 268
Lowell, James Russell, 86, 122, 205
Lowell, Robert, 263

Lovejoy, Elijah P., 28
Lowes, John Livingston, 30
Luther, Martin, 113

McCray, Florine Thayer, 90
Mandarin, Florida, 196
Marblehead, Mass., 178
Mark Twain, 15, 48, 60, 62, 75, 148, 162, 200, 204, 211, 213
Martineau, Harriet, 16, 17
Marx, Karl, 51, 52, 231
Massachusetts Anti-Slavery Society, 33
Mather, Cotton, 26, 56, 180-182, 189, 206, 211, 262
Mather, Eleazar, 182, 264
Matthiessen, F. O., x, 247
Marquand, John P., 233
May, Georgianna, 7, 23, 25
Mayhew, Jonathan, 109, 259
Melville, Herman, 15, 30, 59-60, 69, 75, 79, 106, 241, 242
Michelangelo Buonarroti, 123
Miller, Perry, ix, 54, 105, 172, 181, 190, 192, 246-247
Milton, John, 182, 184, 220
Mississippi, 75
Missouri, 78, 79
Mozart, Wolfgang Amadeus, 112

Napoleon, 220
Nason, Elias, 178
Natick, Mass., 178, 196-201, 203, 204
National Era, 64
New Hampshire, 83-84
New Orleans, La., 32, 37, 43, 45-46
Newport, R. I., 89, 111, 121, 265
Newton, Benjamin Franklin, 124
New York City, 229, 233
New Yorker, 241
New York State, 73
Northampton, Mass., 179, 264
North Carolina, 83
North Star, 33
Nutplains, Conn., 168-169, 235

Oakes, Urian, 211-212
O'Donnell, Father James, 136

Origen, 96, 258
Osborne, Mrs. Sarah, 99
Osgood, James R., 223
Orr's Island, Maine, 146-159

Paris, France, 69, 99
Park, Edwards A., 87-92, 121, 265
Parker, Theodore, 54, 190, 191, 264
Parrington, V. L., 105, 247
Parton, James, 110
Patten, William, 88
Peabody, Ephraim, 53
Pelagius, 96
Pennsylvania, 80
Plato, 70, 123-124, 188
Plutarch, 155
Poe, Edgar A., 21, 79, 130
Puritanism (Calvinism, Edwardean Calvinism, New England Puritanism), acceptance without involvement, 107; afflictions, response to, 26, 98-100, 114-115; American culture, Puritan pattern in, 241-242; American intensity from, 7-8; American mind a product of, 241-242; attitude toward beauty, 69, 70-71, 112, 122-124, 139, 192; calling, doctrine of, 212-213; Catholic Church, response to, 68, 134-144, 232; Calvinists, name of, 92; church membership in, 179-183, 185, 264-265; conversion, 23-25, 92-96, 98, 107, 108-109, 134, 199; courageous opposition to world, 192, 224, 229; covenanted society, 56; covenanters, 67-68; democracy, relation to, 68, 101, 104, 192-193, 234, 237, 238-239; death, response to, 26-27, 84-85, 92-103, 106, 118-120, 126-127, 129-131, 144, 146-153, 186-187, 217; disinterested benevolence, 101, 104, 109; duty, sense of, 42, 157-158, 160, 196, 224; economic and cultural values from, 83-84, 192-193; Episcopal Church, relation to, 165-172, 175-184, 188-189, 232, 236-238; existentialism, parallels, 93, 176; feeling suppressed in, 5-6, 7-8, 112, 127, 230; folk superstitions in, 146-150, 200, 206-207, 214-218; freedom of the will, 23, 94-96, 101, 106, 122, 131-134, 199; Half-Way Covenant, 180, 181; hatred of religion resulting from, 183, 184; individualism developed by, 3-4, 9, 187, 197-198, 238-240; infant damnation, 93-94, 256-257; intellectuality in, 68, 84, 96, 108-109, 112-113, 114, 123, 142-143, 167, 185-186, 187, 188, 195, 198-199, 219-220, 229-230; inwardness, illustrated in Mary Scudder, 118-120, illustrated in Mr. Sewall, 153, illustrated in the Rossiter family, 185-186; logic in, 95, 175, 186-187; lost souls, Lyman Beecher's interest in, 220; love in, 112, 116-117, 120-121, 123-127, 142-143, 208-209, 219; ministers in, 8-9, 77-78, 87-92, 94-95, 100-102, 105-106, 120-128, 132-133, 152-153, 155-156, 169-170, 174-175, 179-184, 186-187, 189-193, 194, 198, 199, 208, 216, 233-236; modified by American democracy, 193; moral realism of, 41-42, 50; nature confirms, 68-69, 113, 143-144, 168; New Divinity (Edwardean Calvinism) satirized, 175; New England doubleness and illustration in *The Mayflower*, 6-11, illustrated in *Uncle Tom's Cabin*, 40-57, illustrated in *The Minister's Wooing*, 108-128, illustrated in *The Pearl of Orr's Island*, 145-154, 156-157, illustrated in *Oldtown Folks*, 179-202, illustrated in *Oldtown Fireside Stories*, 204, illustrated in Esther Beecher, 219, illustrated in *Poganuc People*, 236-240; nondoctrinal Puritan, 229-230; non-Separatist Congregational position, 172, 181; original sin, 95, 98, 106, 109, 131-134, 185, 186, 199, 257-258;

piety, 107; Platonic ladder muti-
lated in, 122-123; Platonic relations of man and woman in, 123-
125; poison to certain minds, 106,
114; poor, treatment of in, 196,
210-211; predestination, 23, 68,
101-102, 168; providences, 207,
211-212; rationalism, 206-207; rebellion from, 94-96, 136-144, 168-
172, 182-189, 235-240, 261; renunciation, 119, 126-127, 142-143;
Renaissance Italian culture, contrast to, 139; retribution, 102,
104-105, 106, 125, 143-144, 182-
183, 186-187; sacrifice, 126, 183;
self-denial, 127; simplicity, love
of, 174, 229; slavery (see also
Uncle Tom's Cabin and *Dred*),
78, 88-89, 121, 192; sovereignty
of God, 92, 101-102, 211-212;
spiritual and material extremes
of New England mind, 193-194;
spiritualism as modifier of, 130-
131; strength from spiritual
bruising, 117-118; submission to
God's will, 26, 94, 98-100, 114-
115, 125-127, 131; theocracy, 56-
57, 175, 181, 234, 237; theology,
108-109, 175, 192; transcendentalism, relation to, 189-192, 265;
Unitarianism, relation to, 8, 136-
137, 161, 190-192, 265; visions,
19-21, 154; wit and humor (*see*
New England doubleness), 48-
49, 100-101, 152-153; worldliness
in disrepute in, 174, 209-210, 212-
213; Yale apostasy from, in 1722,
by Dr. Johnson and others, 169

Quakers, 62, 73
Quinn, A. H., 247

Radcliffe, Mrs. Anne Ward, 110
Ramsay, Allan, 67
Ripley, Ezra, 205
Ripley, Mrs. George, 136
Richardson, Samuel, 14, 17, 30
Rome, Italy, 74, 134, 135-139
Rourke, Constance, 104, 128
Rousseau, Jean Jacques, 166, 187

Sales, Francis de, 139, 232
Savonarola, Girolamo, 137-138, 144
Scott, Sir Walter, 10, 15-16, 17, 30
Semi-Colon Club, 3, 16, 22
Shakespeare, William, 10, 151, 154,
156
Shepard, Thomas, x
Sherburne, Mass., 208
Shreve, T. H., 53
Slavery (see *Uncle Tom's Cabin*
and *Dred*), 13, 33, 41-42, 49-59,
60, 66, 79-81, 88-89, 108, 121, 162-
163, 198
Smith, Seba, 205
Socialism, 54-55
Sorrento, Italy, 135
South Carolina, 71, 80
Spiritualism, 129-131, 163
Sprague, William B., 8, 100, 157
Staël-Holstein, Anne Louise Ger-
maine, Baroness de (Madame de
Staël), 7
Stanton, Elizabeth Cady, 230
Stebbins, Lucy Poate, 13
Stebbins, Richard Poate, 13
Stiles, Ezra, 88-89, 91, 121, 169-170
Stoddard, Solomon, 179, 182, 264-
265
Story, William Wetmore, 74
Stowe, Calvin (HBS's husband),
9, 18, 22, 54, 65, 72, 87, 91, 94,
129-130, 132, 140, 173, 178, 196,
206
Stowe, Charles Edward (HBS's
son), 28, 29, 91, 95, 164-165
Stowe, Eliza (Calvin Stowe's first
wife), 130
Stowe, Frederick (HBS's son), 93,
157, 162
Stowe, Georgianna (HBS's daughter), 102, 163, 267
Stowe, Harriet Beecher: childhood, general description of, 6;
death of mother, 1816, 6, 39-40,
115-116; Nutplains, visit after
mother's death and later visits in
childhood, 168-169, 235-236;
theocracy, collapse of in Conn.,

235; death of Catharine Beecher's fiancé, 1822, 94-95; writes "Can the Immortality of the Soul Be Proved by the Light of Nature?" 3, 187-188, 248-249; reads *Don Quixote,* 15; reads *Ivanhoe,* 15; Byron, reads his poetry, 219-220; Byron, her response to his separation from his wife and his death, 1824, 220; Byron, her interest in as girl, 221-222; "easy" conversion, 1825, and subsequent religious history as girl and young woman, 23, 95; writes *Cleon,* 221-222;

resolves to give up inner world for external one, 1832, 7-8; exposure to regionalism in Cincinnati, 16-17; use of anecdotes of Calvin Stowe and Lyman Beecher in *Mayflower* sketches, 7, 9; "A New England Sketch" read to Semi-Colon Club, 1833, 3; "A New England Sketch" awarded prize in *Western Monthly Magazine,* 1834, 3; writes conventional sketches for money, 22; resolve to live external life fades, 22-27; possible reading of Brownson's "The Laboring Classes," 50-54; capture and rescue of her colored servant, 22; burden of Charles Beecher's fatalism, 23-24; shock of George Beecher's death, 1843, 24; "true" conversion, 1844-1845, 24-25; Vermont interval, 1846-1847, 25; death of Samuel Charles (Charley) Stowe, 1849, in cholera epidemic, 25-26; *Uncle Tom's Cabin* begins at Charley Stowe's grave, 26-27;

reading as preparation for *Uncle Tom's Cabin,* 13-18, 30, 50-54; discussion of Fugitive Slave Law, 1850, 28; meeting with the Rev. Josiah Henson, 20; suggestion by Mrs. Edward Beecher for antislavery book,

28-29; inspiration for *Uncle Tom's Cabin* at communion table in Brunswick, Feb. 1851, 29; various accounts of genesis of *Uncle Tom's Cabin,* 18-22, 29; origin of *Uncle Tom's Cabin* in repetition-compulsion, 103; symbolic action in writing *Uncle Tom's Cabin,* 29-57; economic and social thought in writing *Uncle Tom's Cabin,* 49-57; change wrought in HBS by writing *Uncle Tom's Cabin,* 62-63; writes two letters from Maine for *National Era,* 64-65; begins *The Pearl of Orr's Island,* 65;

religious joy and confidence after writing *Uncle Tom's Cabin,* 1852, 65; writes "Still, Still with Thee," 65; publishes *Uncle Sam's Emancipation,* 1853, 64; visions given as explanation for *Uncle Tom's Cabin,* 19-20; writes *A Key to Uncle Tom's Cabin,* 1853, 18-19, 66; Europe, first journey, 1853, and appraisal of Puritanism against foreign backgrounds, 66-69; meets Lady Byron, 222; works on *Autobiography of Lyman Beecher* at Andover, 69-70; writes "The Old Oak of Andover" as reappraisal of Puritanism, 70-71; Sojourner Truth's visit and story, 72-74; God fades on mountain of victory, 81; writes *Dred,* 71, 74-78; symbolic action in writing *Dred,* 79-85; Europe, second journey, 1856-1857, 92-93; securing of British copyright on *Dred,* 92; Lady Byron discloses reason for separating from Lord Byron, 222-223; concern for spiritual state of Henry Ellis Stowe, 92-93; journey to Hanover to see Henry Stowe, July, 1857, 93; death of Henry Stowe, July 9, 1857, 91; journey to Hanover to view scene of Henry Stowe's death, 93, 96;

vigil at Henry Stowe's grave, 91; "attack of the devil" and apparent reliving of Catharine Beecher's spiritual history, 94-98; temporary submission and feeling of reconciliation, 98-99; visits Maine, 86; writes "Who Shall Roll Away the Stone?" Sept. 1857, 129; symbolic action in writing "The Mourning Veil," Nov. 1857, 99-100; agrees to serial in *Atlantic*, 86; symbolic action in writing "New England Ministers," Feb. 1858, 99-102; dilemma in confronting Henry Stowe's situation in eternity, 102-103, 104-105; resumes writing of *The Pearl of Orr's Island* and again postpones, 86-87; writes *The Minister's Wooing*, 86-87, 90-91, 103-105; discussions with Dr. Park concerning *The Minister's Wooing*, 87-90, 91-92; symbolic action in writing *The Minister's Wooing*, 90-91, 103-128; feeling of reconciliation with Puritanism and writing of "Preface" to British edition of *The Minister's Wooing*, 127-128; Europe, third and last journey, 1859-1860, 129-131, 134; spiritualism, flirtation with at Florence, 129-130; difficulty of submitting to Henry Stowe's death, 131; reading of Holmes's *Elsie Venner*, 131-134; embracing of doctrine of "moral insanity," 131-134; tells stories to Hawthorne on shipboard and possibly discusses *The Marble Faun*, 134-136; spiritual state approximating that of Unitarian converts to Catholicism, 136-137; writes *Agnes of Sorrento*, 134-135, 137-138, 156, 160; tries out Catholicism in imagination, 134-144; symbolic action in writing *Agnes of Sorrento*, 138-144; writes *The Pearl of Orr's Island*, 156-160;

possible use of Mather's *Magnalia* in *The Pearl of Orr's Island*, 262; writes Theodore Tilton concerning second part of *The Pearl of Orr's Island*, 157-158; symbolic action in writing *The Pearl of Orr's Island*, 145, 151-157; visits Lincoln at White House, 162; writes "Reply to the Affectionate and Christian Address," 1862, 162-163; Hawthorne's comment on the "Reply," 162-163; cheered on Lincoln's signing of "Emancipation Proclamation," 163; death of Lyman Beecher, 162; Frederick Stowe wounded at Battle of Gettysburg, 162; Calvin Stowe retires from Andover Theological Seminary, 163;

moves to Hartford, 1864, 162; emergence into new life, 161-165; response to Charles Beecher's trial for heresy, 163-164; becomes member of Episcopal Church, 163-165, 170-172; writes *House and Home Papers*, 173-174; verdict on Civil War in *Men of Our Times*, 55; writes *Oldtown Folks*, 161-165, 171-174, 176-182, 196, 201-202; symbolic action in writing *Oldtown Folks*, 165-176, 179-193; writes *Oldtown Fireside Stories*, 203-206, 213-214, 217-218; sends Fields "The Widow's Bandbox" for *Atlantic*, 203-204; writes "The True Story of Lady Byron's Life," 223-224; writes *Lady Byron Vindicated*, 224-226; literary activity 1870-1881, 227; becomes owner of *Christian Union*, 227; reaction to Gilded Age, 227-233; writes *Pink and White Tyranny*, 227-228; writes *My Wife and I*, 229-232; reaction to "woman question," 230-232; Emily Dickinson, possible knowledge of, 230, 267-268;

reaction to French communism, 231-232; writes *We and Our Neighbors,* 232-233; examines Catholicism as Episcopalian, 232; writes *Poganuc People,* 233-235, 240-241; symbolic action in writing *Poganuc People,* 234-241; career comes full circle with *Poganuc People,* 241; writes "The Author's Introduction" to *Uncle Tom's Cabin,* 1878, 21; Mark Twain's account of HBS in extreme old age, 162

WORKS

Agnes of Sorrento (1862), 134-144, 145, 156, 160, 161, 163, 232, 236

"The Author's Introduction" to *Uncle Tom's Cabin* (1878), 21, 29, 40

"Can the Immortality of the Soul Be Proved by the Light of Nature?" (1823), 3, 187-188, 248-249

Cleon (1825), 221-222

Dred: A Tale of the Great Dismal Swamp (1856), 71-85, 171, 202

House and Home Papers (1864-1865), 173-174, 219

A Key to Uncle Tom's Cabin (1853), 18, 19, 45, 54, 66

Lady Byron Vindicated (1870), 219-226, 227

The Mayflower (1843), 3-11, 18, 63, 65
  "Aunt Mary," 5
  "The Canal Boat," 204-205
  "Cousin William," 6, 8
  "Feeling," 5
  "Little Edward," 5
  "Love versus Law," 6-7, 9
  "A New England Sketch," 3-4, 7, 8, 53, 233, 249
  "The Sabbath," 4

The Mayflower (1855), 70
  "The Old Oak of Andover—A Revery," 70-71

Men of Our Times (1868), 55

The Minister's Wooing (1859), ix, 63, 69, 86-128, 130, 138, 140, 142, 145, 157, 160, 162, 168, 170, 171, 183, 185, 191, 204, 222, 236, 242

"Preface" to British edition of *The Minister's Wooing,* 127-128, 129

"The Mourning Veil" (1857), 99-100

My Wife and I (1871), 227, 229-232

"New England Ministers" (1858), 100-102, 104

Oldtown Fireside Stories (1872), 4, 9, 145, 162, 203-218, 227, 242
  "The Bull Fight," 214
  "Captain Kidd's Money," 206
  "Colonel Eph's Shoe-Buckles," 212, 213
  "The Ghost in the Mill," 206-207, 214-218
  "How to Fight the Devil," 210-211
  "The Minister's Housekeeper," 208, 213-214
  "Mis' Elderkin's Pitcher," 208-209, 213
  "The Sullivan Looking-Glass," 206, 207
  "The Widow's Bandbox," 203-204, 213

Oldtown Folks (1869), ix, 4, 9, 63, 120, 145, 161-202, 203, 204, 218, 222, 234, 235, 236, 242, 264-265

The Pearl of Orr's Island (1862), 65, 66, 69, 86-87, 145-160, 161, 242, 262

Pink and White Tyranny (1871), 227-228

Poganuc People (1878), 6, 145, 162, 164, 221, 227, 233-241, 242

"Reply to the Affectionate and Christian Address" (1862), 162-163

"Sojourner Truth, the Libyan Sibyl" (*ca.* 1862), 72

"Still, Still with Thee, When Purple Morning Breaketh" (1852), 65

Sunny Memories of Foreign Lands (1854), 15, 66-69, 70, 109

"The True Story of Lady Byron's Life" (1869), 223-224

Uncle Sam's Emancipation; Earthly Care, A Heavenly Discipline; and Other Sketches (1853), 64-65

Uncle Tom's Cabin or, Life Among the Lowly (1852), vii-ix, 11, 12-63, 64, 66, 71, 75, 81, 85, 103, 104, 116, 118, 156, 162, 171, 196, 204, 214, 222, 224, 231, 236, 247-248

We and Our Neighbors (1875), 227, 229, 232-233

"Who Shall Roll Away the Stone?" (1857), 129

Stowe, Henry Ellis (HBS's son), 91-93, 96, 98-99, 102-103, 104-105, 127, 129-130, 137, 144

Stowe, Lyman Beecher (HBS's grandson), 104, 128, 255, 257, 258

Stowe, Samuel Charles—Charley (HBS's son), 25, 39, 81, 84, 94, 103

Suckow, Ruth, 258

Sumner, Senator Charles, 80

Sutherland, Duchess of, 66

Swift, Jonathan, 124-125

Switzerland, 68-69

Taylor, Nathaniel W., 220-221

Theocritus, 154

Thoreau, H. D., 10, 11, 75, 87, 154, 156, 174, 210, 224, 241, 242

Thomas a Kempis, 232

Thorp, Margaret Farrand, 247-248

Ticknor and Fields, 145

Tilton, Theodore, 157-158, 160

Tom Shows, vii-viii

Transcendentalism, 87, 106, 189-192

Trilling, Lionel, 105, 258

Trollope, Frances, 13, 17, 30

Truth, Sojourner, 72-74, 83

Turgenev, Ivan Sergeevich, 12

Turner, Nat, 85

Underwood, Francis H., 86

Unitarianism, 106, 136-137, 161, 170, 190, 265

Van Doren, Carl, 110-111

Vermont, 25, 41-43

Very, Jones, 53

Vesey, Denmark, 71

Vesuvius, 143-144

Voltaire, François Marie Arouet de, 166, 187

Waban, Thomas, 197

Wadsworth, Charles, 124, 143, 268

Walpole, Horace, 110

Ward, Samuel G., 118

Wardlaw, Ralph, 66

Warren, Robert Penn, 75

Washington, George, 166, 167, 233-234

Weld, Theodore, 18

West, Elizabeth, 87-88, 255

Westbrook, Perry D., 150

Western Messenger, 53, 54

Western Monthly Magazine, 3, 53

Whicher, George F., ix, 246, 259, 261, 267, 268

Whitman, Walt, 60, 192

Whittier, John Greenleaf, 145

Wilder, Thornton, ix

Williams, Roger, 63, 81, 84

Wilson, Edmund, ix, 49, 59, 62, 241

Wilson, Forrest, 223-224

Winslow, Ola E., 265

Winthrop, John, 172, 181, 185, 211

Winwar, Frances, 225

Woodhull, Victoria, 230

Woolsey, Theodore D., 169

Wordsworth, William, 127, 242, 257

Wise, John, 63

Yale College, 89, 169, 220